Treatise on Laughter

LAURENT JOUBERT

Treatise on Laughter

TRANSLATED AND ANNOTATED BY GREGORY DAVID DE ROCHER

THE UNIVERSITY OF ALABAMA PRESS
TUSCALOOSA

The University of Alabama Press
Tuscaloosa, Alabama 35487-0380
uapress.ua.edu

Hardcover edition published 1980.
Paperback edition published 2019.
eBook edition published 2016.

Typeface: Garamond

Book design: Anna F. Jacobs

Paperback ISBN: 978-0-8173-5963-8
eBook ISBN: 978-0-8173-9055-6

A previous edition of this book has been catalogued by the Library of Congress as follows:
Library of Congress Cataloging in Publication Data.

Joubert, Laurent, 1529–1583.
Treatise on laughter.

Translation of Traité du ris.
Bibliography: p.
Includes index.
1. Laughter. 2. Psychology—Early works to 1850. 3. Psychology, Physiological—Early works to 1800. I. Title.
BF575.L3J6513 1980 152.4 79-16796
ISBN 0-8173-0026-0

CONTENTS

ACKNOWLEDGMENTS

I wish to express my gratitude to the Research Grants Committee of The University of Alabama for the grants-in-aid that have made possible the preparation of this translation. I also wish to extend my special thanks to Professor John Burke of the English Department of The University of Alabama for his valuable suggestions when I was composing the introduction to my translation.

PREFACE

Translations of the literary texts of the French Renaissance have long been at the disposal of the reader of English. Yet, translations of the philosophical or medical treatises that contributed as much to the cultural milieu of an epoch are indeed rare. Montaigne's *Essais* have been translated into English by Florio, Zeitlin, Cotton and Hazlitt, Trechmann and Frame. Urquhart and Le Motteux, Putnam, Cohen, W. F. Smith, and Floyd Gray have rendered the whole or substantial portions of Rabelais's *Gargantua and Pantagruel.* Translation of paraliterary works, on the other hand, has been sparing. Only recently has the monumental contribution of Ambroise Paré been translated into English, that being the sole representative of a vast corpus of scientific prose to have found its way into another language. Laurent Joubert's *Treatise on Laughter,* certainly one of the most interesting texts of this same body of literature, has remained the sole property of readers of French for nearly four centuries.

This is unfortunate, because Joubert's treatise offers us a curious and at the same time stimulating experience: the sensation of moving through another epistemology. Sixteenth-century France experienced a rebirth of learning often celebrated in its prose and poetry. Behind this exuberant cultural activity was an intellectual ferment that frequently manifested itself in the avid study of the recently discovered ancient texts. During the Renaissance truth and knowledge lay in the past, to be found mainly by studying the works of the classical masters: Plato, Aristotle, Hippocrates, and Galen. Certain men of the time were also consulted, but they were usually those who had familiarized themselves with the texts of Greek and Roman antiquity.

The favorite form for this spirit of inquiry was the treatise. In order to "treat" a given subject in accordance with the conventions of the time, one began by culling every mention of the topic in the recently edited Greek and Latin manuscripts. Next came the exhaustive discussion of the subject's every known or even conceivable aspect. It was necessary to observe the traditional philosophical distinctions then in vogue, such as the parts of the soul—intellective, nutritive, and sensitive—or the internal and external senses. Also encountered often in these treatises was the ancient physiological theory of the four humors. Observation, so crucial for the scientific knowledge of our own age, counted for little and, when used, was aimed at corroborating ancient doctrine rather than confounding it. Thus Joubert's ideas can appear quaint, and many of the beliefs held by him and his contemporaries can make us smile. Our smile may well disappear when we wonder which of today's accepted ideas will seem laughable half a millennium hence.

INTRODUCTION

Laurent Joubert was an important figure in the medical world of the French Renaissance. He was born on December 16, 1529, in the old province of Dauphiné in south central France. Information on his early years is sparse, but he was probably educated in his native city. At the age of twenty-one he went to Montpellier, a city renowned for the study of medicine. He became the student of Guillaume Rondelet, himself the chancellor of the Faculté de Médecine. Joubert received his doctorate in medicine in 1558. He soon acquired a reputation as an educator. We read that his students at Montpellier petitioned for his professorship after Rondelet's death in 1556, a mere eight years after beginning his career. Sometime later he was appointed chancellor of the Faculté. In this capacity he attracted the attention of Catherine de' Medici, who called him to be her *premier médecin.* The highest point of his career came when he was made one of the king's own physicians, *médecin ordinaire du roi.* Paradoxically, this well-known doctor of the time died in obscure circumstances in the small village of Lombers on October 21, 1582, not far from Montpellier, the city which had witnessed his rise to fame.

Busy as he was with his professional duties, Joubert still found time to compose several pieces of medical literature. He wrote numerous works in Latin and in French, edited the important *Grande Chirurgie* of Guy de Chauliac, and became well known when he published his *Erreurs populaires,* the subject of considerable scandal because he spoke openly on marital questions and, what was worse, revealed in the vulgar tongue medical secrets previously shrouded in Latin. It was three years before his death that Joubert published what was certainly his most cherished and perhaps his best work, the *Traité du Ris,* the *Treatise on Laughter.*

If we are to believe Joubert's dedicatory letter to Marguerite de Valois, he completed the first version of his *Treatise on Laughter* in Latin in 1560. It was, Joubert claims, the first piece of work to come from his pen. The first of its three books was translated into French by Louys Papon and published without Joubert's knowledge. A copy of this rare work is in the Bibliothèque Nationale's *réserve.* The last two books were translated by Ian Paul Zangmaistre, one of Joubert's disciples, who may have been instrumental in convincing Joubert of the work's possible appeal to a wider readership. Having let his original manuscript languish on his shelves for nearly twenty years, Joubert finally decided to publish an authentic French version in 1579.

Theories on laughter of the sixteenth century never spring solely from one man's mind. They are, on the contrary, deeply rooted in tradition, often reflecting both Aristotelian and Platonic doctrines. Yet they also communicate with the contemporary scene, drawing here less upon philosophical than medical beliefs for material to sustain argumentation. Thus these theories, reiterating reiterations, restate ideas set forth in some of the earliest texts, but they do not fail to put a heavy accent on elements felt to vibrate with a note particularly appealing to certain contemporary ears. Moreover, they often oppose very neatly a current idea or opinion to which the theorist feels compelled to take exception. Such is the case with Joubert's *Traité du Ris.*

His theory was composed during a period of great turmoil in the history of France and of Europe in general. Also at this time man was becoming much more aware of the organic structure of both man and nature. Writers such as Rabelais and the artists patronized by Francis I at Fontainebleau bear witness to this, not to mention the anatomical interests of Michelangelo and Leonardo da Vinci, or the crisp sharpness in the landscapes of Albrecht Dürer. Later, when the Reformation gained momentum, attention was no less focused on anatomy and pathology. Much of the literature of the time records the wars and constant outbreaks of the plague forcing Renaissance man's continued focus on his own body. Medical treatises, such as Ambroise Paré's *Methode de traicter les playes faictes par hacquebutes et aultres bastons à feu* (1545), are no exception, and in this respect also Joubert remains a man of his own time.

In his dedicatory epistle to Marguerite de France, Joubert describes the act of laughter, carefully emblazoning both the qualities of mirth and the human face as it is illumined by them:

> Certainly there is nothing that gives more pleasure and recreation than a laughing face, with its wide, shining, clear, and serene forehead, eyes shining, resplendent from any vantage point, and casting fire as do diamonds; cheeks vermilion and incarnate, mouth flush with the face, lips handsomely drawn back (from which are formed the small dimples called *gelasins,* in the very middle of the cheeks).

He therefore begins with the immediately observable phenomena before penetrating into the more hidden aspects of one of the most admirable of human acts, *amirables accions de l'homme.*

Joubert is keenly aware of the difficulty of the subject matter. Rather than discouraging him, however, this becomes an incentive, making more enticing the study of such a formidable mystery. When the theoretician arrives at the ultimate question, namely, the cause of laughter, he pauses momentarily, wishing to recall to the reader's mind that many philosophers have a good reason for not considering its etiology: searching out the *cause faisant rire* would be in their opinion a frivolous quest. They find laughter inscrutable; too difficult a matter for human delving, it is to be relegated to the realm of "things so difficult they are unknown to man."

Still, Joubert intends to search more deeply. Continuing to amplify his argument, he cites Cicero, Jean Fernel, Alexander of Aphrodisias, Amatus Lusitanus, Jules-César Scaliger, Girolamo Cardano, Girolamo Fracastoro, and François Valeriole, all of whom either admit their ignorance of the subject, or in his opinion fail to advance sufficiently into it. What is necessary, pleads Joubert, is a detailed study, one that would explain, for example, the sudden convulsions of the laugher, and one that would go well beyond all that had been done up to the present. Although the theoretician seems perhaps overconfident here, a certain humility characterizes the final sentences of the prologue; his method will be as sure as it is simple—a straight path from the effects to the cause, with God's help.

Joubert, then, undertakes no less than to explain the mystery of laughter. Needless to say, he is speaking less to the formal cause (as will Bergson three centuries later) than to the material cause. The major difference between Bergson and Joubert is that the former is more concerned with the psychology of laughter while his sixteenth-century predecessor is concentrating mainly on the physiological mechanics of the phenomenon. The theory of Joubert seeks more precisely to reconcile Aristotelian notions tempered by Plato to certain medical beliefs common to the Renaissance. As Bergson will do, Joubert ultimately interprets to and for his century the source and the function of laughter; he wishes to relate its meaning.

This monumental treatise provides us at the outset with categories and examples of the laughable. Joubert makes use of the traditional Aristotelian distinction separating the comic as it is witnessed, or the *laughable in deed,* from the comic as it is recounted, or the *laughable in word.* He then subdivides both of these two major groups by using the senses of sight and hearing as principles in his ordering: "all that is laughable is found in actions (the province of sight) or in words (the province of hearing)."

Laughable actions are further separated according to one of two possible provenances: they are either children of chance or children of conscious purpose. The surprise or chance type can occur on five occasions: catching sight of the shameful parts, seeing the human bottom, seeing a comic fall, noting error in one or more of the five senses, and, finally, witnessing inconsequential loss. The purposeful type subdivides into *imitation* and *practical jokes.*

Laughable speech is also divided according to the provinces of sight and hearing. Thus words can be used for the purpose of *narration,* during which comical scenes are re-created by the inner eye, but they can also be used in a playful way, as is done in puns, in which case they are more specifically aimed at the sense of hearing. Narration is of two types, according to Joubert: *fables* and *anecdotes.* Wordplay can take almost numberless forms, from "lampoons, taunts, sarcasm, derision, scoffing" to remarks that concern "people, places, diverse experiences," and that might be "disgraceful, lascivious, facetious, outrageous, untimely, naïve, fickle, and indiscreet." Joubert sees puns as being closely related to the figures of rhetoric.

These subdivisions and categories, along with their examples, can furnish today's critic and reader with a contemporary vision of comic commonplaces. It is this vision that may prove to be of great value in analyzing comic literature of the Renaissance. Since, as we discuss in a moment, Joubert drew from theorists in several other European countries, and since there was much communication between the nations of Europe for literary, political, artistic, ecclesiastical and medical reasons, Joubert's theory is not necessarily limited to French texts.

On the contrary, certain contemporaneous works from English, German, Spanish, and Italian comical literature might be reevaluated in terms of Joubert's theory. Shakespeare, Robert Greene, and certain aspects of Christopher Marlowe might gain in contemporary comic weight if analyzed in the light of the *Traité.* The same might be true for Hans Sachs, Georg Rollenhagen, and Johann Fischart. Comic elements previously unsuspected because a modern point of reference has been used might be revealed in *Lazarillo de Tormes*, in certain plays of Lope de Vega, Lope de Rueda, Juan del Encina, and of course in *Don Quixote.* Also, Matteo Boiardo's *Orlando innamorato,* Ludovico Ariosto's *Orlando furioso,* Luigi Pulci's *Morgante,* and the *Novelle* of Matteo Bandello might prove to be even more charged with laughing matter for the eyes and ears of the Renaissance reader than is presently acknowledged.[1]

In spite of the utility Joubert's categories afford the modern reader, these formal aspects did not interest the theorist nearly as much as the physiological mechanism causing the convulsions so characteristic of laughter. Indeed, this was the question that intrigued the minds of several theorists of the Renaissance such as Vincenzo Maggi, Girolamo Fracastoro, Ambroise Paré, and Nicolas de Nancel, to name only a few. The source of laughter's convulsions, according to Joubert, was to be found in contrary emotions. For another theorist, only joy could be responsible for laughter. Still another claimed that wonder and joy mixed to cause laughter, but this mixture was, in his eyes, dangerous to the well-being of the laugher. Yet another attributed laughter to mixed emotions, but saw the encounter taking place in the mind and remaining there as a "motion of the brain."

Joubert, like most of his contemporaries, conceived of laughter as a mixture of opposite emotions, joy and sorrow, but he developed the chain of events from that point much more fully. Another characteristic of his conception is that he set the conflict of emotions clearly in the heart, not in the mind. Following Plato, Joubert saw the heart as the seat of the emotions.

But Joubert also borrowed from Aristotle. His basic definition recalls that found in the ancient philosopher's fifth chapter of the *Poetics:* "a defect or ugliness that is not painful or destructive." Can we not see this notion in Joubert's statement that two necessary conditions must be present for laughter to spring into being, "ugliness and absence of strong emotion"? For Joubert, the ugliness that laughing matter necessarily contained incited sadness or sorrow, and the absence of strong emotion corresponded to joy. Furthermore, these contrary emotions stirred the heart in alternating contractions and dilations, sadness causing the contractions and joy the dilations. This to and fro movement was transferred to the pericardium, an organ which anatomy had proved to be firmly attached by a large tissue to the diaphragm. The diaphragm, undergoing the same alternations as the heart, caused the breath in the lungs to be expelled in what could truly be called hearty laughter.

Our immediate reaction to such a curiously mechanical conception of the phenomenon might well be one of laughter. But our levity must not stop us from seeing an important fact: Renaissance mirth, both for Joubert and for the great majority of his contemporaries, does not spring from a single or simple emotion. Rather, it involves ambivalence, and thus proves already to be of a nature difficult to seize.

Joubert, then, borrowed his basic tenets from Artistotle, who had said that the comic mask is ugly and distorted but does not imply pain. But he then cast this esthetic conception in physiological terms, explaining the convulsions of laughter by using anatomy. Shortly after Joubert's time attention would become focused on the psychological aspects of the comic. The scholars and philosophers that follow him, such as Thomas Hobbes, Immanuel Kant, Arthur Schopenhauer, Theodor Lipps,

Henri Bergson, Sigmund Freud, George Meridith, Max Eastman, and Arthur Koestler, were not to break from the mold of the psychological approach.

Because Joubert emphasizes the physiological approach, he offers an unusual view on the subject. Another point of interest is that he does not confine himself to laughter per se. Indeed, he manages to touch upon many other subjects of curiosity and importance as he traces the ramifications of his inquiry. By the time Joubert completes his discussion he has covered many of the medical doctrines enjoying credence at the time. He is not reluctant to express his opinion on, say, the shock that the infant suffers at birth, or the healing virtues of the *bezaard,* a type of marvelous stone that Arab physicians claimed to be the petrified tear of an oriental deer. In Joubert's time an expression such as "an ebullience of spirits" was less figurative than literal. Joubert not only instructs, he delights.

Joubert's thought is different from our own in many respects. His conception of the rules of evidence, for example, differs considerably from ours. Thus, he will not hesitate to use common expressions as proof for a point in his argument on the origins of the emotions: "Now one commonly says 'he laughs heartily,' and not 'brainily.' " This explains for Joubert the source from which the emotion proceeds. One can see from this that he views language as faithfully representing reality. But the leitmotif guiding Joubert's thought is the coincidence of opposites so prevalent in late medieval and Renaissance rhetoric. Consequently, it is not simple joy which furnishes the dynamics of hearty laughter, but joy mixed with sorrow. He also makes use of the common Renaissance topos of setting in antithetical opposition man and the animals: "For experience teaches us that there is no animal that weeps, none that blows his nose, that spits, or that picks wax from his ears." The reason man laughs, Joubert argues, and animals do not, is because "the pericardium is firmly attached to the diaphragm in man, and not in animals." Thus, a number of Joubert's premises may seem naïve, some of his arguments limp, but we read on, often in sheer astonishment that he actually believes what he writes with such conviction and grace.

And Joubert is a superb writer. His style is synthetic, as the practice then dictated. His treatise appeared at a time in the history of France when most of scientific literature was still written in Latin. The long, balanced, and cadenced sentences with numerous coordinators and relative connectors flow with the periodic pulse of classical prosody. However, though his syntax is classical, his diction is not. His vocabulary is a curious mixture of the scientific, philosophical, colloquial, and obscene. At times Joubert will sacrifice precision for style. For example, although a distinction could be made at the time between humors *(humeurs)* and spirits *(esprits),* Joubert uses the terms synonymously as stylistic variants. The same is true for the terms *emocions, passions,* and *affeccions.*

Joubert is at his best as a writer in the introductory portions of his treatise: the dedicatory letter, the prologue to the first book, the preface to the second, and the proem of the third. His letter to Marguerite de Valois furnishes an excellent instance of a Renaissance eulogy. He praises not only her royal person as a whole, but also the parts of her body: the hand, the eyes, the brain. Although the eulogy at first seems to be composed of constant ramblings, they actually serve a definite purpose: Joubert seeks to gain her approval by tying these ends together in the most flattering of eulogistic bows where each element fits intricately into the triumphant conclusion.

Joubert's sources and resources are considerable. His erudition is impressive, as evidenced by his wide-ranging references to classical, medieval, and Renaissance literature. He is at ease quoting Homer, Plato, Aristotle, Vergil, Horace, Ovid, Boccaccio, Ficino, and Du Bartas, and often several of them on the same page. His treatise is a good example of what some have called the extreme gaudiness of Renaissance prose. The words, often appearing to be the product of an unrestrained pen, can seem to swarm. Many sentences emerge as endless peregrinations. Nevertheless, Joubert is always in control of the syntax as he pursues the expression of his ideas through several relative pronouns and coordinating conjunctions.

My attempt in this translation has been to render clearly Joubert's thought while preserving as much as possible his sentence structure, images, and vocabulary. There seemed to be very few taboo words in sixteenth-century French, for all the words that the French Academy and later codes of decency sought to banish appear freely in comical as well as in medical texts. Clinical terms existed but they were not necessarily preferred over the more colloquial. Thus *cu, merde,* and *baiser* were judged suitable, and so I have used their earthy English counterparts.

There are two sets of notes. Superior letters refer the reader to the bottom of the page; superior numbers refer to notes placed at the end of the treatise. The lettered notes are Joubert's or Zangmaistre's, and appeared marginally in the 1579 edition. These are usually additions to or explanations of the argument. I have kept the alphabet used in Renaissance typography, which omits the letters *j, v,* and *w.* The numbered notes are my own, serving to clarify briefly names and concepts less familiar to today's reader.

The following selected bibliography directs the interested reader to further study both of comedy in general and of Joubert and his milieu.

Amoreux, P. J. *Notice historique et bibliographique sur la vie et les ouvrages de L. Joubert.* Montpellier: Tournel, 1814.

Dulieu, Louis. "Laurent Joubert, chancellier de Montpellier." *Bibliothèque d'Humanisme et Renaissance* 31 (1969): 139–67.

Eastman, Max. *The Sense of Humor.* New York: Charles Scribner's Sons, 1922.

Escarpit, Robert. *L'Humour.* Paris: P.U.F., 1967.

Grant, Mary. *The Ancient Rhetorical Theories of the Laughable: The Greek Rhetoricians and Cicero.* Madison: University of Wisconsin Press, 1924.

Greig, J. Y. T. *The Psychology of Laughter and Comedy.* London: Allen & Unwin, 1923.

Koestler, Arthur. *The Act of Creation.* New York: Macmillan, 1964.

Mauron, Charles. *Psychocritique du genre comique.* Paris: Corti, 1964.

Rocher, Gregory de. *Rabelais's Laughers and Joubert's "Traité du Ris."* University: University of Alabama Press, 1979.

———. "Le Rire au temps de la Renaissance: Le *Traité du Ris* de Laurent Joubert." *Revue Belge de Philologie et d'Histoire* 56 (1978): 629–40.

Screech, M. A., and Ruth Calder. "Some Renaissance Attitudes to Laughter." In *Humanism in France,* edited by A. H. T. Levi. London: Manchester University Press, 1970.

Sypher, Wylie. *Comedy.* Garden City: Doubleday, 1956.

TRAITE´ DV RIS,

CONTENANT SON ESSANCE, SES CAVSES, ET merveilheus effais, curieusement recerchés, raisonnés & observés,

Par M. LAVR. IOVBERT, Conselier & Medecin ordinaire du Roy, & du Roy de Nauarre, premier Docteur regeant, Chancelier & Iuge de l'vniversité an Medecine de Mompelier.

ITEM,

La cause morale du Ris de Democrite, expliquee & temognee par Hippocras.

PLVS,

Vn Dialogue sur la Cacographie Fransaise, avec des Annotacions sur l'orthographie de M. IOVBERT.

A PARIS,

Chez Nicolas CHESNEAV, ruë S. Iaques, au Chesne verd.

M. D. LXXIX.

AVEC PRIVILEGE DV ROY

Βίβλος Ἰουβέρτου φύσεως ἀπεμάξατο πάσης
Εἰκόν᾽· Ἰουβέρτου δ᾽ εἰκόνα πᾶσα φύσις.
Ἰωσήππου Σκαλανοῦ.

C'ét à dire, de mot à mot.

Ce livre de Ioubert,
Ha exprimé l'image
De toutte la Nature:

Et toutte la Nature,
Ha exprimé l'image
De ce mæme Ioubert.

TABLE OF CONTENTS OF THE *TREATISE ON LAUGHTER*

THE SECOND BOOK OF LAUGHTER, CONTAINING ITS DEFINITION, ITS TYPES, DIFFERENCES, AND DIVERSE EPITHETS 65

THE THIRD BOOK OF LAUGHTER CONTAINING THE PROBLEMS AND PRINCIPAL QUESTIONS ONE CAN ASK CONCERNING LAUGHTER 91

To the Most Excellent and Virtuous Princess Marguerite de France, Queen of Navarre, King's Daughter, only Sister and Spouse

FROM LAURENT JOUBERT, HER MOST HUMBLE AND MOST AFFECTIONATE SERVANT HEALTH AND ALL PROSPERITY

Madame,[1] I have at times discoursed on the dignity of the organs of the human body, of all the most perfected, and leaving aside the heart (commonly considered the prince of our members) I used to put into the contest the brain and the hand. I would say for the brain that it deserved first prize because it is in the highest place and especially because it gives to the rest of the body movement and feeling, by which we differ from the plants, and a rational sense, which puts us far ahead of the animals.

For the hand I used to allege that only man is gifted with it, except for the monkey, who imitates it, but this is not a perfect hand. As for the brain, it is common to all the animals unless they are too imperfect and very small, although something is given them that corresponds to it. The difference could be that man has a brain larger than that of any other animal his size; but the greater and the smaller do not make for a difference in kind. It is still a brain of like substance, consistency, form, aspect, color, and division of its parts, and is just the same in an ox, a horse, ass, pig, sheep, dog, etc., as in man, except for its temper, which is the principal thing. But hands, animals have none. For the hand was as if owed to the wisest animal in order for him to explain, express, and effect the conceptions, designs, and enterprises of his soul. And so we say with Aristotle that the hand is the instrument which precedes all instruments.

I would then make the brain reply that the hand is but its servant, for it is the brain that moves it and makes it undertake what it dictates on the basis of its own invention or learning. Art is more worthy than the instrument: just as music is more excellent than a harp, painting than a brush, and sculpture than a chisel. Now reason, which resides in the brain, is like the art of all arts inasmuch as it invented them all. Wherefore the brain will be more excellent than the hand, which is but the instrument of the arts. Anaxagoras was gravely mistaken when he said that man is the most wise because he has hands.[a] For it is not because of his hands that he is wisest but, on the contrary, he got his hands because this was fitting for the wisest animal.

Yes, but it is the hand that masters and accommodates all animals to the service of man, even the mightiest and the fiercest, that renders the soil fertile and harvests its fruits, and that is the instrument of all trades, useful in the necessities, commodities, or recreation of man. The hand makes geometrical and astronomical instruments, with which one measures the far-off heavens and lands. It paints, engraves, writes, and makes understood near and far what would otherwise be unknown. It makes us speak with the dead who preceded us by several thousand years, and to those who will follow afterwards until the end of the world, by means of books. The hand touches everything; everything passes through the hand, known and unknown.

Still, one must always come back to this point: the brain commands and the hand obeys. So the brain must be considered the more excellent part even though it is very common and more similar in man and in animals than is the hand. Joined to this is the fact that the hand is not of a complex construction compared to the brain, which represents a marvelous machine in the diversity of its parts and is of a most admirable handiwork. Add to that (if you please) that man cannot live without the brain, and can well live without hands. Likewise, the illness of the brain harms the entire body, but that of the hand is of little consequence. And so the brain wins the contest.

But it does not for a long time remain the peaceful possessor of primacy among the parts. For its neighbor the face suddenly stands in its way and forms opposition to it. The face has good reasons for itself, and I shall touch upon a few of them. First, no animal but man has a face, properly speaking; and he has the most perfect face there could be, namely, a round one.[2] Next, only man carries it high, looking towards the sky as if into his mirror, for he sees and recognizes himself in it, which is not the case with animals.[3]

Moreover, the face of man is most excellent in that it is not covered with hair, scales, or feathers, as it is improperly said of the face of an animal.[4] And for this reason the face of man is appropriate for all its changes, like a chameleon, to make manifest and put into evidence the passions and internal movements, a condition truly human and praiseworthy. For man, being a social and civil animal, ought not to have his affections so hidden that one might not discover them, otherwise his conversation would be feared as being too clever, dissimulated, fraudulent, traitorous, and of evil properties. But since he is open-faced, and raised up, it is not possible for him to conceal totally what he has in his heart, clever, feigning, cunning, shrewd, and crafty as he may be. It is in the face that all the affections imprint some mark and sign of their movement, being like the face of a clock on which the hours are marked and indicated by its hands, the gears and movements being hidden within. And who is (I ask you) the Proteus who can dissimulate so well that in no way is there shown in his face the joy, the sorrow, the hope, the defiance, the love, the hatred, the envy, the malice, the compassion, the jealousy, the fear, the

a. Galen, *On the Usage of the Parts,* Book 1.

shame, the anger, the contempt, the disdain, etc., when his heart is greatly moved or his brain hammered by it? It is impossible that the affections, when vehement, not be revealed by some change imprinted in the face. For this reason this part is to be more esteemed and cherished than any other, just as one loves and holds high in esteem an open person that is naïve, without falseness and dissimulation.

And where lies the beauty which makes us fall so humanly in love and be so taken with each other that because of it we desire the union of the Platonic Androgyne?[5] In this man differs singularly from the other animals which, without any discretion or choice over beauty or ugliness, become infatuated with the first mate they encounter, as soon as they are stimulated by nature and excited to copulation. But man, a rational being who must control and regiment all his actions with proper measure and good order, and with judgment, was in need of diverse subjects upon which he might employ his choice and his discretion. To these correspond the different types of beauty, imprinted in the face principally, which make men and women reciprocally fall in love in such a way that each thinks that he or she has met the most beautiful. This is a very great feat, worked by an admirable craftsman who has placed in this part some secret of contenting something or other in everybody: a secret incomparably more marvelous than that of those who paint a picture with eyes looking everywhere, as if they were focused only on one of those who are looking at it, and follow him constantly. Not thus is one in love with the brain, the hand, or any other part of the body.

Also, how many different types are there among faces, split up into a great number of different kinds? Yet in all of them are seen particular beauties that latch onto (in a manner of speaking) subtly, steal away, and ravish, the heart of those who are tenderly disposed to love: a large, wide, and square forehead that is smooth, clear, and serene; eyebrows neatly bowed and thin, as if done with a small stroke of the brush; eyes wide open, gay and shining; nose thinly formed; a small mouth with coralline lips; a short and slightly cleft chin; high cheeks with pleasant dimples in the middle; round and delicately rolled ears; and all this accompanied by a lively, white and vermilion complexion. Does this not have greater power to move a heart and attach it to this object than does a lodestone to ravish unto itself the iron around it through a miraculous attraction?[6]

In this nobel part lies the principal difference between beautiful and ugly persons, for with the face covered the rest is practically the same, even though Paris wanted to see the three goddesses completely naked in order to appreciate better their beauty.[7] This is also why one usually keeps the face uncovered, as is most reasonable, unless one does not want to be recognized. For by the hand (which also is often uncovered) or by the other parts, one is not recognized. Is it not a masterpiece of the Creator to have made our faces infinitely different one from another? The brain, the heart, the lungs, the liver, the stomach and the other internal parts, the feet, the hands, the shoulders, the chest, the nipples, etc., can be similar in different persons, so much so that one could not find any difference; but of faces where will two be found that are alike in every respect? And if two such faces are found, is it not considered a most astounding thing? In the animals of the earth, of the water, of the air (there is none of the fire),[8] what corresponds to the face is the same in each species, or very nearly. Wherefore I rightly say that it is a masterpiece of the Creator to have infinitely diversified the face of man in order to show the excellence of this creature, model of the entire creation.[9]

Also, art, which imitates nature, does not concern itself with the other parts when it wishes to represent or scale down a person. One is content to paint or sculpt the face as the total or principal mark of this individual. For there is where you read who it is, not any less than if he were written. This is not, however, the origin of the common expression "One reads the man in his face,"[b] for it is necessary to understand this correctly as meaning the affections and the manners. As for the affections, we have shown that they are very noticeable in the face. This is why Saint Jerome very aptly said that the face is the mirror of one's thoughts, for very often without one's saying a word the eyes reveal the secret and confess what is hidden. With respect to manners, one must not scorn or reject what is said about them by the physiognomists, who stop at the traits of the face more than at any other member. And that these are not observations wholly empty and frivolous (as can be those taken from the hand in chiromancy), the authority of the great Aristotle, who wished to write about it, suffices to verify them. In this the hand gives way immediately to the face.

It was very reasonable, then, for the face to be uncovered and raised up, as much because of its excellence (just as one willingly exhibits what one has that is most beautiful) as in order to respond better to the human condition: sociable, civil, not fierce or fraudulent, so that one might recognize people's nature, manners, and emotions. The other parts ought to be covered and most of them so well hidden that one is most ashamed to expose them or even talk about them, unless for a very good reason and out of necessity. Animals have nothing to hide since they have no shame, or to speak more correctly, they already have everything covered (for their fur, scales, or feathers cover everything) and do not even have the part corresponding to the face uncovered. This is just as it is in wild men, who are hairy in the face, and rightly so, for since they are not sociable animals they do not have to show through changes in the face their internal affections. The hair hinders this, covering all the skin, so that no change in color or of the traits can be seen in answer to their joy, sadness, anger, malice, rage, or other passion.

Also, the emotions are not noticed in people who have very deep complexions because of a rough, rustic, and savage disposition. We mean here by *complexion* the thin skin (called epidermis in Greek and cuticle in Latin, otherwise given the term *flower* or *efflorescence* of the skin, normally more delicate in the face than elsewhere) that receives and projects the colors of the humors underneath, as when it is fresh, sharp, and clear. For the humors tint it easily with their colors: red, blue or pallid, dull, citrine, leaden, blackish, changing constantly like the crest of an Indian rooster. Thick and rough skin, on the contrary (called a dull complexion), or when dirty and filthy, or black and charred, like that of the Moors, does not project the

b. *In facie legitur homo.*

color of the diverse humors nor does it change in any way with the diverse passions and affections, not any more than if it were covered with scales, feather, or hair. This is why no changes are witnessed in such people as far as the face is concerned, not any more than in wild animals.

But those who have a very clear and transparent complexion because their skin is very thin (as it usually is in fat people) are very *changing,* that is, their complexion often changes for but a slight reason; wherefore women are usually considered to be more beautiful. It is also in them that we observe and hold in higher esteem than in men a delicate complexion, as is fitting. For man, born to work in the city and in the fields, to the exercise of peace and war and every tedious trade, is subject to the sun, the evening chill, the wind and the rain, on the sea, on land, and in all sorts of distress. Woman is born into tranquility, and in the shade, under the protection of her house, which she is to carry as does the snail or the turtle. And it is most fitting for her to be careful about her natural beauty in order to give pleasure respectably to her husband who, finding recreation in her company and acquaintance, diminishes and erases with it the injuries received in his toils and labors, gently relaxing the tension of his mind. This is why God created woman, the companion of man, prettier, lovelier, placing in her the careful desire to preserve her beauty so as to be more desirable with it.

Now her beauty consists mainly in having her face very much uncovered, revealing all its parts to our eyes. Man, when he reaches the age of virility, loses the freshness of his cheeks, his mouth, his chin and of his throat on down to his chest because of the hair that covers them. In woman these parts continue being agreeably smooth and glabrous, that is, without hair, except in some with rough and dark complexions, called *mannish,*[c] who are found to be so strange when their beard has grown out a little that there is a vulgar expression: "Salute a bearded woman from afar with three stones in your hand." If, therefore, man alone among all the animals has his face clearly uncovered, and because of it is more beautiful, frank, and sociable, then woman, who has it still more uncovered, is to be judged more beautiful, frank, and natural in showing and indicating by it her diverse affections, and consequently more sociable, approachable, companionable, and gracious, less feigning, simulated and secretive, less deceiving, crafty, malicious, traitorous, and wicked. These are qualities and conditions that are most human, virtuous, and amiable, proceeding from a sincerity, a simplicity, an easiness, gentleness, and delicate tenderness.

There, Madame, are some of the great dignities and preeminences in favor of the face, which make it deserve first place among all the parts of the human body, if it does not displease the brain and the hand. Shall I add to this that not only the above-mentioned passions or affections which are otherwise called perturbations of the soul, and sicknesses of the mind, but also (a more difficult thing) the greatest sicknesses of the body are read in the face? Such is elephantiasis, commonly called leprosy, which has its most definite symptoms (we call them unequivocal) in the

c. In Latin, *virago.*

face. Similarly, scarlet, colic, and hectic fevers, along with other miserable destroyers of the body give their poor victims a Hippocratic face. Doctors so call the face described by Hippocrates of him who because of the vehemence or length of some illness has a pointed nose, sunken eyes, prominent temples, cold, withdrawn and slightly drooping ears, the skin of the forehead stretched and dry, the color of the whole face black, dull, pallid or leaden.[d]

But more than all of these parts, the eyes give a more certain indication of the vivacity or of the languor in our strength. Because of this the common man even has hope that a sick person will recover as long as he has good eyes, that is, clear and lively. And to come back to the subject of grace, beauty, and gentleness, which are in these organs beyond and above the extent to which they are in all the others of the face, what is there in the world that is more gracious and pleasant to see than beautiful eyes, laughing, sparkling, and casting more fire (beyond comparison) than the finest diamond? Is there a diamond of a more beautiful clarity than that of eyes full of shimmering spirits darting and lancing out from all sides? Is there an emerald or a turquoise more beautiful to behold than an eye, green or blue, when it is joyous and gay? All the precious stones of the orient will lose their luster compared to beautiful eyes unless a sordid and bizarre mind does the judging. And when such eyes serve a soul that makes them move now joyously, then pitifully, shamefully, modestly, or lasciviously in order to express its internal affections, then there is something that will ravish a man even more, and constrain him to the will of this soul.

And what about laughter? It is about time we said something about it. Where is its principal throne? Is it not in the face, and especially in the eyes which it moves so freely that nothing else surpasses it? Is it not there that it shows itself and appears most favorably, rendering these parts more than charming? Certainly there is nothing that gives more pleasure and recreation than a laughing face, with its wide, shining, clear, and serene forehead, eyes shining, resplendent from any vantage point, and casting fire as do diamonds; cheeks vermilion and incarnate, mouth flush with the face, lips handsomely drawn back (from which are formed the small dimples called *gelasins,* in the very middle of the cheeks), chin drawn in, widened, and a bit recessed. All this is in the smallest laugh and in the smile favoring an encounter of much grace, amidst salutations, caresses, and greetings.

And the kiss, which is the most explicit symbol of love, the most charming of the decent fruits of love, and by which is accomplished a sort of conjoining of souls—is it not of the face? One kisses the hand, the knee, the foot out of honor and respect, symbolizing submission and servitude, but among equals, comrades and friends, people have always kissed the forehead, the eyes, and the mouth, all parts of the face. It is finished, then. The face has won every contest and is awarded the primacy of the parts of the body. There is no more debating to be done.

But if the other parts call out for it, I shall submit the matter to you, Madame, who have a sense of judgment no less solid than that of the wise Solomon, and under

d. *Prognostics,* Book 1, Section 9.

which I shall say, only to resolve my argument and bring it to the end and conclusions to which I was tending throughout this disquisition, that there is no part in our body as excellent and admirable as the face, and that laughter (effect of the most human passion there is) is wonderfully shown on it, as on the indicator and dial of all the affections. For this reason the face is most illustrated and miraculously well adorned. And so it is very reasonable that the act proper to man in the fourth mode (as the dialecticians say) which makes him differ from all the other animals, be housed in the part which is proper to man, properly speaking.

Now, since the face is ordinarily more beautiful in woman than in man (for as the divine poet and philosopher Du Bartas sings:

> she has a more laughing eye,
> A more delicate complexion, a more attractive forehead,
> A chin free of hair, a less harsh speech),

and since her constitution is more delicate, softer, and more passionate, her manners gentler, more benign and amiable, her condition gayer, more joyous and sweet, laughter in her is also more proper, more fitting, and more gracious, expressing her great gentleness and humanity.

This could somewhat draw me to dedicate this work to the female sex out of simple convenience, but I have more reason to consecrate it to you particularly, Madame, because this subject exceeds the normal capacity of women and (I dare say) of men of only mediocre knowledge. The subject of laughter is so vast and deep that few philosophers have attempted it, and none has won the prize of treating it properly. I have gone a little further, yet I am not boasting to have satisfied even myself, so I am much less able to content others who are more careful. I am hard put but to explain the causes of the great change that laughter brings about in the face. And so I am also finally forced to turn over this study to some mind of an excellent perfection, residing in a body of such constitution and temperament that the divine mind will not be in any way impeded in it.[10] It is necessary to have in this matter an angelic, superhuman, studious, inventive mind with exquisite judgment and marvelous memory, which will be able to delicately burnish, polish, and finish what I have roughed out. And to whom could I better hand over this beautiful study than to Your Majesty, of a sublime and heroic nature, to whom I present it in most humble reverence, as if to the person in the world who is the most perfect and accomplished in the talents necessary to delve into and to resolve each and every great difficulty? The assiduous study of philosophy and mathematical sciences (your great recreation) has so enlightened your soul, chasing out the usual darknesses of error and ignorance, that the most obscure and hidden things are by you easily discovered and drawn out of the deep well of truth.

This subject seems light, but it is very grave and worthy of being treated better than by my dull mind in order to penetrate deeper into its mysteries. To do this, a more purified, more subtle, and sharper mind than mine, both by nature and by discipline—and above all a person of great authority—is necessary in order to convince others of his conclusions, such as Your Majesty.

And when I imagine and contemplate the French nation, comprehending women as well as men, and especially those who have in our time a reputation of great knowledge, wisdom, and judgment, even among princes and princesses, lords and ladies, who are today of a large number in this kingdom (thanks, Madame, to your grandfather, Francis the Great, justly called the father of the arts and sciences, who has chased ignorance far from letters, far from his house), it seems to me that you are the face of it all, the most delightful part of the entire body, as I have deduced. Your brother the king[11] (my sovereign lord and good master, most benign, clement, humane, magnificent and liberal who ever was) is the head of this figurative body. Your mother the queen[12] is the brain who has guided her children kings with their sceptres and crowns with such prudence, vigilance, diligence, dexterity, fidelity, and magnanimity that Her Majesty has earned perpetual praise, recommending to all the provinces of the earth the happy success of her most heroic enterprises in the most calamitous times that ever troubled this kingdom. Monsieur[13] (your brother) is the hand to whom the king gives all power and management.

To the face laughter is owed the most evident, the most certain, and most fitting mark of humanity. It is therefore to Your Majesty (o excellent face of the French nation, the most admirable part of the body) that this little commentary on laughter must be presented, giving homage to it because of what it possesses. Madame, you have the reputation of being among the most beautiful princesses of Christianity, but I have only to make a mention here of the virtues that correspond to the divine traits of your face, on which, if I dared, I would compose a glorious piece according to the way I see it. But I fear being taxed for superfluity in a thing which requires neither proof nor witnesses. For the serenity and clemency of Your Royal Majesty, its most humble benignity, the splendor and vivacity of your mind, illuminating this kingdom, and shining to the four corners of the earth, its grace and most heroic generosity, all make celebrated the name of the third MARGUERITE DE FRANCE (pearls of inestimable value)[14] all the way to the Antipodes.[15] The eloquence, the sweetness, the silver tongue, accompanied by a profound wisdom and sound judgment, evident in her grave remarks, and by admirable prudence (the ornament of good common sense), the roundness of her conscience, proceeding from zeal, piety, and a most Christian devotion, producing infinite works of charity, the purity, sincerity, and innocence of life, the candor and natural shame, all make your soul perfectly beautiful. I remain silent about the other virtues, each and every one of which courts you, is among your affairs, your favorites, your guards.

Oh most happy King of Navarre, to have met his other half.[16] Happy his kingdom and country, which will be governed and maintained from now on by these two souls, so well conjoined and united that they seem but one in that there is but one will and one refusal, with reciprocal affection in the mutual duty of sacred marriage. Oh most happy tie (as it is sung by the noble Du Bartas):

> Oh chaste love, who fuse with your ardor
> Two souls into one soul, and two hearts into one heart.[17]

May God fill you with his grace and holy blessing, giving you the desired beautiful lineage and succession,

> Being reborn in your sons, who have the means
> To make eternal here below the blood of the Navarres.[18]

Madame, I shall conclude after apologizing for the roughness of the language you will find in this *Treatise on Laughter.* Its style is graceless and unrefined, and it may seem a strange and improper thing to present it to Your Majesty. Please realize, then, that this is the first work I ever wrote in my life, and doing it I imitated Zoroaster who, coming into the world began with laughter in being born, as I did in writing. Now I wrote it in Latin while spending time at Montbrison.[19] Monsieur Louys Papon (the younger son of the great Papon, light of our time in jurisprudence) translated the first book furtively and had it printed more than twenty years ago. The other two remained forgotten among my commentaries until Monsieur Ian Paul Zangmaistre (a young German from a noble house in Augsburg, and my adopted student), finding them in my library, borrowed them secretly in order to practice his translating. When he since brought them back to me I praised him for his enterprise, which has brought me to recognize their worth and no longer to keep them hidden. I found his translation faithful and in conformity with my meaning, but a little rough and uneven with respect to the language, which I nevertheless did not want to change so as to give him more courage and confidence upon seeing these books published in his own translation. I also remembered what Horace said:

> The thing does not wish to be ornate;
> It is enough that it is taught.[e]

This is why I did not fear presenting it to Your Majesty, Madame, who understand these things well, being the princess who seemed to me the most apt to esteem and value properly this beautiful subject, just as to you also is due the singular sign of all humanity. I have always wanted to have a way of humbly serving it, and honoring it with some of my work that might be acceptable to it. If I have succeeded with this one, I praise God, begging him always more devoutly that He grant me the grace to respond in measure to the greatness of my affection.

Given in Paris this first day of the year 1579, according to astronomy, which opens it with the entry of the sun into its Arietine house.[20]

e. *Ornari res ipsa negat, contenta doceri.*

The First Book of Laughter,

CONTAINING ITS CAUSES & ALL ITS ACCIDENTS

PROLOGUE

Hesiod,[a] author of the *Fabled Findings*, and a heaven-sent philosopher,[1] wishing to show that bewonderment over the workings of nature engenders curiosity and, ultimately, knowledge of their causes, ingeniously imagined[b] Iris[c] to be the daughter of Thaumas in order to demonstrate that whosoever is not struck by a marvelling and by an intense desire to know will never delve deeply into things nor, consequently, ever discover anything. Why is this? Simply because it is from fretting and from frequent meditation, through industrious, continued, and extreme labor that we come to understand clearly.

For ignorance in the soul is natural and, in spite of what Plato says,[d] is only chased out by doctrine gaining entry through the exterior senses into the soul which, so they say, is rendered more or less docile by the substance and complexion of the body, of which it is forced to make use in all of its undertakings. Whence it is that those who are most conditioned to make their souls all-wise have a natural desire to know the essence of things, moved by a praiseworthy curiosity, by doubts that arise and prick the mind. Those who are less refined, and for whom the body is a hindrance, fail to penetrate deeply into things; they stop at the surface, their sense[e] unable to go beyond. Then there are others who passionately desire to know, but lacking initiation in philosophy, are unable to succeed. For philosophy is the sole method of solving every difficulty; it is a divine gift bestowed upon man, this marvelous working of the soul (as Plato used to say) surpassing all functions of the flesh.

Thus, congenital ignorance is the common lot, and most worthy are those who are incessantly spurred by doubt and curiosity, ever desirous of knowing, and thrice happy are those who have been blessed with the ability to philosophize well, and to contemplate. The vain and presumptuous, as if leprous, remain insensitive to their imperfections. Impudent and quick to decide, they are untroubled by doubt, which

a. Hesiod wrote on the race of the Gods, interpreting through fables his Theology.

b. Hesiod, in verse 265 of the *Theogony*.

c. Iris signifies contemplation, and Thaumas wonder.

d. Plato said that our souls were by nature knowledgeable, and that our knowledge was nothing more than a remembering.

e. The interior sense must penetrate into that which the exterior presents to it.

would provoke thinking according to the laws of reason. This is why their sickness is considered incurable,[f] troubled as it is by such contrariness, and refusing any remedy. The sound and beautiful minds, on the other hand, fearful, docile, and already well formed, cease not to deepen and to will to penetrate into the most hidden secrets of nature, as much for their own enjoyment as for having something over which they might better praise God,[g] thus showing his grandeur through these marvelous effects which inspire contemplation.

It is perfectly true that there are things so difficult and hidden that we confess openly to be unknown by man,[h] and that he cannot discover their cause, be it ever so diligently and methodically sought, such as the thunderbolt and those things which miraculously issue from it. So it is with all that we attribute ordinarily to the property of essence and unfathomable nature, since these are the principal actions of their forms, proper unto each. The cause of these virtues, faculties, powers, or efficacy, are called temper and complexion. These latter, the result of a certain proportion and diverse mixture of the four elements in such a particular manner that they are not found[i] in any other, cannot be fully grasped by our understanding. Thus it is said to be impossible to give a more evident cause of their effects than their own natural property. For this property springs from the quality of the simple and basic[k] elements, and due to the weakness of our minds we are unable to understand just the exact proportion that there is of each of the four elements as they join together to compose a given thing. This is why we marvel to see a magnet or lodestone drawing iron to itself, as amber would a wisp, or a torpedo[l] or tramble numbing a fisherman's hand, even without his touching it. A remora, a very small fish, not only slows down (as the name signifies) a ship pushed by high winds and hardy oarsmen, but detains it and stops it short. A lamprey does likewise, if we believe Aristotle, along with Rondelet's[3] experience in the matter.[m]

But let us turn our attention from these effects which the ignorant can doubt to more familiar ones of which the condition is no less admirable and strange. Why do the rending of a sheet, the smashing of stones, the stroking backwards of the beard of an awn make our teeth tingle?[n] Why is it that if somebody happens to yawn those seeing him are scarcely able to keep from doing likewise? How is it that fruit puts our teeth on edge, and that purslane[4] is a remedy for it? Is there anything more awesome than iron being drawn by a magnet, or choleric humor[o] by scammony,[5] or

f. Arrogance causes them to be unaware of their ignorance, and to not desire to learn.

g. The end of all contemplation must be God.

h. Causes unknown to man.

i. The Greeks call this idiosyncrasy, which Galen confesses to be unknown to man.

k. These are the four elements.

l. The numbing power of the torpedo travels all the way to the fisherman's hand in the line.[2]

m. See his work *Concerning Fish,* Book 13, chapter 2.

n. Such is not the case with everybody, but with some, who shiver upon seeing or hearing this.

o. The author has since changed his mind, affirming now in these paradoxes that medicines drive out humors.

food by each part of our body? All these effects inspire wonder, and have caused much confusion among the most subtle of our philosopher-physicians who are, in the last analysis, bound to agree upon the common obstacle of properties.[p] Thus we are able to understand that Nature wanted to hide some things, in order to have herself more highly esteemed, in which our sluggish minds, dulled by the body, are not able to anchor.

This is why it is most praiseworthy to want to investigate[q] these things, and to leave nothing unsounded, following the path of the ancients, using their methods and adding to them our new variations.[r] But inasmuch as we prize those who by their strong curiosity have advanced us considerably and have in their study sifted diligently the occurrences of such great marvels, I am astonished that not one of these noble authors who have gone before us has undertaken the search for the causes which move us to laugh, considering that it is one of the most astounding actions[s] of man, if one examines it closely. Indeed, who would not be amazed upon seeing in an instant the entire body thrown into motion and shaking with an indescribable stir for the pleasure[t] of the soul (so it would appear), were we not already so used to it–so much so that one scarcely takes notice?

It must therefore be something phenomenal,[u] since with violent force it is able to generate such a vehement and sudden commotion. Quintilian[6] said this of it: "Laughter has an extremely great power which cannot be resisted. Most often it slips out of us and is not to be contained. It not only forces both the face to confess and the voice to declare our feelings, but its violence shakes and sets the whole body in motion, oftentimes diverting and overturning the importance of our concerns, dissipating hatred, and mitigating anger. It restores the mind overworked by cares, turning it away from dismal thoughts, satiating and renewing it after a great and tormenting burden, as it chases out all melancholy. Sick people have been cured by this sole remedy." These are marvelous effects, and all brought about by an impulse so proper to man that the definition of him necessarily includes it.[x]

I admit that the primary occasion[y] of these effects is empty and light, all the more so because tumblers and playful wits have no other purpose than to make us laugh. But we find the act most enjoyable and desire it most deeply on account of the pleasure it brings. For we are so naturally drawn to delight[z] that all our designs have it as object, as a sovereign good. This is why, as we know, a thousand different

p. In scholastic medicine, this is called the asses' bridge.

q. The philosopher has rightly said that the knowable is far greater than the known.

r. We are as children on the shoulders of a giant, able to see what he can, and a little more.

s. It indeed had to be so, in order to be fitting for the most astounding of animals.

t. The quality of this pleasure will be described in chapter XIV.

u. The magnitude of the effect corresponds to the magnitude of the cause.

x. The definition of man (according to some) is a laughing, reasoning, and mortal man.

y. The primary occasion is the laughable object; the second is intrinsic, as will be declared hereafter.

z. Delight is the privation of trouble or sadness, which we try to avoid by every possible way.

pastimes are sought and taken up by everybody, whence the invention of games, public and private, triumphs, banquets, farces, comedies, morisques, masquerades, dances, music, and every other manner of making merry.

In addition, the pleasant and facetious man shows that he has a clever mind, with great advantages in civility and ease in speaking. This is why Lycurgus, otherwise most severe in his laws, not only permitted the Lacedemonians the use of upright games, but commanded them specifically to partake in them, and raised a statue to the god Gelot,[aa] considering it necessary to recreate moderately and to put to rest the ardent alertness of the mind. Likewise Cleomenes, who never allowed in his republic any tumblers, buffoons, comedians, or musicians, found it good nevertheless that the citizens have a good time among themselves, with lampoons, jeering, and mockery, all of which sharpen the mind. And after all, Democritus, so perfected in wisdom (as is witnessed by Hippocrates) that he alone was able to make all the men of the world wise and prudent, laughed as a rule. And if he is thought to be mad because he put out his eyes, I answer that he did it in order better to give himself to contemplation, as Aulus Gellius said, or so as not to see women and be turned away by carnal concupiscence, as Tertullian has written. And perhaps he was of the opinion that by this he would become more fat,[bb] which is most helpful in engendering laughter. Whatever the cause, he lived 109 years, being dissatisfied with nothing. Heraclitus the weeper, on the contrary, always sad and upset, frequented the desert, lived on herbs and other foods that only sharpen the appetite, so that finally weakened and undone, he died hectic in the hide of an ox, in which state he was devoured by wolves, and found in the fields not recognizable as a man.

Since, therefore, laughter is the principal sign of this frisky pleasure that we like so much, which counteracts old age,[cc] is common to all, and proper to man, I am most astonished that the diligent ancients, scrutinizers of causes, have omitted the investigation of its origin, working a great deal more to find the reasons behind things which touch us less and are in far less regard. Why do we not stop to consider the familiar, common miracles that we carry about, and are able to examine closely and at leisure? Why have they not tried to understand the motive and the cause producing laughter, as much a secret as anything else? Perhaps it is because it cannot be understood, being too closely joined to its form and (as the philosophers say) coming directly from it. For this reason they are all in agreement, and have resolved that no other cause can be sifted out,[dd] esteeming almost frivolous such a search, seeing that the source is hidden under the very species, which is why it deserves the name of an occult property. The author of the *Book of Apparent and Secret Movements* (which is falsely attributed to Galen) proclaims that he knows nothing about it, when he says: "I do not understand how laughter begins its motion when the armpits

aa. Gelot in Greek signifies laughter, or a laugher. Apuleius at the end of the second book of his *Golden Ass* relates that the Thessalonians used to adore the god Laughter.

bb. Thus, to fatten capons better, their eyes are put out or covered.

cc. It is said commonly that to laugh and to be joyful stops one from getting old.

dd. That is to say, it is an occult property.

are tickled, or when something laughable is heard or seen. I do not know how it moves and shakes the whole body with a violence such that it is impossible to keep from it, despite whatever means one might employ to stop." Alexander of Aphrodisias[7] agrees with this, writing in the prologue to his *Problems,* that it is an inexplicable question, why one laughs from being tickled under the arms, on the sides, the bottom of the feet, etc. Cicero (who is no less prized for his philosophy than for knowing how to argue eloquently) in the second book of the *Orator* is of the same opinion, saying: "What is there about laughter, what moves it, where is it, and what is its nature that it flows so promptly that even if we want, we cannot restrain it? Just how it seizes the sides, the mouth, the veins, the face and the eyes, Democritus[ee] will inform us, for that is in no way connected to our purpose, and if it were, I should not be ashamed to be ignorant of it, seeing that those who might promise to do so would never be able to explain it." Moses the Jew,[8] a physician, in the penultimate and last chapter of his book, basing himself upon the authority of Galen, believes that it is impossible to uncover the cause of laughter springing from the matter of trivial things, or from any other, and even less that which is brought about by tickling the armpits and the bottom of the feet. By such testimony it is evident how difficult this undertaking seemed for the ancients, even impossible to bring to an end, such that if we had a little less courage, we should not dare to take upon ourselves further inquiry into it.

But why should we not be able to find the causes of these effects which have their source and foundation within our very selves? Is it any more difficult than to understand by unaided reason the essence of our soul? Not as I see it, and still its faculties, actions, and works demonstrate to us its nature when we are led, as if from hand to hand, to the explanation of these secret and innermost mysteries,[ff] perceived by none of the senses. And so I think that the condition, force, and emotion of laughter can be understood, since it is intrinsic to us, manifesting itself on the outside. For there is no thing within us which, after a careful and well-founded inquiry, does not become evident. Being confident about this, I have constantly cultivated the desire[gg] to form an argument of such excellence, hoping that if I am not able to draw great honor because of it, at least I shall be pardoned by those who know how difficult it is, so much so that the ancients have not dared to touch it. As for those of our own age, Jules-César Scaliger[9] writing against the subtleties of Girolamo Cardano,[10] and Girolamo Fracastoro[11] in his book *On Natural Concord and Discord,* both of whom are great philosophers and excellent physicians, working to other ends, spoke about it. François Valeriola,[12] a very learned, elegant, and humane personage who has served medicine well, treats this subject at greater length in one of his *Narrations.*[hh] But again, he does not advance far enough into the matter,

ee. Because he made a profession of laughing.

ff. From visible things and other sensible ones, we come to know invisible and secret ones.

gg. It is said in a common proverb that in great things it suffices to have had the will, or to have strived.

hh. *Narrations,* Book 2, 4.

satisfactorily explaining all the effects and the sudden convulsions which, with no small wonder, brought about in me long ago the desire to search out in every detail and to go further than have those named above. I had planned to do this work before having seen their writings, and in putting my hand to it since that time, I have borrowed nothing from them,[ii] neither method nor argument, in order to arrive at it by myself (if I am able), all the while trying to do better. I shall not boast of anything other than keeping in this quest to a path so straight, so sure, and so simple, that I shall not be lost, with God's help, certain to find all that I ask.[kk] For from the start I shall inquire into the subject matter: At what do we laugh? Then from this I shall know which parts of the body are first to receive its effect. Knowing then where laughable matter abuts, and where the emotion lies (the internal cause of all its accidents), I shall easily be able to enlarge, through the particular changes which are manifested outwardly, in order to know the occasion of it. And then I shall be at the end of my undertaking, obtaining the sought end that one contemplates at every beginning.

CHAPTER I
WHAT IS THE MATTER OF LAUGHTER

Every well-ordered study begins with those things that are the most known,[a] and from there as by degrees, from the lowest to the highest, conducts us to the understanding of the most intricate and difficult. The most known things (those which each man understands and accords) are accepted by the populace, and such that they can never be denied. What aids much in proving something is the putting forth of propositions so evident[b] that they cannot be refuted, and from these to deduce as much as possible. So it is with what we are attempting: to show from general acceptance what is the matter of laughter.

With respect to this, matter is commonly considered to be the object itself, and that which brings about such an effect; as when one wishes to say that there is no occasion for laughter, one says in common parlance: that is no matter for laughter. Now, this object, subject, occasion, or matter of laughter is related to two senses, namely sight and hearing, for all that is laughable is found in actions or in words, and is something ugly or improper, yet unworthy of pity or compassion.[13] This is a bit obscure,[c] but by means of induction and examples, we shall make it simple, by making this genus known particularly, through its species.

ii. Very often reading stifles a good imagination. Other times it amuses excessively, and upsets a better progression of thought.

kk. The means for finding the causes of laughter and of all its accidents.

---

a. All knowledge (says the philosopher) is made up of what is already known.

b. One must always base oneself upon that which is freely accepted, and on which there is agreement.

c. This is what must be shown and clarified first, since it is not granted at first sight.

CHAPTER II
CONCERNING LAUGHABLE ACTIONS

What we see that is ugly, deformed, improper, indecent, unfitting, and indecorous excites laughter in us, provided we are not moved to compassion. Example: if perchance one uncovers the shameful parts which by nature or public decency we are accustomed to keeping hidden, since this is ugly yet unworthy of pity, it moves the onlookers to laughter. For nothing leads us to commiseration but that which comprises some sort of danger, which opens the way to compassion. If the chest, the arms, or the feet are uncovered, there would be nothing to laugh at, because it is not considered ugly or indecent to expose these parts of the body to view. Also, laughter will not come over us if an ugly thing is followed by commiseration, as when a man's virile member is wished removed, either against his will or with his consent, in order to avoid a greater evil; it is not possible that we laugh, due to the unhappiness that follows such an act, over which pity surprises and arrests us in order to contemplate, stunned with displeasure, such an operation.

It is equally unfitting to show one's arse, and when there is no harm forcing us to sympathize, we are unable to contain our laughter. But if another suddenly puts a red-hot iron to him, laughter gives way to compassion unless the harm done seems light,[a] and small, for that reinforces the laughter, seeing that he is properly punished for his foolishness and unpleasant foul deed.

All these acts are unbecoming, and we laugh at exposing the shameful parts when done without necessity or restraint if there is no harm involved. If one is forced to do it, and from this should come pain, if at first we laugh, unaware of the injury, finally, struck with compassion upon learning of it, we stop laughing entirely and say with repentance: this is no laughing matter. So much, then, are these two conditions, ugliness and absence of pity, necessarily joined.[14]

For the same reason, seeing someone fall in the mire, we take to laughing, because it is very unseemly and without any danger which might draw us to sympathy. So much so that the more indecorous the fall, the greater the laughter. I call it indecorous when it is not ordinary or expected: for the surprise has much to do with it. Thus it is that children and drunkards fall often, and make us laugh: but we will laugh incomparably more if a great and important personage who walks affectedly with a grave and formal step, stumbling clumsily on a heavy stone, falls suddenly in a quagmire. That is very uncomely and does not inspire pity unless he happened to be our relative, ally, or dear friend, for we should then be ashamed and have concern. Still more unbecoming would this be if it happened to him among much company, and more yet if he were richly clothed and odious about it. But there is nothing so disgusting, and that causes less pity, than if this same personage is unworthy of the rank he holds and of the honor one gives him, if he is hated for his pride and excessive arrogance, resembling a monkey dressed in crimson, as the proverb has it. And who, seeing such a man stumble stupidly, would be able to keep from laugh-

a. Light, if there is only a scald and nothing serious comes from it.

ing? If one falls into the mud from very high, we scarcely laugh,[b] because from such a fall comes to us the suspicion of danger, for one fears that there may have been injury. Or if suddenly we laugh at this, we are not thinking of his injury, but of the fall, which cannot be pitied since it is improper and ridiculous not to be able to keep on one's feet, falling like a drunkard wherever one may be. It will be still more ugly if the fall is in the mud, due to the filth that aggravates such unseemliness. Nevertheless, if some time later any injury received becomes apparent, laughter ceases, and sympathy follows. Such and similar accidents are seen daily, and all have in common that they come about unconsciously and unwillingly. The fall shows this very well, for if one falls down on purpose, or wallows in the quagmire, he will provide a meager amusement. Also, not everyone laughs upon seeing the shameful parts: in fact the most severe will reprehend sharply anyone who unabashedly and knowingly exposes them. It must happen unexpectedly, such as seeing them through an open seam of the breeches.

After this type of laughable matter comes the other, done with full consciousness and on purpose, which is also unbecoming and makes us laugh over novelties that are pleasant as well as improper and unworthy of pity. Such is the case if an old man plays in the streets as would a child; or if an extremely well-known and imposing person, after drinking much wine, dresses up in a strange manner; or if a fool imitates a wise man in dress, in gesture, and in speech. All this makes us laugh because there is no harm to merit sympathy. Similarly, if a man who became frenzied or maniacal says and does some strange things, we cannot keep from laughing until we think about the great loss of his senses and understanding he has suffered.[c] Then we experience compassion because of the misery, and more still if this misfortune does not come through his own fault.[d]

Another type of laughable matter is inconsequential loss brought about by foolishness or lack of attention, such as when one would complain about losing a sparrow, some nuts, or similar things, over which children become sad. Also, this type of laughing matter is more from simple childishness, and their innocence moves us to laughter when they complain much about little, for this is found to be unseemly without moving us to pity. Likewise we will laugh at him who has broken a glass, because the damage is slight, the stupidity greater. Stupidity is unbecoming and unseemly; the loss does not enlist sympathy: this is why one laughs. But if this glass, or some other thing that has been broken, were of great value, we would laugh at first and until the loss was realized. From then on laughter ceases, as much because we regret the ill fate of the person guilty of the mistake (if he is in danger of being punished), as because of the displeasure we normally have upon seeing a rare and prized thing awkwardly smashed to pieces. All this can make us sad and move us to compassion.

b. The first thing one imagines in a fall is that one comes to injury, for which reason there is no laughter.

c. The loss of possessions is nothing compared to the loss of health or especially of the mind.

d. Through his fault is when it is due to a poor diet. Thus one pities more one who has the pox without having rolled in the straw.

Very close to this type of laughable matter are the tricks we play to ridicule or to upset others, but it is always light, and in fun. If for example, when somebody is unaware, we undo his clothes, or if we throw water on somebody who was not expecting it, or if we put another to the task of looking for something of small importance that we have hidden, and similar numberless tricks we play facetiously and so purposely on others that there is no real outrage, displeasure, or harm, although there may well seem to be. These tricks would be meanly done, and with malice, if they were done seriously, but the levity keeps them laughable. Nonetheless, often from these games come great and dangerous quarrels because those to whom they are addressed take them in an ill manner. Then laughter ceases, when it seems to us that there is offense and injury in them. Whence it is that he who received it deserves sympathy in not being one who can endure the outrage.

Next come all the deceptions, snubs, or impostures one perpetrates. Here it is a matter of being careful about the place, the time, and the persons; otherwise these are not laughable, but mean and vicious, especially if the deception is in important things, such as someone's selling brass for gold, tin for silver. The deception we acknowledge as being laughable is lighter, and such that it cannot be ill interpreted, done among friends and companions, or inferiors, who cannot really be upset or ask vengeance. This is why one must choose the persons.

Now these tricks are commonly played on all the senses, and cause us to laugh because it is unbecoming, due to a lack of attention or judgment, to see ourselves greatly misled since, if we had been thinking the least bit, they could have been avoided: such as if somebody wanted to touch an iron he does not know is hot, and burns himself; or if ice breaks under the feet of one who foolishly thought that it was thick; if one takes shit for honey. All these things are laughable because it is easy to test and to find out if our senses judge correctly.

Taste is similarly deceived in several ways, both as a sort of touch and as organ of odors, and we laugh at the person who burns his tongue on very hot soup, or at his spitting it out, because it seems improper to us not to test the heat beforehand (to do as he who spewed out his soup did), and to pounce boldly on the food and devour thoughtlessly in the manner of a glutton. Taste is also misled when one has somebody else eat something bitter, or of equally bad quality, yet having the appearance or covering of sweetness and goodness.

Sight is abused particularly over empty promises: and laughable ugliness consists of imprudence or foolishness in believing everybody so easily and firmly, putting much faith in words that could easily be doubted. We do not sympathize when the deception is harmless and simply laughable: as when we are promised the sight of a beautiful young woman, and just as we are aroused, we are shown a wrinkled old lady with one eye, a runny nose, a thick and kinky beard and underslung buttocks, dirty, smelly, drooling, toothless, flat-nosed, bandy-legged, humpy, bumpy, stinking, twisted, filthy, knotty, full of lice, and more deformed than ugliness itself. Here there is truly something to laugh at, seeing ourselves made fun of in this way. Numberless similar impostures are employed, based on credulity which makes up the unseemliness or deformity required in all laughable matter, for to deceive the senses in another does not move us to laughter, even if it is not a matter of deception properly speaking, but rather of not perceiving and sensing what had been expected, through whatever sense it might have been.*

The sense of smell is abused, properly speaking, if stinking odors are presented to it as being sweet, and less strictly speaking also, when a bouquet is given to smell perfumed with euphorbia or hellebore as if it were with powdered violet or cypress. For from the odor we begin to sneeze so hard and so long that it is funny. One is also deceived in this matter of flowers when hidden in them is something pointed that comes and pricks the nose upon approaching, at which we laugh very hard. For we find it absurd and improper to be affronted as it were, especially in what could have been avoided, if only we had exercised the least bit of caution: and this does not justify any compassion.

Hearing will be misled in awaiting for a long time, because of another's promise, a joyful and charming song, or the delectable sound of some instrument (things that it finds pleasant), if afterwards there are neither words nor melody worth listening to. We could very well attribute to this sense all manner of credulity,[e] because persuasion takes its entry through it. But all other errors do not pass through our hearing considered as instrument of sound, but fall strictly on that part of the soul responsible for judgment, neither more nor less than the preceding impostures, if one wishes to speak correctly. For our senses do not fail in recognizing their object: we laugh only over the imagination's being falsely convinced, which we find unbecoming and unworthy of pity when it is over a thing of no great importance: so much so that vain and foolish emotions fall into this section, such as the banter that bumpkin lovers maintain in their endearments, the empty hopes with which they nourish their souls, the mad melancholy some give themselves over to, and any emotions proceeding from a mistake in judgment, and without any conviction other than one's own. This comes from a natural imperfection, a weakness of mind or of character: as can be seen in those who, due to pusillanimity, are too fearful, daring not to go out in the night, afraid of shadows and ghosts; some flee from a rat, others would not touch a worm, in dread of being bitten. Seeing such reactions, we laugh at their cowardice (an inept and unpitiable thing) when there is no reason for true fear.

I think that I have collected and reduced in short all that is considered laughable, unless we add the grace, the composure and the gestures, which often move us to laughter. What I have enlarged upon concerning the other senses that receive impostures deals completely with things seen and done, and I am gathering them into one chapter. The great variety of material has forced me to prolixity, and, wishing through diverse examples to explain more familiarly how ugly things, unworthy of sympathy, are what we laugh at, I have put aside the strict rules of logic in forming my divisions. It is sufficient to have professed and deduced what constitutes the genus of all laughable matter.

*This is not deceiving our judgment (for it discerns correctly what is proposed to it), but our patience and expectation.

e. Thus is faith through the ear, as Theology says.

CHAPTER III
CONCERNING LAUGHABLE REMARKS

The sense of hearing receives laughable matter proper to itself, and matter pertaining to the sense of sight. By the latter I mean those laughable deeds which are recited as having been done and witnessed, and which during their narration seem to be before our eyes; whence it comes that we do not laugh at them less than if they were actually seen. Such are all the acts described in the preceding chapter, or very nearly, for be they abuses, errors, foolish acts, or other unseemly deeds, provided they are recounted straightforwardly, we laugh at them almost as much as if they were being done before us. To this type, then, belong fables and facetious tales like Poggio's,[15] and the stories of Boccaccio, of which those telling of the infidelities that wives perpetrate on their husbands we find most conducive to laughter, because it seems unfitting, without inspiring compassion, that a man be thus deceived.

The raw material of the laughable in speech is drawn from lampoons, gibes, derision, mockery, and remarks that are stinging, biting, equivocal, ambiguous, and which spring in any way from error. All come from scorn and derision, which when serious and of consequence become harmful, but when light remain laughable. There are a thousand ways to make humorous comments based on people, places, occasions and diverse experiences, and they take the form of remarks that are disgraceful, lascivious, facetious, outrageous, untimely, naïve, fickle, and indiscreet. They take their principal form from the figures of rhetoric, or manners of speaking common to poets and orators, such as amphibology, enigma, comparison, metaphor, fiction,[16] hyperbole, pretense, allegory, innuendo, beausemblant,[17] and dissimulation,[18] and others put forth by the rhetoricians. Of these I find the funniest the ability to render tit for tat, and for a taunt, to come back with a clever reply.

As for their usage, we make these remarks so that others, or we ourselves, will be laughed at: others, if in a mocking tone we take up, refute, mock, or abase what they say; ourselves, when we say something a bit absurd, either on purpose or without thinking, and when we disappoint the expectation of the listeners or take what was said in the wrong way. One would think that in this there is no artifice, and that everything (leastwise in the main) is done naturally. In reality Nature is not alone in making a person clever and subtle in making humorous remarks, but some have such grace and presence in speaking that another saying the same thing would not be as funny, and in touching upon occasions and things that happen, these qualities are so efficacious that with them a bumpkin will be able to be clever by returning the barb to him who first sent it. Besides, all is more noble in defense[a] than in provoking: but this should not stop us from knowing how to send back a lampoon that would make a very fitting reply.

But in what way do these mockeries, puns, stinging words, and gibes make us laugh? Not in any way other than through a certain ugliness or deformity, unworthy

a. Since we are permitted to ward off the insult, we take pleasure in seeing the same done to someone else, and not to us.

of pity;[19] and they become all the more laughable to the extent that we pay close attention to the place, the time, and the person, as we have said above. Aside from this, the confident demeanor of the speaker can add much luster: often even a remark is funny only if the author does not laugh or if the remark is made quickly, and if it does not seem prepared, or made-up elsewhere, lewd, haughty, or unfitting for the time and place. For one must clearly realize that, in banquets and familiar chats, frisky remarks befit people of low social class, and gay remarks befit everyone. One must never irritate those who are dangerous to offend, because of the quarrels that might result, or a shameful reparation: for there is nothing to laugh at when imminent danger incites compassion in us. Nor is it funny to mock a suffering and miserable man (unless in such a calamity he were evil and arrogant), but is of a great inhumanity to make fun of the miserable on whom we should take pity.[b20]

Laughable remarks, therefore, are little subtleties, railleries, puns, equivocal expressions and similar things said in recounting or replying to another, without touching on things of importance or honor. All have some sort of deformity: for we find it unseemly to be mocked, and to have said or done something reprehensible. We laugh not only at stinging remarks, but also at all others made without thinking, said stupidly, foolishly, in anger, spite, or silly cowardice. It is not necessary to bring examples for these, nor for the preceding types; being so common to our speech, they are able to be recognized easily by all.

It is enough to have shown with facts, through ordinary induction, that all laughable matter shares one point in common: namely that there is no pain, danger, undoing, or outrage, even though at first it may seem so, but there is some unseemliness and ugliness, unworthy of sympathy. What I have thus declared by reasoning and examples,[c] Cicero confirms with his authority when he says that laughter springs from a certain ugliness or deformity as though it were its source, in such a way that there is not much difference between laughter and mockery. And true enough it is that often we cannot easily tell if one laughs simply from gaiety or in mocking another. That all derision[d] corresponds to something indecent is unnecessary to prove: it is heard often enough if one only listens. The only thing remaining is to note certain necessary conditions in the area of laughable matter, and we will have greatly advanced our enterprise in finding the true object and matter of laughter.

CHAPTER IV
OBSERVATIONS ON LAUGHABLE MATTER

Laughable actions and remarks do not always make us laugh; it is either because they lose their charm, being otherwise quite funny, or because they do not make their way into our mind. Their pleasantness and delightfulness is lost when they do

b. On the afflicted one we must not add affliction, as the wise man says.
c. Book two of the *Orator*.
d. If the derision is well-founded, it is a just reprimand.

not come in the proper time and place, or are so often repeated that they tire us, or are not prompt and sudden, a required condition above all in matters of speaking, for the quickness adds to their arrangement.[a] Now in all laughable matter there must be something new and unexpected, beyond what is hoped for very intensely. For the mind, suspended and in doubt, reflects imaginatively on what will be coming, and in facetious things, the end is usually quite the opposite of what is expected, which causes us to laugh. Even if such an event had been suspected or foreseen, or else if one had seen and heard it, nevertheless in recounting and redoing it, we laugh because the reiteration presents it to us as being freshly said or done.

When laughable matter does not penetrate into our mind,[b] it is either because we are not attentive, having our mind elsewhere, or because we do not understand it. One cannot be aware of laughable matter without seeing it take place or hearing it spoken of; one may also be present, but thinking of something else. When a sharp pain weighs upon us, it will cancel out our attention, and will have more power than the laughable matter. The same will be true of a bothersome worry that hammers the brain. This is why we see that in vain will something funny be presented to sad, grave, and severe Cato,[21] to Heraclitus the weeper,[22] and similar sour-faces. For dullness is the poison that blasts and snuffs out laughable matter. For these, unless it is evident, it is not understood; it is as if it were told too softly, or in an unknown language. And how can they be expected to laugh at it if they do not grasp what it is about? If the remark is rich and ambiguous, those that understand it will laugh, the others will not. If a man is among Germans, Basques, or full-fledged Britons, and does not know their language, he will be able to hear them talking and laughing in stitches without being able to do likewise because he does not understand why. And if perchance he begins to laugh, it will certainly be on credit, and due to a natural accord[c] which often moves us (exciting the appetites) to imitate our fellow men; or, more precisely, he will laugh without knowing the occasion of it, since, not understanding why yet seeing the others laugh, as if it were at nothing (because for as much do we take the unknown), he laughs at the laughers. It can also be said that we find a dissolute and immodest laughter ugly, and because of this ugliness we find the others laughable, since upon seeing people laugh moderately and not too long, scarcely will we laugh as they do, so long as the cause is not made clear.

Sometimes laughter does not come suddenly, because we are slow to understand an obscure, difficult, complex, or ambiguous situation or saying that occupies the mind for a time as it contemplates the matter, or if we laugh at it, it is really coldly. But finally, understanding the reason, we begin to laugh at the matter now gone by. This is very similar to a laugh we have because we remember something funny from several months ago. For memory puts before the eyes what one has seen in the past, and it is able to move the senses as would a thing present.

These, then, are the two principal interferences that stop laughter from being moved by its objects, namely, not to perceive them, and not to grasp them. On the

a. Quickness is like the sauce that gives the appetite to laugh.

b. This is the other part of the division of required conditions.

c. As in seeing somebody yawn, we yawn; and sometimes we piss out of fellowship.

contrary, we laugh sometimes at what is not at all laughable, but seems so to us. And in fact it very often happens that our eyes are sorely mistaken, causing a false laughter that ends as soon as we discover the truth. Similarly, in ambiguous remarks there is error, which makes us laugh, even if they are grave and serious, because we take them in the opposite way and equivocally, or because we like to distort the phrase thus. This is why we can laugh much at what is not laughable, and why we will not always laugh when the matter is laughable and comes up.

Up to now we have deduced and by several means shown the object of laughter to be, if not an indecent, an ugly and ridiculous thing excluding any pain, danger, or discomfort, which would move us to pity. For the grave and serious acts that are deformed to the point of causing pity are not considered laughable, and what is only ugly never makes us laugh if it is not accompanied by some gaiety. Having thus limited and circumscribed all laughable matter, showing its true and sole object, it is time to inform ourselves how laughter is caused by it, and which part of the soul is first moved by it. For all the movements of the body, both secret and apparent, are the work of the soul,[d] which governs and manages it. Then we shall see through which instruments laughter is formed, and whence come the marvelous effects of the passion of laughter.

CHAPTER V
WHICH PART OF THE BODY FIRST RECEIVES THE OBJECT OF LAUGHTER

If it was difficult to find the genus and the species of all laughable matter, it will be much more so now to search out the part of the body it touches first of all. For previously we did not need to verify what we said since it was accepted by commoners and uneducated people, who would recognize as laughable all that we have proposed; it was necessary only to put them forth and, to formulate the argument, show how they all come together and link among themselves. But now it will be necessary to use keen judgment in inquiring diligently into that which is still not well resolved, even among the most learned:[a] that is, which part of the body first receives laughable matter.

Here is where we must labor, and there is toil and much difficulty. This is no longer a question of frolicsome and vain remarks that make us laugh; it is grave, serious, and such that scarcely will we arrive at it after long research, for the effect is most marvelous, having thoroughly hidden its cause. For which reason if in this matter I do not satisfy completely the sensitive minds, I hope my arguments will at least be credible; the greatness of the undertaking will serve as an excuse for me.

d. The soul is the worker, the body is the instrument of all acts, save the contemplative ones.

a. This is informing through art and method, when division and collection are used.

The principal problem[b] lies in that the object of laughter seems to touch and to belong more to the brain (to the part receiving all that the attentive mind seeks out) than to any other: seeing that it is the foundation, base, and source of all the senses receiving such matter. The heart, on the contrary, wishes to make it its own, and attribute it to itself by right, being the seat of the passions, because laughter seems to spring from some emotion. Now to better clarify the problem, and to proceed more methodically in the matter, it will be necessary to begin immediately with what all admit and grant,[c] and from there to clear a path in order to make our way little by little through the difficulties, determining the unknown from quite common things, so much so that having arrived at our end we may have knowledge of what we desired so greatly.

Everybody sees clearly that in laughter the face is moving, the mouth widens, the eyes sparkle and tear, the cheeks redden, the breast heaves, the voice becomes interrupted; and when it goes on for a long time the veins in the throat become enlarged, the arms shake, and the legs dance about, the belly pulls in and feels considerable pain; we cough, perspire, piss, and besmirch ourselves by dint of laughing, and sometimes we even faint away because of it. This need not be proven.[d] I take it for certain and approved by all; and it is in fact what draws us to this investigation, which must now be roughed out.

The emotion causing the above-mentioned sudden and diverse movements can only lie in a major part having command over the body, for the less noble particular parts that do not hold an honorable rank do not have the power to constrain and make the others share their own movement, but rather they serve the more worthy ones due to an ordering on Nature's part, who has ordered these things as she sees fit. The master parts, then, are the brain, the heart, and the liver.[e] As for the brain, it has such authority that the sensing and moving parts depend upon it, and recognize their common nerves. It is the muscles (which are noted as the only instruments and organs of movement) that depend on our will, which resides in the brain. If, therefore, the nerves and muscles are obedient to it, all movement we perform by order of the will will appertain to it by right. There are other movements that are natural and involuntary, such as that of the heart and arteries moved by it. The heart owes to Nature alone the continuous and indefatigable movement it undergoes along with the arteries. The liver does not move about in the least, but it indeed has the power to move within itself, in attraction, expulsion, and distribution of the humors; these latter change places, but not the organ by which they are moved. For which reason it is only the first two parts,[f] to which we attribute movement from one place to another, that are able to debate and quarrel over their preeminence in the movements causing laughter in us. I do not see how they could be adjudged to the

b. Cause of the problem, and proposed difficulty.

c. One must always base oneself upon what all or the most learned grant.

d. One need not prove what is perceptible, one has only to observe it.

e. One might add the testicles: but they are not necessary for life or the basic existence of man.

f. The first two are the brain and the heart.

heart inasmuch as it does not govern the muscles; for the widening of the lips, the shaking of the arms, of the breast, and the other movements can be accomplished only through the nerves, which obey only the brain. The arteries have nothing to do with it, although (on occasions) they are for the duration moving more than ordinarily. But we shall give our opinion in this matter in the third book.*

It is, therefore, to the brain that such agitation appertains, by means of the nerves it lodges in each muscle. Indeed so, but, its movements are only voluntary, and those seen in laughter arrive in spite of us. For it is impossible to hinder them when there is something to laugh at, or to stop them sometimes once they are in motion, except with great difficulty, even with reason ordering it. Moreover, we assign to the heart, and not to the brain, all the emotions, among which if laughter does not figure, it at least is declaring the presence of one of them, which it uncovers suddenly. I would even dare say that the act of laughter follows and makes known one of the emotions in the same way that rejoicing is a sign of pleasure. For perhaps[g] we shall place under another sort of emotion the cause of laughter. But in order better to deduce this fact, we shall explain briefly the soul's faculties, from which all our actions proceed; and in doing this we shall find to which of these principal parts all the emotions must be assigned. Then, when it will be proved how laughter, as accident, is connected to a few of the passions or emotions, the principal area[h] of its occurrence, which is what we are seeking, will no longer be in question.

CHAPTER VI
DIVISION OF THE SOUL'S FACULTIES

Medical doctors divide the powers, virtues, or faculties of the soul into three parts, namely, the animal, the vital, and the natural, distinctly assigning to each one a part of our body as its seat and regiment. The natural reigns in the liver, the vital in the heart, and the animal in the brain.[23] This is to say no more than if they claimed that the soul (otherwise entirely of one piece) practiced such functions in said parts, as the reason why it can do nothing without its corporeal instruments.[a]

Metaphysicians speak of other powers which can be reduced to the preceding: these are the vegetative, the sensitive, the appetitive, the motivating, and the intellective. The vegetative, the only one in plants, is also in animals under the natural. We put under the vital the appetitive or desirous, the sensitive, and the motivating. The animal includes the intellective, which is proper to man. This is

*Chapter XII.

g. Perhaps, he says, for laughter does not come from joy alone inasmuch as there is displeasure mixed in. Still, the emotion that provokes it draws more upon joy.

h. For the principal area will be the part that is responsible for such an emotion.

---

a. To do nothing, except contemplation, must be understood. The soul still has need of its corporeal instruments, since there is nothing in the intellect that was not first in the senses, as the philosopher says.[24]

how the five come down to our three, and have no further advantage than to explain and reveal more distinctly the essence and the functions of the soul. For this reason, wishing to clarify my argument neatly, I am going to pursue this division.

The vegetative faculty[b] is the cause of three things: nourishing, growing, and reproducing. The sensitive has two types of workings: one through the external senses, one through the internal. The external are five in number: sight, hearing, smell, taste, and touch. The internal, at least according to medical doctors, are three: common sense, cogitation or thought, and memory. Those who wish to assign more do nothing but explain in greater length the said faculties, adding to common sense the imaginative, to thought the speculative, and for fifth retaining reminiscence. These interior senses are in the brain: the exterior ones likewise have from it their power, due to the presence of the nerves, which are like conduits.

The third division[c] of the soul is the desirous, covetous, or appetitive, as we said above. It does much more than the others in the area of our subject, so we shall have to spend more time in peeling it down. To describe it, it is said to be the one that, aided by knowledge, pursues or flees objects. Three conditions are attributed to it: one natural, the second sensitive, and the third voluntary. Natural appetite could be reduced (so it seems) to the above-mentioned vegetative; but it is necessary to understand it differently here than there, namely, in the sense of simple inclination without effect, for the natural appetite, which we shall treat now, comes after knowledge and can be guided somewhat by reason. The sensitive appetite is with the senses, as its name indicates, and is of two types, one through touch and the other without touch. From the first comes pleasure or delight, and pain or suffering, both through the intermediary of the nerves, although they in no way proceed from thought nor do they obey reason. For think as much as you will that one of your appendages is wounded, you will still not have any pain; likewise it is not possible to be joyous when one is in pain, much as reason might wish it.[d] The desires or appetites not connected to touch necessarily follow thought or cogitation and are nothing more than movements of the heart, through which we pursue perceived objects. I say that they come from cogitation inasmuch as it teaches us, whether correctly or falsely, to avoid what displeases us and to pursue the agreeable.

Such motivators are properly and well named: emotions. The principal of these are joy, sorrow, hope, fear, love, hate, anger, pity, shame, impudence, zeal, and envy or malice.[e] They are also called passions, troublings, or perturbations of the soul in that they come from an appetite that does not proceed from reason. As to their instrument or seat, there is disagreement among the authors. For Plato places all of them in the heart, except for love, which he relegates to the liver so as to put it under the

b. This division is the most formal, and follows that of the metaphysicians.

c. He says division in the sense commonly used in metaphysics and medicine, to designate virtue or faculty. For strictly speaking, the soul, being indivisible, has no divisions.

d. Then all one can do to help reason is to restrain oneself and to disguise it, letting on in no way, not any more than if there were no pain.[25]

e. He says malice, which the Greeks called *pichairecacie,* when pleasure is taken from another's misfortune, and displeasure from his good fortune.

vegetative: whence comes the saying that the liver constrains us to love. But he is mistaken, unless he misuses the term love for simple inclination[f] and natural appetite to reproduce one's kind. For the other sort of love is a movement of the heart, no less than is hatred, its contrary, which (without question) comes from there, and not from the liver. Now contraries always spring from the same area, which is why they are incompatible, so much so that the one hinders or repels the other. This is why it is better to assign love to the heart, and follow the general consensus that every emotion is attributable to it.

We could also prove it in this manner:[g] if the emotions are neither in the brain nor in the viscera which serve the vegetative, they will be in the heart. If they were in the brain, they would not be able to infringe upon its other functions; but we see often that judgment reproves such passions, and is powerless to arrest them. This is because another agent constructs them, and because they are caused in a place quite distant from the brain. This is why Medea would say:

> I know well what is better, and approve of it,
> But I nevertheless follow out the evil deed.[26]

For the same reason it is not possible to find them in the vegetative, since the natural appetites, such as hunger and thirst, are not appeased by thought or logic, which the emotions sometimes do obey.

And after all, our senses tell us clearly that they are proper to the heart, when in them we feel it move undeniably. Under the effect of joy it expands thirstily, as if wanting to receive and embrace the object presented, whence it sends forth joyfully its blood[h] and its humors. With hope, the same is no less the case, for there is an almost identical movement in the imagination over some future good as over a present one. Sadness and fear, as contraries to the preceding, beset the heart in a contrary manner. Love has considerable affinity with hope, but is a more ardent emotion in which it seems that the heart almost itches with the desire to draw to itself a good (either truly such, or in appearance) in order to enjoy and delight in it. In anger there are two movements, for in the same instant the heart becomes angry over the offense and also would chastise the author of such an injury. Hatred is a chronic anger. These two latter emotions are contraries of amorous passion. Shame has a movement similar to anger, for the shameful guilty person scolds himself silently for the mistake, stupidity, or misdeed he has committed, and seems to punish himself for it or at least blames himself, fearing the opinion of others. Under such an emotion we put compunction, or verecund shame, which is a natural habit or tendency to fear failure, and one rebukes himself with spite when under its effect. Its opposite is impudence. Envy is nothing other than sadness, but over the fortune

f. This natural inclination is from the vegetative faculty (as he said above) which is the only one found in plants; and plants reproduce their own kind.

g. They must be in one of these three, or in the testicles, which are considered principal parts and responsible for some of the emotions. But this is included under the vegetative.

h. This can be witnessed from the color in the face that comes from it.

of others. Zeal[i] is an emotion mixing love and anger, resembling jealousy. Malice, made up of hate and joy, completely contrary to zeal, befits properly those who rejoice over evil coming to good people, and good falling upon the bad.

Now in all these troublings or perturbations one feels very clearly that the heart is moved, pressed, or shaken, now constricting, now dilating, according to the effect of the emotion. Furthermore, the movement of blood which comes about in the majority of these troublings shows us clearly that they affect the heart. What shall we say of the common consensus attributing all these conditions to it and not to the brain, as is discovered naturally, or else from learned elders? We say commonly: his heart is joyful, sad, timid, shameful, amorous, pitiful, merciful, evil. But this is not said of the brain.

All these movements and emotions of the heart can, therefore, be assigned to the heart, and it can be concluded that it is moved in two ways: one is by the emotions we have just presented in our argument, the other is the ordinary one[k] that it continues constantly to have by expanding and contracting. Both are natural and proper to it; proper, I say, in that they are not found in the other parts, and are naturally instinctual, springing from its own fibers. These are heart fibers, very dissimilar to muscle fibers, both in strength and in material, and by which the heart is naturally made to move,[l] along with its arteries, without the will ordering it. And for this very reason these movements are considered natural, because there is no violence, and they are like functions or effects produced naturally by themselves. And how should they not be so named, when in more moderate emotions only the heart is acting?[m]

As for the ordinary movement, no other proof is necessary. For no one doubts that this is not its proper and natural movement. Nor must one doubt its emotions, for this we have sufficiently proven, showing that the movement of the passions has its source and beginning by nature. But since they proceed (as we said) from the sensitive appetitive faculty, by knowledge or imagination, this faculty necessarily precedes the movement of the heart. And yet we say that one does not covet the unknown,[n] for in imagining an object, and judging it good or bad, the humors, agitated by our noticing it, affect the heart, which as though hit and struck, is moved, desiring or disdaining the object. These movements incite the alliance of such natural forces as these in order to pursue knowledge of the object. Thus, the causes of emotion which are called efficient, will be both the objects and the heart, since these perturbations spring from the heart and are in it, as they are in the subject, each one having some matter[o] apt to move it. Love has beauty, be it true or

i. It is a mixture of love and anger, so much so that one hates that another partakes of the same object.

k. Its ordinary movement is its continual pulsation.

l. It moves naturally, as do all other movements that do not depend on the will or that spring from untrained inclination.

m. Only the heart is acting when the emotion produces no exterior effect.

n. *Ignoti nulla cupido,* says the philosopher.

o. The matter is the object itself, as he will explain immediately.

apparent; anger, an injury; fear, a danger; and the others, some other, according to their differences.

We have put an end to the dispute over the emotions, which come from the sensitive appetitive faculty, that is, from the sensitive appetite, from which laughter seems to have its source. I would stop at this point if it were not necessary to found the argument better which leads me to continue into the remaining faculties of the soul. For if we forget the least one, some suspicious person will be able to calumniate, saying that the cause of laughter (the main object of our search) is therein. Let us therefore explain, in the order we have followed, the rest of the faculties so that no one might suspect a false argument or sophistic deception. And when after peeling down the others, we find nothing that could be the chief agent in this matter (we shall however be able to extract something useful for our purposes), we shall return to the first ones, as one returns to the path one had abandoned to follow some other route where a better passageway was thought obtainable.

CHAPTER VII
CONCERNING THE OTHER PARTS OF THE SOUL

We said that the third part of the desirous faculty is that which reasons, accounts for speech, and aids understanding. It is, properly speaking, nothing other than the will itself. Now understanding is so closely related to the internal senses that it is unable to perform its functions without their aid.[a] Besides that, since the will is blind, it is forced to consent to the movements of the heart, although the will does have an individual choice and some small power in ordering the arrest[b] of the external members. So much so that with respect to the heart it is like a child on the back of a fierce horse that carries it impetuously about, here and there, but not without the child's turning it back some, and, reining in, getting it back on the path.

To understand our argument better, it is necessary to presuppose that there are two ways to govern: one is as master, where one simply commands; the other is civil or political, where with authority one points out obligations. Reason governs the heart in the second way when with its advice it moves or calms the emotions, and if the heart resists the bit, reason has recourse to the first means, through which it can order the external members to do its bidding. This is the sovereign power by which reason or will controls the motivating faculty, forbidding the eyes, the tongue, the feet, the hands, and other parts to obey in any way mad or evil desires. The will is, therefore, free in its own right, and is able to choose or refuse the right thing, having as obedient subjects two faculties: the sense appetite (which abides in the heart) and

a. Unless it is pure contemplation; but even then there must be humors, which are corporeal instruments.

b. It orders their arrest and that the execution not follow when based upon philosophy, which is natural in few.[27]

the power of movement.[c] This power never refuses any of the will's orders; the sense appetite does not obey immediately, and often contradicts the will, employing long arguments and various thoughts, after which it sometimes happens that the diverted will yields to the emotions. For it is not so contrary to the heart (unless there be something repugnant) that it allows it nothing.

The fourth faculty of the soul is (as we were saying) to move all the members, and to move about, for which the instruments are the nerves, muscles, and tendons. It has two immediate causes, namely, purposeful imagination and desire, to which the nerves are obedient in an admirable natural confederation, pushed by the moved and circulating humors. Animals have a triple movement, one natural, another voluntary, and the third a mixture of the first two. Natural movement does not commence or cease with our will, wish, or fantasy; but as soon as an object presents itself, if nature is strong, these movements come about naturally, by virtue of the fibers and bodily heat. Thus, the stomach takes in food, and the heart is moved by the humors. Voluntary movement begins with our bidding, following the imagination. The third type, which is mixed, handles the rejection of excrement from the bladder and the bowels, but not respiration, which is entirely voluntary, as Galen[d] has proved.[28] The four above-mentioned faculties have need, necessarily, of corporeal instruments, without which they can do nothing.

The fifth is named by metaphysicians the inorganic, since it is able to function without organs, although the internal senses aid it in presenting their objects. For it has its own action,[e] and some of its movements are separate from the body. It is divided into two parts: one is understanding and the other will. The effects of understanding are three: the first is called apprehension of individual objects; the second, thought, deliberation, and judgment; the third, reminiscence and memory. This faculty has as its object all[f] that is. The term *will* is ambiguous: we take it here as a faculty, or division of the desirous and cognizant soul, more dignified than the sense appetite, and sovereign and free in its operations when understanding presents it with something. Its functions are: acceptance, refusal, and the betwixt and between, when we hesitate or are in doubt.

Aside from this, the will performs two actions: one is called inclination, wherein, on its own, without dissimulating and without ordering, it disdains or covets something ardently, as the miser who desires nothing more than money, and puts his whole mind to it. Under such a heading it seems that one could put all the emotions (I mean to say under the grand desirous faculty)[30] and not only the sense appetites; however, seeing that these evidently move the heart, and come about

c. Voluntary movements are performed through the muscles and nerves, which obey the will completely, be it reasonable or not.

d. In the second book of *The Movement of Muscles,* where he relates that a servant died by voluntarily holding his breath.

e. This is why it is recognized as immortal, for the other souls can do nothing without the body.[29]

f. All that is in heaven, on earth, and between them, and even that which is universal, separate from individual objects, and the object of the understanding.

without warning, and that the effects of the inclined or ardent will do happen little by little, without our feeling the movements in them, there is a great difference here, and we must not confuse these two appetites. The other action of the will is a controlling of the internal faculties, and of itself, but not in the same manner. For the fever-struck, forced into thirst, will wish only to drink: the will does not agree and orders the motivating faculty not to present what is desired. In the healthy, strong, and magnanimous, the heart fears death, such that it beats down somewhat the will's endeavor; yet, when the object sought gives it new strength, the will forces the heart a little to be moved by such a good, and to diminish its movement toward cowardice. Under these controlled actions are also put shams and dissimulation.

This, then, is what seemed necessary to me: to treat the soul's faculties (in the explaining of which I was prolix in spite of myself) because from it we must extract what we shall treat concerning that faculty causing laughter; for if the foundations are not solid, the entire edifice is easily tipped over.

CHAPTER VIII
TO WHICH OF THE SOUL'S FACULTIES LAUGHTER MUST BE ATTRIBUTED

The faculties of the soul, since they are diverse, cause a great variety of effects in animals, which differ from plants in their feeling[a] and movement. And, because laughter needs these two effects, and inasmuch as plants are deprived of them, laughter is adaptable to animals alone. Thus, having dismissed and foreclosed the vegetative faculty, this effect will only befit one of the four remaining.

Now, this effect cannot be from the sensitive faculty because neither everything that we see, hear, smell, taste, and touch, nor the internal senses, move us to laugh. Would we then not have to laugh ceaselessly, and be Democritus,[31] if the laughable were the object of the sensitive appetite? Yes, unless it be taken for a part of the desirous faculty. For above we proposed three areas of appetite: namely the natural, sensitive, and rational, and of which the first seems to approach more the vegetative (which we have just excluded), except that it is more elevated.[b] Nor can laughter be under the rational, that is, the sensitive intellectual faculty, because very often it comes about in spite of the will, as when we are unable to stop or restrain it. This is why it will be proper to the sensitive faculty, which animals alone have, principally in that part causing the emotions, joy, sorrow, and the others. For it will never be believed that laughter springs from the inorganic understanding (even though it is proper to man, just as is laughter) if it cannot be reduced simply to sensitive knowledge, especially since very often it contradicts the will.

a. And more in their feeling than in their movement, for there are sea animals whose movement is doubted.

b. The natural appetite in animals is more elevated than it is in plants.

Therefore, we shall affirm that the principal cause of laughter is contained under desire, which, without the sense of touch, follows the imagination and obviously moves the heart, inciting it to various emotions.

CHAPTER IX
THAT LAUGHTER COMES FROM AN EMOTION IN THE HEART AND NOT FROM THE BRAIN

We were endeavoring above to prove that the power to laugh should be put among the passions of the heart, but we shall confirm this better with the following reasons. First of all, this power could be lodged under joy, since it follows or accompanies laughter. For one never does see the sad and unhappy laughing; it is as if laughter were a sort of joy. Another more convincing argument is that in laughter we distinctly feel the heart move, something proper to the emotions. One can also adduce the common way of speaking which often serves as credible proof in things of great importance, having authority for bygone observances and handed down to our own time, valued by the most learned who first taught the nations, fashioning their language and tuning it to a natural meaning which is itself a half-knowledge.[a] For it is quite necessary to admit that common people are normally instructed by learned people through mutual conversation, and that from it they retain many things that are not considered worthy of committing to writing, seeing that they have already been made public. Now, we say commonly: he laughs heartily, and not brainily, thus denoting the place from which the risible emotion proceeds.

All these reasons prove well that laughter does not come from any other place. Someone (perhaps) will object to us by saying: "Well, in the beginning of this book you showed that the laughable will have no effect if it is unperceived. From this it follows that the heart is not the first touched. For laughable matter is no sooner perceived by the external senses than it comes to our consciousness, after which it is received by the heart. Now, such a perception is the office of the brain. For which reason we shall say that the brain feels first the emotional state, and causes the movement of laughter (especially seeing that it commands all movement by means of the nerves) and that after it the heart is informed of it all, over which it becomes joyful. The heart is not aware of this before all the others, as it is of its own feelings."

This is the problem that could be raised, and we shall answer immediately that all the emotions must be taken notice of, and it is important that they are proper to the heart, and not the brain, which is in no way moved by them. What? Is one not to be aware of the injury before the heart is moved to anger? The senses perceive first of all their objects, which from there run to solicit the faculties that are in various parts of the body, such as, in the heart, the angry, the joyous, the sad, and others that are similar. For the object moves the faculty. It is true that all enters the brain which is

a. There is a natural knowledge which is not learned in schools, but through common conversation with the learned.

the first and common receptor, but the objects of the faculties presiding in the heart transport themselves instantly to the heart. We never laugh without knowing the deed or the word, and no sooner do we learn it than we begin to laugh, so rapid[b] is the communication between the parts of the body.

The act of the brain perceiving such things, therefore, is only that of a common receptor, since it does not take the laughable for laughable, which belongs more properly to the heart. Thus, joy is not in the brain, even though it receives the joy before any other thing that could excite it, but it is not moved by the joy because it does not understand it first off by itself as rejoicing. I mean (first off and by itself) that some time later the brain can discern joy and know it as such when it feels the heart move. For from this the brain learns that what it gave passage to, without knowing anything else about it, is cause for joy. That the brain is last to know is easy to prove, even from the fact that judgment is not seated in it, and[c] that the heart is moved by emotion. For the matter of the passions flows through the instruments of the brain only as through conduits, and penetrates so quickly into the heart that the brain can be ignorant of it, and unaware of it before the emotion and the stirring of the heart have begun. The emotion in progress cannot remain unknown to the brain, which from then on starts to consider whether it is reasonable for the heart to be so moved. If it seems proper, the brain consents and takes part in it; otherwise it advises the movement to stop. To this advice the heart sometimes adheres, and calms the emotion, obeying in a political fashion; other times there is not a reason that can prevent it from being ravished and carried off by the brutal emotion which is very often so violent that it constrains the will to intervene at the same time. This is due to the great violence of our emotions and the close alliance of the soul's faculties, so much so that we are apt to say that the first[d] movements are not under man's power. Now, when reason sees itself disobeyed (if it does not wish to consent to the heart) it commands as master one of the other faculties so that it will not have to follow such movements. This is the motivating faculty, which serves reason as a slave, and never contradicts its orders.

Through these reasons and examples we have pointed out sufficiently that laughter must spring from an emotion proper to the heart, even if the particular object of laughter at first touches the common receptor.[e] It cannot be inferred from this that the office of its faculty is in the brain, which we shall better be able to make understood by something very analogous: it is in the workings of one of the other faculties. All believe it to be certain that the principal and proper function of the liver is to make blood, which it does not accomplish without matter fitting for the task being brought in from elsewhere, for since it does not move about the least bit, it is unable to go get it. For this reason nature has placed conduits through which is

b. It is like the gears of a clock. They all move together but differently, and all from the first gear, which moves all the rest.

c. *And,* that is to say, *easier than.* Thus the external senses, which go to the common receptor, are nothing but conduits furnishing passage to different types of objects.

d. The first movements form a surprise when the object is violent and sudden.

e. At first, or upon first contact, following what was said.

brought the chyle from the stomach: these are the mesaraic veins. Now, if some one, impressed by this, wanted to attribute sanguification to the veins, insofar as they are first to receive material for blood, would that not be considered strange? It is all the more so to give to the brain the emotions peculiar to the heart[f] because the mesaraic veins can at least tint the chyle a sanguine color, and perhaps all the veins of the body are taught by nature to sanguify, but the liver does it best. The brain, however, receives laughable matter without being stirred by it, and without changing or transmuting it, for just as it is presented to the brain, it arrives instantaneously right in the heart. There is, therefore, no sound reason to prove that the brain is first to apperceive the laughable.

But to come back to what has been demonstrated, and making it serve and uphold the present argument, we conclude that there are two causes for every emotion: the object carried to the heart through the sense organs, just as though through conduits, and the heart itself, from whose force come forth all these movements, and are there as in their cause. What is said generally of all the passions must be applied particularly to the emotion causing laughter, for it has its own objects over which the heart is moved. It is not simply gaiety, as in joy, nor is it only the disturbing thing, as in sadness, but what is properly called laughable. This needs no further proof, and we have only to consider whether such an emotion might be a type of joy (as we said in passing at the beginning of the chapter), or whether it will have a place separate from the others.

CHAPTER X
THAT THE EMOTION CAUSING LAUGHTER IS NOT SIMPLY ONE OF JOY

Our argument begins to delve into what is the most useful, touching the best of the matter. The past has taught us what laughing matter is, provoking[a] in the soul a certain faculty which is responsible for laughter. We also said that this faculty resides in the heart as do the other emotions. There remains only to know what it is, and how it is to be named. I do not doubt that it will be one of those that we have already mentioned: joy, sadness, hope, fear, love, hate, anger, pity, shame, boldness, zeal, envy, or malice (for that is all of them), or that it will be included under one of these, or that it draws upon several. It is not simply joy, as we shall deduce later, although it is closer to it than any other. For one does not laugh out of sadness, hope, fear, love, and so forth; but facetious things, which seem joyous, pleasant, and enjoyable—be they seen or heard—in delighting us, make us laugh. So much so that

f. The author has ever since followed this opinion, and has made of it a Paradox in his first Decade.[32] But he has much stronger arguments than this for it.

---

a. To provoke means to move, to excite, and, as it were, to needle. We therefore say that objects move the faculty.

the risible emotion could well be a kind of joy; one would even say that it is one and the same, since the matter is so similar.

Seeing, however, that one can be joyous without laughing, and the laugher cannot be without joy, these must be different emotions, or one must extend further than the other. It is impossible that they be contraries, since their effects are similar. It is better to say that joy has the greater extension,[b] and that the object or matter of the two, with the emotion wrought in the heart, is similar generally, but, particularly, has its object and proper movement, which will be easily understood if we compare them. The object or matter of rejoicing is a serious thing that brings pleasure, gain, profit, usefulness, or some other true contentment. The matter of the emotion causing laughter is only foolish, playful, empty, and often deceiving, turning around things of no importance. He who will want to consider this closely will see this difference; furthermore, they are sometimes so mixed and confused that the two matters will be in one object, without one's being able to discern them, unless it be the more or less serious rejoicing. From this one can understand their great affinity, since they differ only in that joy is over a more serious and grave matter, and laughter, over a lighter and more foolish. So much so that we shall be able to set up two kinds of rejoicing in order to facilitate our argument: one will be over serious things, the effect of which is named joy, just like the emotion; and the other over foolishness, whence comes laughter. The latter has no name of its own, the former is simple rejoicing, which has considerable modesty in all its movements. For the foolish type is dissolute,[c] debauched, and lascivious. So much so that, besides the difference in objects, there is also diversity in the emotions of the heart; and in this are these two emotions particularly dissimilar, as we said above.

Also, inasmuch as laughter is caused by something ugly, it does not proceed from pure joy, but has some small part of sadness, in such a way that it follows two contraries, one of which is superior to the other in its efficacy. In order to make my idea, foundation of this whole argument, better understood, it will be necessary to state separately what the role of joy is, and what comes about through sadness, and finally the effects of the risible faculty, which we believe to participate in both, for the simple must be sifted before their mixture[d] and compounding.

CHAPTER XI
WHAT COMES PARTICULARLY FROM JOY

In true and simple joy, the heart, struck by what seems enjoyable to it, expands thirstily, as if to embrace the object presented. In this dilation, it is unable to keep

b. Joy has the greater extension, for under it is contained laughter, and the container must be greater than the thing contained.

c. It is dissolute and immodest in Cachin laughter, from which the wisest and most experienced often cannot abstain.

d. This is the doctrinal order, which is called composite order.[33]

from pouring forth great amounts of blood and still more humors, whence appear in the face the evident signs of rejoicing. These[a] are: an open countenance, a shining, clear, and taut forehead, sparkling eyes, reddening cheeks, and a drawing back of the lips. All these accidents show clearly that a great quantity of humors gushes upwards and, being retained by the skin, is the cause of this change. For it is the nature of the moved heart to place[b] in the face some sign of its emotion. The radiant eyes glow from all sides, sparkling and casting fire like diamonds for fullness of so great an amount of humors which come up to them. The face widens, swells, and is embossed, becoming better colored by the sanguine vapors and by the buildup of humors that the skin holds captive. For if it were not for the thickness of the skin that stops them from escaping away, they would soon be dissipated and would not cause these effects.

The same reasoning demonstrates why the forehead is more taut, clear, and shining. In short, the entire face is beautified in joyous and contented people, due to a certain glow and delightful vivacity which the humors, fluttering through the skin, produce. The mouth is slightly drawn back, fashioning in the cheeks pretty little dimples, named Gelasins:[c] this is due to a contraction that the muscles undergo through repletion, since the face is filled with humors and sanguine vapors that build up there when the heart dilates. For the dilated heart is either unable to retain them, or willingly it sends them forth to welcome the delightful object. But it is more probable[d] that the heart is unable to stop them, due to its excessive opening up, seeing it does not employ reason, for otherwise it would think more about the safety of its own life, and would never allow, to its great detriment, such waste and spending of humors normally suffered by those who die of joy. For the strength of the heart is overcome by such prodigality when, expanding too much, it is unable to retain some for its own provisions. Of this Galen used to say: "The strength of animals does not issue from such violence or ardor in joy, as in anger, but, on the contrary, if it had beforehand some vivacity, in that case it is completely lost, since, released through an excessive joy, it abandons the heart, is dissipated, and becomes faint. For this reason (he says), some people, too pusillanimous and of little courage, die of a great rejoicing." He himself interprets this lack of courage elsewhere, saying: "Some die of weakness and faintheartedness that issues from the mouth of the patient's stomach, others of bitter pain, strange fear, or excessive pleasure. For the soul is easily dissipated in those who have little vigor and who, being ignorant, know not how to resist, mitigate, and break the violent movements of the mind. Among such people, some die of sadness, but not suddenly, as from other things. The magnanimous man is never overcome with cares, or other troubles of the mind

a. Signs of joy appearing in the face.

b. The face is like an indicator, or the face of a clock, showing the interior movements of its gears.

c. *Gelasin,* word for word, means laughing; the front teeth are likewise nicknamed because they show in laughter.

d. It is certainly more probable, for if it were a question of going out to welcome, the heart would not be a part, but an entire organism, reasonable and civil.

that are stronger than sadness, because he enjoys powerful and assured strengths of soul, and his emotions do not have great vehemence, and so forth."

The makeup of the heart is of great importance in this matter; for the feeble, weak, and loose heart is not as fit for retaining the humors when it is upset, whence it happens that those who have such a one are unhesitatingly cowardly. The hardy and valiant, on the contrary, have a small, thick, nervy, tight and manly heart which easily keeps its humors closed up. Such are the dog, the lion, and other courageous animals. This is the opinion of Aristotle, who says: "Fearful animals are those that have a large heart: the hardy and assured ones have a medium or small heart. For the feeling that comes as a result of fear is natural to an enormous heart inasmuch as, due to its largeness, it does not have enough warmth,[e] and the small amount it does have becomes cold in such a large vessel."[34] It is, therefore, probable that such were the hearts of those said to have died of a sudden and unexpected joy, as Pliny wrote of Chilon of Lacadaemon, who died of happiness upon seeing his son come in triumph from the Olympic games.[35] Sophocles and Denys the Tyrant of Sicily also died of joy when they heard news of their victories in tragedies.[36] A mother, seeing her son return safely after the battle of Cannes, contrary to a false report she had heard, expired out of great joy. In our own time the Duchess of Vic-fezensac in the county of Armagnac, at sixty years of age, when told her daughter was dying (in order to withdraw from some company), died suddenly upon arriving and finding her well and sound. It is also said that Polycrites,[37] a noble lady, died of an unexpected pleasure, and Phillipides, the writer of comedies,[38] for having beyond his expectation won the prize in a literary contest. Aulus Gellius tells that a man named Diagoras gave up the ghost before his sons' eyes and in their hands when he saw the three youngsters, one a boxer, one a pancratist, and one a wrestler, victorious and all three crowned the same day of the Olympics.[39] The great Valerius wrote that two women died, each one upon seeing her son return against all hope from a battle.[40] It is not, however, surprising that one lose his life over such a happiness since every day we see very weak[f] people faint from a small joy; for this fainting is a partial death.

I think that I have sufficiently proven that in joy there is dissipated a great quantity of humors and good blood, which makes the heart's feelings show in the face. If one asks the source of such a harmony, we shall reply that it is due to the softness, tenuity, or delicacy of the face, which suffers every change easily, along with its great diversity of parts in which various changes take place, and also because the indicators and signs of the feelings are more apparent there than elsewhere. I grant that the humors flow in all directions throughout the body, but the greater part flow upward to the face in their lightness. There, retained for a time by the skin, they emboss it, draw back the lips handsomely, make the eyes sparkle, the cheeks redden, and cause other effects which clearly point to joy.

e. It must be supposed that the natural warmth is slight, as in melancholic animals. For man, who has much natural warmth, also has a larger heart than other animals his size.

f. It is, properly speaking, delicacy and softness, to which women are much more subject than men.

CHAPTER XII
WHAT COMES PARTICULARLY FROM SADNESS

Just the contrary of what we deduced to have come from joy marks sorrow, which drives down the humors, and amasses them inwardly there, where those that had been spread out in the eyes and throughout the face withdraw also. Whence it happens that the face[a] shrinks and withdraws (as if it were fleeing) and becomes pale; the nose seems to lengthen, the mouth is preceded by the lips, which thicken and swell but go limp, due to the absence of the material which had filled the muscles that set up and hold the lips in place. The forehead is all wrinkled, the brow heavy, dense, and thick for the same reason. The eyes, darkened and dull, have lost their sparkle and gay vivacity, remaining sullen and stopped by a great weight, having lost what made them shine[b] and move. This change is caused by the retreat of the humors towards the heart, where they concentrate as if to comfort and assure it; or rather they hold in disdain and horror, hate, and flee the reason for the trouble.

And because of this, just as in joy, many die suddenly from a great sadness, when their little soul,[c] weak in itself and pressed with a great emotion, is instantly extinguished and suffocated. For the extinction proper imitates the nature of this feeling coming from coldness; the suffocation results from the affluence of blood which races back to the principle of life.[41] These two types of movement are found somewhat in joy as well as in sadness; for the natural warmth, in order to maintain itself, needs to keep taking in and giving out air, which the heart enjoys, sometimes expanding, sometimes contracting. If the heart becomes too dilated, it is unable to shrink in time; this causes it to keep too long a time its thick smoke, which stifles the heat. When it contracts excessively, it is unable to open itself up again soon enough to take in fresh air, and so the heat is extinguished. For it is not enough to expel the heated air, or take in the fresh; it is also imperative that the two actions succeed one another. If one takes too much time, loss of consciousness follows, and if still more time, death.

These effects of joy and sorrow are greatly aided by the substance of the heart. For the soft, tender, and slack heart opens up beyond measure when a great pleasure comes along, because it lends itself easily to such a syncope, caused often by joy, a bath, or hot air. The hard and tight heart, on the other hand, will faint promptly away less from happiness than from being upset. For the hardness (especially joined with heaviness) resists loosening, and favors excessive suppression.

a. Signs of sadness appearing in the face.

b. These are the humors and natural warmth which render the body frisky, as is the case with portliness.

c. Little soul, diminutive of soul, as is said in Latin, *animula,* to signify its delicateness and weakness.

CHAPTER XIII
WHAT IS PROPER TO HAPPINESS AND LAUGHTER

The effects of joy and of sorrow are so clearly evident that they need only to be mentioned, without other proof. We have, therefore, only taken the trouble to give the reasons behind their principal accidents, which are the signs of these feelings, manifested in the face.

It is now necessary to know how laughter is formed, what proper movement it has in responding to its proper object, what it draws from joy, and what it draws from sorrow, if it is true that it participates in both, as we have said above. As for the change in the face, laughter[a] expresses more the traits of joyousness than of joy itself; so much so that one could say that it manifests greater feelings and signs of contentment than does simple joy. For not only does it draw back the mouth, but it uncovers the teeth and makes the throat open; it widens, swells and reddens the face, deepening the Gelasins (which are the dimples in the cheeks) much more than does joy, and so fills the eyes with humors that they glisten fully and tear. From this we can understand that the heart is greatly moved in laughter, much more so than in happiness, and yet in the same fashion. One clearly feels it flounder about while laughing; and that this is due to its expanding, as it does in joy, the similar effects sufficiently bear witness, for all proceed from the humors and sanguine vapors which rise to the face from the heart. The extent of the effects which follow it shows most clearly that the agitation is very rapid and vehement, since besides those mentioned above (which are more conspicuous in laughter than in joy), laughter has some others peculiar to itself, such as the interrupted voice, the bouncing chest, the extremely tense stomach muscles, the arms, legs, and the entire body moved, shaken and tossed about, with other strange effects which we shall mention later.

If, therefore, the opening of the heart in laughter is so remarkable that there is an excessive loss of humors, how is it that one does not die from laughter sooner than from a sudden happiness? In the smallest laugh more humors are consumed than in the greatest rejoicing, if it is true that the indicators[b] noted in the face, and which bespeak both laughter and joy, come from a widened heart whence spring their material causes. What? Those who die of joy lose all their humors, yet one does not see them laugh. Nor is the material lacking that imparts to the face the great characteristics of laughter. If, therefore, one does not die from laughing at length, and if those who die of pleasure do not laugh, even though their heart dilates extremely and loses all its humors, something else must enter in to produce laughter besides these two causes which, by themselves, turn out the soul sooner than a laugh would.

This will guide us to the other difference that separates the essence of laughter from that of pure and simple joy. The first one lies in the object, as we have already

a. For the accidents of laughter are more noticeable and vehement.

b. If there is greater opening and widening, there is greater loss of humors. From this it follows that one will die sooner of laughter than of simple joy.[42]

demonstrated, and the second will lie in the movement, which follows the diversity of the matter, and is so peculiar to laughter that I judge it to be the principal of these differences. Laughter is born of two contraries, one of which hinders the other from being excessive, and this is the reason[c] that one does not easily die of laughter. But this matter, due to its difficulty, deserves to be delved into, and we reserve it for the next chapter.

CHAPTER XIV
THAT LAUGHTER IS COMPOSED OF CONTRARY MOVEMENTS DERIVED FROM JOY AND SORROW

The emotion of laughter, as we have shown, comes from an empty and foolish joyousness. From this we concluded that the heart is moved over laughable things in a manner different from that of real and simple joy. For in the latter there is only a dilatation with great loss of humors; in laughter this movement is restrained by yet another, which stops all the humors from being emptied out immediately. These two movements together will constitute that movement which we claim to be the peculiar difference in laughter's because, being joined to the conditions of its matter, and to its accidents, it perfects its essence. It must be that this movement is composed since it proceeds from a double emotion,[a] just as the cause of it is also double.[43] For laughable matter gives us pleasure and sadness: pleasure in that we find it unworthy of pity, and that there is no harm done, nor evil that we consider of consequence. The heart therefore rejoices over it, and expands just as it does in real joy. There is also sadness, because all laughable matter comes from ugliness and impropriety: the heart, upset over such unseemliness, and as if feeling pain, shrinks and tightens. This displeasure is very light, for we are hardly upset over what happens to others when the occasion is slight. The joy that we have knowing that there is nothing to pity (other than a false appearance) has more effect on the heart than does the light sadness. If such a thing were in the smallest way to happen to us we would be much more upset, and because of that we would not be able to laugh (for it is necessary in laughter that the pleasure be greater than the sadness); but for another we are less worried.

This is how laughter is made up, of the contrariety or battle of two feelings,[b] holding the middle ground between joy and sadness, each of which in their extremities cause loss of life. Laughter can therefore be called a false joy with false displeasure, being a participant in both that retains the nature of neither. Whence it provides man with recreation, having been given him for his great pleasure, because

c. Why one does not easily die of laughter.

---

a. It must be that the emotion is double or mixed, just as is its object.

b. Each of these two emotions, joy and sorrow, by themselves and if extreme, cause loss of life.

it is far from extremes,[c] and nature likes the middle way. For this very reason one does not die from laughter,[d] for there is not such a widening of the heart as there is in extreme joy (nor, consequently, such a loss of humors) because it is suddenly taken aback by the shrinking. These contrary emotions which protect the heart from weakness and too great a dissipation succeed one another rapidly, and are maintained in this state; as long as the matter of laughter lasts, be it in speech, in action, or in thought, so does laughter continue.

Our senses do not distinguish these contrary movements because they follow each other so rapidly that they can be grasped by reason alone, from which we also learn[e] that laughter lasts as long as the object presented has its two conditions, and ceases when what had at first been laughable changes quality. For if the ugliness becomes excessive and some compassion remains, the heart will only have the movement belonging to sadness, which is simple contraction.

It is now necessary to see how the heart moves, and brings about with its movement the strange effects that we see in laughter. This will be the beginning of the explanation of the causes that we are searching.

CHAPTER XV
OF WHAT MOVEMENT THE HEART UNDERGOES IN LAUGHTER

We have cracked the nut, as one says in the proverb; we are getting to the meat and are at the most beautiful part in the treatment of our subject. We have pointed out all that precedes the act of laughter: it is the laughable matter, carried first by the conduits of the senses to touch the heart, which, in turn moved by the laughable, is stirred alternatively by sudden contrary movements. It is now necessary to state what results from it, how we laugh over it, which instruments form laughter, what is the cause of all its accidents—even of the change in the face, greater than in any of the other emotions. For all have their mark: fear and sorrow, a paleness; anger, joy, and shame, a blushing; and so forth with the rest. Laughter's mark is so evident that it cannot be hidden, as much because of the size of the indications as because of the violence of its commotion.

But let us get to the reason. When an object, pleasant with facetiousness and sad with ugliness, is presented suddenly, the heart moves very rapidly and unequally because it wishes to make two contrary movements at the same time, namely, one of

c. Man is the most temperate of all the animals and as if in the middle of all extremes. For this reason it was necessary that he be moved only by a passion far from all extremes.

d. He says this as if in passing, or as a common saying, for at the end of the third book he will show that some have died of it.

e. Reason teaches us that two contrary movements cannot be made together, but that one must cease before the other begins.

joy and the other of sorrow. Each one is short in that it is suddenly interrupted[a] by its contrary, which undercuts it; still, the dilatation outlasts the contraction since in all laughable matter there is more pleasure than pain. One follows the other so closely that it is possible for the heart to move about suddenly, and insofar as they hardly wish to be overcome, but rather fight to see who will go the fastest or who will be the master of the realm by depriving his adversary (whence it comes that they become mixed together), they could not be told apart if reason did not distinguish them. For two contraries cannot be together in the same place at the same time, and still retain their original strength and qualities.[44]

As for the senses, they only perceive a great upheaval working in the heart. Nor can they see the movement of the pericardium, which is shaken more than usual. This is the sheath or cover of the heart, which surrounds it on all sides without pressing it or adhering to it, and is so wide and roomy that the heart moves about at ease inside it, performing its ordinary systole[b] and diastole. But when it is greatly moved, it cannot spare its sheath from likewise being stirred and shaken, as is understandable. Whoever would like to test it has only to open the breast of a live animal, where he will be able to see at once how it works itself. For it is not the heart that first presents itself to view; it is hidden in its pericardium,[c] which alone we see move, shaken from the inside. It might also be that, naturally and without constraint, the heart and its little box work this way, but observation cannot tell. We understand only through reason and logic that the heart has a roomy pericardium that is not connected to it, so that it can move about inside in complete freedom. When it is greatly moved, as it is in the animal whose breast is being opened, everything is in commotion.[d] Is it not reasonable that it thus comes about through an emotion that troubles the heart, through a contrariety that causes laughter?

The pericardium, therefore, will be moved and shaken with the unequal and frequent movement of the heart. This is where all the stirring begins that is seen in laughter. It is from the reveling and fluttering heart which, like a mainspring, transfers to the other parts its frolicsome passion.

a. They interrupt each other reciprocally and blend together, as in the blending of the elements, so to speak.

b. Systole is the tightening, diastole the dilatation of the heart, just as in the pulse of the arteries.

c. Pericardium means "around the heart." It is its sheath, or capsule and box.

d. Everything is in commotion, that is, the heart and its sheath.

CHAPTER XVI
HOW THE DIAPHRAGM IS SHAKEN BY LAUGHTER

The pericardium, moved by the heart, pulls on the diaphragm to which it is thoroughly connected in men, quite otherwise than in animals,[a] as can be seen through anatomy. And this is (in my opinion) the reason, or at least one of the principal ones, why only man is capable of laughter.[45] It is, then, very easy for the heart to push the diaphragm and to coerce it according to its feelings since it is thus conjoined to it by the pericardium.

The diaphragm is the instrument of normal respiration, which never ceases, not even when the others are resting. Its substance, form, and place show how much it is apt and prompt in following certain movements, by which it lets itself be led easily, consenting to and obeying the heart. It was also necessary for the heart that it not be too tightly bound to any part, but rather loose and suspended, thus accommodating movement, and that it give easily so as not to impede or restrain the heart in the least in its great troublings and movements. Nature has indeed placed reason above, which commands the passions; yet she wished that the heart have no restraint in the breast. It was necessary, therefore, to free it or to connect it to other parts that might be able to follow its movement quickly when there would be need to do so. For this she has well provided by fashioning the diaphragm in such a way that it moves according to the whims of the heart, but not in the same manner.

In order to understand this point better, one needs to know about the function of the diaphragm, which we shall learn from the manners and kinds of respiration. Galen puts forth two of them: one is normal or effortless inspiration and expiration, and the other is violent. The violent kind comes from the intercostal muscles (of which the internal expire, and the external inspire) along with others rooted in the chest and in the lower abdomen. Normal inspiration is caused by the diaphragm alone, which is able to widen the chest enough to take in air when there is not a great need of it. Normal expiration does not need any muscles: it happens when all of them cease, and when gravity alone[b] presses down the chest. This is Galen's opinion, who nevertheless says elsewhere that the muscles of the epigastrium work at it also; but this serves us little now, and it will be examined better later. For the moment we are contented to know that during expiration the diaphragm rests and does nothing from its own movement. It then becomes much looser, for in order to expand the chest and cause inspiration (which is its proper function) it stretches on all sides and becomes very taut. When it is not able to do so any more, it begins to draw back and pull into itself, only to stretch out directly afterwards. The stricture comes in

a. Principal instrument of laughter, of which the other animals are deprived, insofar as they have no need of it, being deprived also of the risible faculty.

b. This is not to say that expiration is purely voluntary, or that the chest goes back to its former state, but the voluntary movement is greatly aided by the weight of the expanded body.

expiration, due to the shrinking of the chest or to the action of the epigastric[c] muscles. The diaphragm, finding itself thus loosened, is unable to resist the heart's movements and so it also is shaken. When it is very taut, the heart cannot make it move, or does so only with difficulty, since the diaphragm is performing a task extremely necessary for the whole body, as inspiration is, and it is understandable that it resists the heart with great vehemence.

Thus, if laughter springs from these movements, it will never be formed except in exhaling. Experience supports this argument also: for we never laugh except during the contraction of the chest, and when all the air spent in laughing has been emptied, one hastens to breathe in more. During this time it is not possible to laugh except with great difficulty, and in small bursts, but it is necessary to wait for the expiration immediately following, in which laughter continues. Consequently, in inspiration the diaphragm does not yield to the heart whereas in expiration it is at its disposal. The heart, therefore, troubled by contrariety which is caused by the frolicsome joy conceived from the laughable matter, since it is able to move the loose and slack diaphragm, shakes it. This is during the time when the diaphragm draws back little by little and pulls in to its center. Then the trembling motion of the heart works the diaphragm in such a way that the chest is compelled to move along with it at the same pace[d] (even though the chest falls inward again and again, tumbling freely) because it is connected to the diaphragm all around. From this proceeds also the cause of the lungs' being pressed in a similar manner, characterized particularly by the sound of the air that is forced out, which we wish to discuss with the help of some familiar examples.

CHAPTER XVII
THAT LAUGHTER CAN BE ILLUSTRATED BY THE EXAMPLE OF BELLOWS, AND OF THE TREMBLING PARTS

Because examples illustrate conveniently what is sought, and because through a like[a] we better arrive at an understanding of another, in order that we might continue this treatise according to the best means of instructing possible to us and by the same explain clearly our idea, I shall make bold to show through familiar examples what I have proposed.

Bellows are used to light a fire by spreading apart their sides, leaving a vacuum between them which by natural necessity becomes filled with air. It comes in

c. These are the muscles that are called abdominal, and are ten in number. They serve in respiration and in the rejection of excrement, whence it happens that one sometimes pisses and shits from laughter.

d. At the same pace: this is because it made it go along with it, and work at its own rate.

---

a. The argument of the like is not irrefutable, but it instructs familiarly and makes the hearer more apt to understand the principal point better.

through certain inlets made in a place that has against it on the inside a loose flap which refuses the air an exit once it is sucked in. When we wish to empty the air by pressing together the two sides of the bellows, we force it to exit through a single hole with such violence that it makes wind. And if we want this air to be pushed out jerkingly as if broken up, it will come out cut up and will make an analogous sound. Bellows are made in the image of the chest, and just as it does not move except by means of the muscles, so too bellows can do nothing without our hands, which dilate and compress them. In free inspiration the diaphragm corresponds to the hands; in the violent kind, the other muscles assisting in it do. Whence, just as the consciously[b] jerking hands break up the compressing of the bellows, causing a broken sound, so does the diaphragm worked by the trembling of the heart compress the lungs and the chest. This is what I was talking about in the foregoing chapter, and what the example would make clear.

But since we have spoken just above of tremors to which the condition of the diaphragm could be compared, it is necessary to explain in what sense we mean it. This trembling results from the weakness of the faculty causing the movement: the faculty[c] raises up the parts as best it can, but since it is weak the great weight of the chest overcomes it. This battle is the trembling, over which most often the faculty[d] dominates. In an almost similar manner, we are saying that the jumping movement of the heart stops the diaphragm from drawing back freely, and impeded in its drawing back, the diaphragm undergoes a kind of trembling. For the heart is trying to constrain the diaphragm to a movement much like its own while the latter is attempting to finish its undertaking, which is to contract the chest. The victory finally rests with the diaphragm, the compressing virtue of which has a greater power, seeing that in spite of the resistance the heart gives it, it draws back bit by bit. During its widening the heart has no power to stop it, so necessary a thing is inspiration.

We have much advanced and profited from having found the source of the risible faculty, showing through simple reasonings how the heart is moved by such a condition, working upon the aloof diaphragm. For these are the principal instruments of the act called laughter, or laughing. Nonetheless, the heart is felt to be the master worker, and author of all the accidents; the diaphragm is the coadjutor, or the organ by means of which they come about, as I shall from this point on discuss in detail in what order they are produced, taking care to put first those that are essential, and that are found in all laughter as ordinary, simpler, and easy. Then we shall point by point pursue the others, which spring from greater violence and are found only in excessive laughter. For one must always begin with the most common things, and from there pass on to the less frequent, and those which come about rarely.

b. It is conscious when they do it purposefully.

c. The faculty, virtue, or power to move is impeded by the weight that it is unable freely to command.

d. The faculty, or power, dominates when, however it may come about, it moves the parts about, this way and that.

CHAPTER XVIII
HOW BY LAUGHTER THE CHEST IS SHAKEN AND WHENCE COMES THE BROKEN-UP VOICE

Galen in his treatise on the movement of the muscles says that the chest by its weight alone, and without being pulled down, lowers, shrinks, and goes back to its former position when the diaphragm (after having dilated the chest in order to gently suck in air) contracts back little by little.[46] Elsewhere he states that the muscles of the abdomen govern this action, since they are clearly felt to contract in each expiration.[47] The latter opinion seems the better, but be that as it may, only the epigastric muscles are involved in this when the heart has no new movement that would augment the necessity or hinder the normal movements of respiration, which is what happens in laughing. For the diaphragm, drawn by the heart, loses its freedom and power to pull in normally when the chest relaxes and, shaken by a disordered movement, it contracts the chest also in jerks, willy nilly.

One must not be surprised that the diaphragm (which is during this time felt to be lower than it normally is), forced by the heart, does violence likewise to the chest which obeys it. For it would otherwise be in great danger of bursting or of overstretching. This is why, besides the abdominal muscles, the internal intercostals serve also this function and aid the diaphragm so much that the chest follows along with ease and gives it no adverse hindrance or resistance. With less intense laughter, in which the diaphragm is scarcely shaken and little restraint will suffice for the chest, few muscles take part; but as for the epigastrics, they never cease in even the smallest of laughs.

It is, therefore, certain that the need to breathe is augmented by laughter, and consequently the chest must be more greatly shaken. From this comes the fact that the voice trembles, namely, when the lungs give way, pressed upon by the ribs which are tightening; for with each contraction the lungs expel the air they had taken in. If the compression is continuous and without repetition, nothing is heard, or else only a well-sustained voice; if it is broken up, the sound of the voice will also be cut up, as we have demonstrated above with the example of the bellows. A small laugh of only a partial jiggle does not produce the open mouth or the torn voice. There is only a bit of a sound passing through the nostrils, caused by a force and an impetuosity which drives out the air more hurriedly than in normal expiration. This effect or accident is one of the principal ones, as is the preceding one, for since laughter is never unaccompanied by the shaking of the chest, it is, then, impossible that one not hear the air coming from the mouth (or at least the nose), making a spasmodic noise. This is what causes it to bear the epithet *tremulous*—most fitting, given its natural condition.

CHAPTER XIX
WHENCE PROCEED THE OPENING OF THE MOUTH, THE STRETCHING OF THE LIPS, AND THE WIDENING OF THE CHIN

The third of the inseparable accidents of laughter is the stretching of the thinned lips with the widening of the chin, never lacking in even the slightest laugh. In the greatest or most sustained there is besides these the opening of the mouth. And as for the causes, they have no greater difference than that of greater or lesser degree. They are not very easy to find, and this is the most difficult part of our work; we do have, however, some principles that will serve as a basis for our proofs. These are the conclusions drawn after having thoroughly debated the drawing back of the mouth, which comes from the joy. For since these two emotions[a] have considerable affinity with each other, they share this common trait.

Now, we have proven that joy causes a medium stretching of the lips by virtue of the humors and sanguine vapors which pour forth from the heart and rise to course through the muscles of the face. In laughter, aside from this stretching, there is some plying of the mouth which is necessarily proof of a more powerful condition since there is in its movement greater vehemence. Upon the opening up of the heart in laughter, a great quantity of subtle matter is lost which in rising fills the muscles of our cheeks and causes a certain convulsion in them, of which Galen speaks: "Since voluntary movements are made sometimes through muscles made taut and contracted towards their source, and sometimes due to their being full of humors that rush into them, the convulsion comes about normally. For air, vapor, or humor can be generated in them, which will make them swell, and so on." These words show us very clearly that the muscles filled with the humors are able to undergo convulsion. Yet how could they be filled in laughter since the sudden contraction hinders the effusion of humors, in which lies the great assurance that we talked about earlier? What the dilatation, overtaken with compression, is unable to do on one occasion, it accomplishes on several through frequent repetition, and perhaps even less spirits are lost in laughter than in joyousness. It is true that, occurring as it does in this way,[b] the heart does not tire as much as it does in joy, where the humors are lost all of a sudden. Yet this explanation does not suffice to prove what we are maintaining, but rather will remain suspect, and seem contrary to what we have already shown.

It is necessary to have other proofs from anatomy, since these facial expressions are caused by muscles that move during laughter without our knowing it, in spite of ourselves, without the order of the will; for they obey the impetuosity of an emotion that is natural and not voluntary. The cheeks have their movement from four muscles at each staddle. The first is formed out of the fleshy membrane which is so well lined with filaments that it becomes muscular. Its principal base is in front of the neck on the bone called the clavicle and on the upper joint of the arm, from which it extends all the way up to the cheekbones. This is the governing master of

a. These two emotions, that is, joy and laughter.

b. Occurring in this way, that is, in an interrupted manner that relieves considerably.

the movements made in the cheeks, lips, and the anterior skin of the neck. It is the one that can flatten the chin and draw it down (where, due to its weight, it is somewhat inclined) when the chest, heaving with laughter, shakes and moves it. Or, if it does not have the power to open the mouth completely, it at least will flatten the lips somewhat with its contraction.

"What?" someone will say. "In a small laugh, when the chest is not in so strong a commotion that it is able to prevail upon this muscle, there is plying of the mouth, which could not come about through the action of said muscle without considerable attraction.[c] Moreover, in continual fevers, pleurisies, asthmas, and several other ills where much respiration is required, the chest must move with all its power. We clearly see, therefore, that the chest must then rise and fall, shaken with painful violence, along with the shoulders and the arms, all of which endure hurt and strife. Now it is probable that the above-mentioned muscle, since it is rooted high in the chest, is also attracted. Yet none of this plying of the mouth is seen. If the sick hold their mouths open, it is most often voluntary in order to breathe in more easily, and not involuntary as when laughter is violent." We can, nevertheless, assert that it is proper and natural that this wide muscle, being pulled upon a little in laughter, remains in such a state (as occurs in convulsions, as long as the action lasts),[d] due to certain necessities. These are the necessity to breathe, and because, inasmuch as during laughter air is expelled forcefully and then quickly drawn in again, it was better for our convenience that the mouth remain open. For through the narrow passage of the nostrils it is not possible for such a large amount of material to exit easily and quickly, nor for provision for more to reenter suddenly. This is why this muscle keeps the mouth open wide as though yawning until the end of the laugh, and why it is moved, pulled from the chest, either because filled with humors, or because of both these causes together.

This first muscle[e] moving the cheeks would not alone suffice for such a function without being aided by the others. The second comes from the upper jawbone on the cheekbones, and is attached to the upper lip. The third comes from the lower jawbone and goes to the lower lip, and by means of it the chin is greatly flattened. The fourth is found in the cheeks, in the part that we swell up, reinforced by a portion of the muscle that draws the nose from the sides. It is necessary that the opening of the mouth and of the lips come from these muscles, moving them when we wish outside of laughter, and in laughter, but in spite of ourselves, with the jaw sometimes lowered and sometimes drawn up. In heavy and dissolute laughter, which is called cachinnation, the throat is opened so much that it is able to stretch; in medium laughter there is a medium opening; in the smallest the teeth touch and are barely uncovered, or the lips, very flattened, are over them. All this is due to a muscular contraction, great or small, causing the effects; and from it comes the

c. Considerable attraction, he says, meaning that this muscle was violently attracted, not only filled with vapors.

d. Laughter constrains the mouth to remain open for a considerable duration.

e. Enumeration of the muscles of the lips and cheeks.

gelasin[f] befitting so much the cheeks of modest laughers. Gelasin is this pretty little dimple of which Martial[48] says:

His is the face less gracious
Who has not the gelasin joyous.

By the same means the widening of the chin is accomplished, wherein in some people a great cleft is seen. Aside from the above-mentioned reasons, the causes of yawning show us that the affluence of the humors and vapors into the parts surrounding the mouth is able not only to draw back the lips but even to open them widely, dilating the jawbones. For one yawns (as Galen says) when there is continual distention with opening because of certain vaporous and thick humors retained in the muscles.[g] If, therefore, we are constrained to have the mouth open while yawning until such vapor is dissipated, then in laughter, which brings about the same accident, will there apply the same cause, except that the humors which fill the muscles in laughers are more subtle than the vapors causing yawning. Whence there shall come this difference: that the least yawn will open the mouth as much as the greatest laughter. Aside from the above-mentioned causes, one taken from experience can be put forth which shows clearly the source of this facial expression. When one pushes a little while moving the bowels, or if one has a bellyache due to the diaphragm's contracting against the bowels (which are considerably pressed upon by the epigastric muscles from the sides), one plies the mouth just as when laughing. Why is that? Because of the diaphragmatic contraction. For when it draws into itself in order better to push against the bowels, and to force out of them what is harmful and unpleasant, the chest remains low and constrained, the respiration vague, and there comes about a grinding of the teeth, with a stretching of the lips, as if one were laughing. Just the same thing happens with other pains in whatever part they may be, if one does not want to cry out, but endure the asperity of the pain patiently. Then one does likewise as with intestinal pain, for the diaphragm contracts, halting respiration,[h] as if thinking that with its constriction it could push out what is hurting us. Excessive weeping over some great sadness causes a similar countenance, so much so that whoever would see and hear it only would scarcely be able to distinguish whether one is laughing or weeping. Consider two men in a painting, one of whom is laughing so hard that he becomes completely undone, the other flails about horribly, complains and weeps large tears; even if the work is finely done you will not know to which to assign pleasure and to which sadness, so much are the faces alike in these two passions.

From this argument we gather first of all that laughter partakes of sadness (as we have always said) since the plying of the mouth serves in one as in the other; secondly, that severe pain and sadness cause the diaphragm to contract, the chest to shrink, the belly to go in and respiration to be suspended, all of which are the

f. *Gelan* in Greek means laugh, whence gelasin, which is the sign of laughter.
g. Book Three of the *Difficulties of Respiration*.
h. This is why when in pain one holds one's breath. See Aristotle, Problem 9 of Book 27.[49]

common accidents or effects of laughter. These effects are noticeable, but their causes are most obscure. One can say that the diaphragm, moved by the heart (for the heart is the author[i] of the movements that follow an emotion), makes several other muscles harmonize themselves to its movement, and have friendship or compliance with it. Anatomy teaches us that the different parts depend upon one another, and those which are upheld or conjoined in mutual liaison have mutual consent.[k] For all the parts of the body feel the pain and the pleasure that is in the liver, the heart, and the brain, through the intermediary of the veins, arteries, and nerves which come from them; but the mouth of the stomach sympathizes particularly with the brain, more than other members outside the head, and the brain with the mouth of the stomach, due to the large and very sensitive nerves which surround it.

Now all the nerves which move the diaphragm come through the neck and make up the greater part of the fourth couple (augmented and reinforced by the fifth), from which come also those moving the jawbone.[l] This is why the diaphragm, upon being wounded and communicating the spasm immediately to the nerves of the fourth couple likewise, causes the lips to be drawn back and the mouth to open convulsively, showing a false appearance of laughter, called canine. By the same means we prove that the arms are shaken in uncontrolled laughter, inasmuch as the seventh pair of the nerves of the nape is servicing them completely, with the exception of a few filaments which go to the head, neck, and diaphragm. By an accord of the copulation among motor nerves, therefore, the diaphragm, moved and shaken, can move other muscles to consent, and cause the plying of the mouth seen in weeping as well as in laughter. It is the most marvelous accident there is in it, and of which the cause is most obscure; but we have forwarded it so much that if one or the other does not suffice, both together can make such a great commotion.

We have found the cause of all that follows medium laughter, the inseparable things and the ordinary accidents, namely, the agitation of the diaphragm pulled upon by the heart, the jostling of the chest, the pulmonary compression, the broken noise of the voice, all of which appertain to it. Finally, the stretching back of the lips and opening of the mouth when the laughter continues more than a little while. Laughter can nowise be without all these accidents, for they are of its essence, proper to it, always accompanying it and increasing in observable extent as the laughter is more dissolute and approaches cachinnation. Aside from those mentioned above come still others proceeding from yet greater vehemence, which we shall now treat.

i. The author is the heart, his minister is the diaphragm.

k. There is double consent: both common and particular.

l. The lower jawbone is meant, for the upper is immobile in nearly all animals except the crocodile.

CHAPTER XX
HOW BY LAUGHTER ARE MADE WRINKLES IN THE FACE AND AROUND THE EYES

When laughter is modest, born of a light occasion, the lips stretch back to a medium opening; when it is dissolute or of long duration the throat opens wide and the lips draw back to an extreme. For the agitation of the heart follows the force of the object proportionately,[a] and all the accidents of laughter are more apparent when it lasts very long. And because of this, laughter becomes ugly, improper, and lascivious, letting go excessively and tiring the muscles, which are then unable to draw up the mouth and put it back in its right position, due to which it remains indecently open. This in effect follows cachinnation, no less than the wrinkles in the face and around the eyes. For they commonly appear in those who willingly have a fat laugh when the muscles above the mouth contract upward and the others downward, so much so that because of the laughter one shows who has the prettiest teeth. Due to this contraction, the skin must wrinkle in the cheeks and in the two corners of the eyes. For the muscles (which are quite thick and numerous), pressed upon and contracted in several places, make diverse wrinkles among which is the beautiful gelasin. In the exterior corners of the eyes the wrinkles are more common and natural than elsewhere due to the thinness and softness of the skin, in spite of the fact that the wrinkling of the cheeks stops there upon meeting that of the forehead when its skin stretches down to make it wider. At this point the two join and make an infinity of wrinkles that are very visible and (depending on the dryness) lasting, and from which those who are getting older form the first wrinkles.

From this argument we are able to understand why young girls are warned not to laugh foolishly, and threatened that they will become old sooner.[b] This is also why dissolute and too continued a laughter causes an ugly countenance because of such opening of the mouth, from which come many wrinkles in the face. In children, due to the tenderness of the skin, these wrinkles are gone as soon as they are made: they do not last. But with time, as the skin becomes dry, the continual wrinkling in the same place keeps them imprinted. Whence it happens that fat people become more wrinkled in old age than the others: not only because once the fat is lost their skin withers, but also for having excessively and willingly laughed. For fat people are very sanguine (if their stoutness comes, as we believe it does, from an abundance of blood) and such people[c] are naturally joyous, foolish, and laughing. This is why it is not strange that those who have a tendency to wrinkle arrive at wrinkles sooner through too much laughing and get from it the better share of them.

a. Even without a great object some are dissolute in laughter, which comes from a weakness and stupidity.

b. Why young girls are forbidden to laugh.

c. He demonstrates this in the Third Book, chapter IV.[50]

CHAPTER XXI
HOW IT COMES ABOUT THAT THE EYES SPARKLE AND TEAR

The eyes sparkle in joy (as we have said above) because they are full of clear and glistening humors which shimmer as they take flight, seeking all about an exit, just like a bird in a cage. In a small laugh the same is true for the same reason. For the humors, moved into agility, create in laughing eyes a joyous splendor, but not such a distinct one as in continued or lascivious laughter, because the extent of the causes heightens the effects. This glistening is the principal sign of joy and delight. For one may well feign being joyous by assuming in the mouth and the rest of the face a countenance of contentment through the usage of the muscles which, obedient to our will, shape it; but the sparkling of the eyes cannot be successfully[a] imitated at our bidding in that it follows the widening of the heart and the effusion of humors, which lie not in our will if the occasion is not present.

From the outset I called this glistening the principal sign of joy since it could not be dissimulated or falsified, coming more from nature than from artifice. Some people have shining, gay, and lascivious eyes naturally, which are so full of humors that sadness cannot dull them. Thus, a sparkling eye does not always imply a joyous heart, since it can be so ordinarily; it nevertheless does plead well that the soul is hardy, joyous, and inclined to pleasure, loving all kinds of recreation. And in fact, the people that have gay and lively eyes are willingly pleasant, merry, jovial, and do not develop melancholy by themselves.

Concerning the tears that laughers shed, it is necessary to know that one weeps of sadness when suffering presses the eyes and the adjacent areas with constraint, squeezing out[b] their humidity. Joy, on the other hand, dilates and opens the pores, from which the humors are able to flow and fall in the form of tears. Or (which is the principal reason), the tears are engendered from the vapors and humors which this part of the body, due to its softness, receives abundantly and then thickens into water with its coldness, just as the brain makes its distillations. For the eyes are obviously cold.[c] All these causes together make laughers' eyes tear, and we have shown clearly that they participate both in pleasure and in pain. There are some people that tear at the slightest laugh, as I do, and such people perspire profusely from the head, and have a great supply of humors in the eyes. Others are slow and hindered in it, not weeping so quickly from laughter, pleasure, or sadness. Yet hardly any are seen who do not shed a few tears after a long laugh.

a. Successfully, he says, for there is an evident difference between true and feigned joy.

b. See the reasons of Alexander Aphrodisias, Problem 29 of Book I, as to why one weeps both from joy and sadness.[51]

c. The author has since changed his mind, for today he holds that the brain and the eyes are not like all other spermatic parts, and that water is engendered in them as fat is elsewhere, by the density of the tissues.

CHAPTER XXII
WHY THE FACE FLUSHES AND THE FOREHEAD AND NECK VEINS SWELL

After just one or two laughs one does not change color unless one blushes easily; but when the laughter lasts a long time the most pale become red due to the quantity of humors and sanguine vapors which rise little by little. The parts of the face moved augment its tinting with their agitation. Besides this, impeded respiration, seeming difficult and considerably broken up, makes the face redden as anyone can experience by holding his breath.

These same causes make the veins in the forehead and neck swell more than usual in those in whom they show and who laugh for a long time. For the vapors and the humors, filling the vessels[a] which give them passage, enlarge them considerably because of the great pressure in them. Hampered respiration evidently causes this also, because of which the entire neck swells up unbelievably in some people, due both to laughter and to hampered breathing.

CHAPTER XXIII
HOW LAUGHTER CAUSES COUGHING AND THAT WHICH WAS IN THE MOUTH TO EXIT THROUGH THE NOSE

Very often one laughs for so long a time and with such great vehemence that the lungs become heated and melt their mucus, which then tickles, stings, and irritates them, and forces coughing in order to eject it. Other times this is caused by a drop falling from above into the lungs when the head feels heated and when a quantity of humors has been recently engendered from vapors, and when these humors which were already there become pervasive.

It is for the same reason that one coughs from laughing, having something in the mouth which, because of this disorder, falls into the bronchial tube. The coughing due to this becomes very disagreeable and lasts until that which is in the respiratory passage comes out.[a] During this time the coughing works the chest about, convulses the entire body, shakes the brain and moves it in such a way that, the roots of the eyes being troubled, they weep, swell, and seem to have to come out of the head. If the stomach is full of food, and one is the least bit inclined to vomit, this great upset empties everything from it. Such accidents happen commonly to those who while sipping or drinking are made to laugh, because it is very easy for liquids to flow into the gullet.

a. These vessels are the veins, where the pressurized blood causes this tension.

---

a. The cane of the lung, called the tracheal tube, can not bear to have anything occupy its canal.

Besides the above-mentioned effects there is another which is very common (if not proper)[b] in this occurrence: that of coughing out through the nose what is being drunk,[c] or if the mouth has not yet taken anything in, the nose's excrement alone. The reason for this is that one sips by sucking and drawing into oneself the liquid which, passing through the mouth, goes straight down to the stomach through the esophagus. During this action, inspiration is accomplished through the nostrils, and as long as one can hold one's breath the swallowing continues. For one is not able to expire or breathe out and suck in at the same time, as the proverb says.[d] If, therefore, during this, laughter presses upon us, it is necessary to cease inspiration completely since laughter never comes about except in expiring, as we have sufficiently proven. It is then necessary to force air out suddenly and in great amounts. If the air finds the mouth occupied, it jumps up through the nose which is the next closest passageway, and comes out with such impetuosity, because of the narrowness of the straits, that all that it meets is forced out.

CHAPTER XXIV
WHENCE IT COMES THAT THE ARMS, SHOULDERS, THIGHS, FEET, AND ENTIRE BODY CAN BE MOVED BY DINT OF LAUGHING

In chapter XIX we said that the arms are moved and shaken in excessive laughter because the seventh pair of nerves in the nape serves them in their entirety, except for a few strands going to the head, neck, and diaphragm. Such communication can suffice to make the arms, and the shoulders (all of which are intimately connected), harmonize with the diaphragmatic motion.

But there are numerous other occasions which are in no wise less important. These are the muscles moving the arms, which come from the chest. The first is rooted in the sternum and in the first half of the adjoining clavicle. The second proceeds from the other half, from the upper arm and from the tip of the shoulder. The fourth comes from the spines of the pectoral vertebrae, from the sixth on down. The shoulders, in a similar manner, from which hang the arms, have certain muscles coming from the chest.

It is, then, easy to understand how, when the chest is shaken by dissolute laughter, one sees the same arms and shoulders shake, and shake in such a way that they cannot be held back. And what also? The thighs undergo jouncing because of it, the feet dance about, and the whole body goes into a heap due to a consent of the forced and contracted muscles of all the parts. For all of them uphold each other, and all are connected together through nerves, ligaments, and tendons.

b. This is not proper to laughter but rather to coughing brought about by the initial shaking with which coughing begins immediately.

c. This is called Nezareth wine, inasmuch as it comes from the nose.

d. *Nemo potest simul flare et sorbere* (No one is able to simultaneously inhale and exhale), says the Latin.

CHAPTER XXV
CONCERNING THE PAIN FELT IN THE ABDOMEN FROM TOO MUCH LAUGHTER

The agitating of the diaphragm and the working of the epigastric muscles, which stretch thick and fast, often cause one after a long laugh to feel pain in the abdomen, as if one had been beaten with rods. For the diaphragm, almost completely shot with nerves, is highly sensitive, and has very sizeable nerves from the sixth pair, which make it feel so keenly that when it is ill it has the same symptoms as the brain.[a]

Besides the diaphragm, there are several tissues and membranes in the abdomen which are exquisitely sensitive. These are all connected and stretched due to a single cause during laughter with a tension so great that they approach being torn. The liver hangs from the diaphragm, and because of its heavy weight labors considerably in such an emotion, and does injury to the other.[b] The liver has scarcely any pain, not more than it has feeling. The spleen, the bowels, and similar viscera of the body's kitchen undergo the shock of the neighboring parts. In short, everything is in a great commotion, unleashed so violently that the belly thinks it is going to burst, and suffers from it greatly. But the principal locale of the pain is in the part under the belt, in the area of the diaphragm, which suffers more torment, and feels it much more, than the other parts.

This is why we press both hands on the stomach to ward off this pain, as if to restrain the agitation of the diaphragm, the cause of such a disorder. And in fact, this does help; for it arrests the bowels, stopping them from easily giving way to the diaphragm which is pushing down on them. It beats upon them by contracting, and if they do not give way because of lack of room, it is forced to diminish its movement. Thus, we notice that the laughter dies down, or at least the pain in the abdomen (coming from the continuing of the laughter) diminishes and passes when one presses hard against the stomach; for that affords considerable relief to all the viscera. Similar pain, and from a similar cause, comes to those who run a long time on foot or on horseback, and who have no better remedy than to use a bandage, and squeeze the stomach tightly.

CHAPTER XXVI
WHENCE IT COMES THAT ONE PISSES, SHITS, AND SWEATS BY DINT OF LAUGHING

At the neck of the bladder there is a round muscle which girds it all around like a ring, closing the passageway to the urine when it is contracted, and for which reason

a. Thus, the ancient Greeks called the diaphragm *phrenes*, that is, thought and understanding.

b. The liver does injury to the diaphragm due to its great weight.

it is called the sphincter.[a] The anal bowel has a similar one with the same name forbidding issue of the fecal matter so long as we wish to retain it. In order to void these excrements, it is necessary to make such muscles open by means of others which are stronger and which obey our will. These are the epigastrics, eight in number[b] not counting the diaphragm, which press in from all sides all together and push against the bowels and the bladder with such violence that the sphincters give way, no longer able through their contraction to prevent those vessels, ordained to receive and keep for a time these superfluities, from discharging them (if we wish to consent to it) as soon as they become disgusted with them.[c] For it lies within our will to make the sphincters stop their contraction, which is their unique function, instituted for retention; and expulsion of the excrement is accomplished by the natural forcing of the bladder and bowels, aided nonetheless by the constriction which the epigastric muscles effect, with the diaphragm.

It is, then, likely that when these muscles press a long time and with much violence, soliciting the bowels and the bladder to give up their contents (as it happens in laughter), if there is a quantity of liquid matter, all escapes us indecorously. For the agitation and jouncing is so strong that the sphincters are unable to resist, especially when after a long duration they become loose and weak, like the rest of the body, losing all strength.

As for the sweat (the third type of excrement which laughter forces to come out), it is easier to provoke it than those mentioned above; yet I put it last in order to proceed by degrees down to the weakness of fainting, and to death, if it can come from laughing. For these accidents commonly follow a notorious evacuation. Now perspiration comes after a long laugh, either out of the entire body or out of the face alone, in some people easily and quickly, in others later and more slowly. It is caused by the agitation and general commotion, which excite the humors and dilate the pores of the skin, neither more nor less than does hard labor. But the face especially sweats[d] profusely from a big laugh because of the moisture of this part of the body, which is adjacent to the brain, and because of the softness and sparseness of its skin, with the affluence of the spirits and sanguine vapors that rise up into it and are able to make a lot of water, either on their own or with the humors.

a. Sphincter signifies compressing, tightening, and restraining.

b. Sometimes ten, counting the two small ones called the appendages of the uprights.

c. They become disgusted with them when the excrements begin to displease, by their quality, quantity, or both.

d. Why one sweats more from the face even though it is a thin and unfleshy part is debated by Aristotle in the second problem of Book 36.

CHAPTER XXVII
THAT ONE CAN FAINT FROM LAUGHING AND WHETHER ONE COULD DIE OF IT

Sometimes laughter lasts for so long a time that, because of the great emotion and stress, it seems that the lungs will burst and no longer be able to provide for respiration because they cannot move as fast as the heart. Nor is the diaphragm able to help draw air in adequately, and all the muscles of the chest are already very weak. You would say that everything is broken, crushed, and torn: the sides and the abdomen ache. Whence it often happens that the muscles, troubled in this way, having lost their vigor and fatigued by the long ordeal, are no longer able to hold the body up, so much so that from having laughed so hard one is forced to lean on something for fear of falling down or tipping over backwards, for one has no more strength; laughter is displeasing and one is overworked. In this there is enough to faint over, with the loss of humors and the lack of respiration. For with such emotion the heart heats up unduly and the lungs do not suffice in cooling it since they are beyond comparison slower than the other[a] in moving, so that one nearly asphyxiates if the laughter continues. And this is when death occurs, if death can come from laughter: which is what I did not yet want to grant, even though I have demonstrated how it is possible to die of joy, through the dilatation of the heart and such a great loss of humors that there does not remain enough to sustain life.[b] But with laughter the contraction cuts in quickly on the dilatation and makes the heart spend its humors and vapors more carefully (not all at once), in which salvation lies.[c] But can it not also sometimes happen that, with the augmenting of the causes of fainting from the violence of continued laughter, death result wholly from it? Along with difficult respiration, will there not be a great loss of humors if it persists for a long time, without the heart's having time to renew them? What is at once dissipated through extreme joy should be lost over several successively repeated dilatations, which, notwithstanding the succeeding alternating contractions, waste a great deal of humors and natural heat, and which cause sudden death in those who have a link between soul and body that is easy to break.

Yet, we rarely see people die[d] from much laughing unless it is due to tickling. I heard of a young man whom two girls were tickling importunately to the point that he no longer uttered a word. They thought he had fainted until, thunderstruck, they realized he was dead, asphyxiated. But I still do not wish to admit that true laughter proceeds from tickling, such as we have described it, and less yet that laughter which comes from bruising the diaphragm, as Hippocrates, Aristotle, Pliny, and other

a. Than the other, that is, the heart. Also its perpendicular position makes it more mobile beyond comparison.

b. Chapter XI.

c. Salvation lies in the careful dispensing of humors. For in whatever the circumstance, Nature cannot bear sudden evacuation.

d. See what we said in the third annotation in chapter XIV.

great authors have said. Such laughter is of another kind which we shall consider (if it please God) in the second book,[e] where we shall show all its different aspects.

This first book is long enough, during which without wandering here or there, and keeping constantly to the thread, we have shown the matter, faculty, form, and all the accidents of laughter, explaining them through their causes. I do not think I have omitted anything essential. But in order to understand it better, I am in favor of briefly recapitulating and recalling to memory at the end of this first book all that we have said in it. For from there we shall take up the subject of the definition of laughter, which will furnish a beginning for the book which follows, in which we shall answer several objections or reprehensions one could make concerning what we have put forth, the whole being of our own invention. There we shall also amply treat tickling, and whether it is as proper to man as is laughter, and explain six problems on tickling. Also, along with other arguments worthy of annotation,[f] we shall tell how saffron can cause one to die laughing. Then in the third book I shall delve into several difficulties and very beautiful questions such as why man alone is able to laugh,[g] whence it comes that some laugh more than others,[h] and some while sleeping,[i] that fatter people laugh more willingly,[k] that laughter does not occur before the fourth day after birth,[l] and wherein we shall speak also of one who was born laughing, of others who never laugh, and of those who are said to have died laughing without having been touched by anyone.[m] There we shall see why it is said that the spleen causes laughter,[n] and several other good arguments which will be very interesting.

RECAPITULATION CONCLUDING THE FIRST BOOK

Laughter, then, is provoked by deeds or words which have the appearance of ugliness and are not worthy of pity, except perhaps at first blush.[a] It is necessary to notice them, and that they be understood, otherwise laughable matter cannot have its effect, and is not able to move the soul if it does not penetrate into the internal senses.[b] There it is not recognized as such, but only received as are all other perceived objects.[c] For the senses are but doors or windows through which entry into the soul, hidden within, is gained. The soul is of a single piece, simple, indivisible, and without distinguishable parts, and because of this, objects move it in its entirety; but, since several functions are able to be performed by it, several faculties or powers

e. Chapters IV and V.
f. Chapters II and III.
g. Chapter I.
h. Chapter IV.
i. Chapter X.
k. Chapter XIII.
l. Chapter IX.
m. Chapter XVI.
n. Chapter VIII.

---

a. Chapters I, II, III.
b. Chapter IV.
c. Chapter IX.

are attributed to it, which it in fact exercises and practices by means of the instruments fitting to each. Whence it is that philosophers assign such power to such member, as if they meant that the soul, affected, tempted, or moved by the objects (which have made their way to it through the windows of the body), shows here and there in diverse parts what it is empowered to do, operating diversely through diverse instruments, as it happens to be easiest for each.

The soul thus moved, then, by the laughable matter, excites the member most accommodated to express its feelings, which is the heart, true seat of the emotions.[d] The heart rarely obeys reason, but rather against both our will and our judgment, it becomes perturbed like an animal. The faculty which presides in the heart is called the sensitive appetite deprived of touch, and is not in the brain although the brain receives its object.[e]

The risible emotion approaches closely that of joy; nevertheless there is a difference, as much in their matter as in the movement of the heart, because joy comes from something serious and causes only dilatation;[f] laughter springs from foolishness, due to which it adds contraction to the movement, so that laughter has two contrary movements, one made up of delight and the other of sadness, but the dilatation always exceeds in laughter since the matter is more pleasant than miserable.[g] The heart, moved in such a manner that the soul experiences this pleasant emotion, is hardly able to release such a great quantity of humors that death would follow, which in joy does often happen.

The heart is accustomed to revealing all the emotions by some change in the face.[h] During joy it gives very clear and obvious indications, for from the humors and sanguine vapors which rise up, that portion which fills the eyes makes in them a clear sparkle; the other portion remains in the skin, embossing and giving color to the face.[i] The lips draw back charmingly, due to the muscles pulling back as if in a contraction, caused by the abundance of humors.

Laughter has all these accidents in common with those of joy. Its own are the same, augmented, although there is not a greater dissipation of the pervasive matter, for other things assist it.[k] For the heart, moved impetuously in alternating contrariety, shakes its sheath, called the pericardium.[l] This latter does not fail to pull abruptly on the diaphragm, to which it is connected with a strong membrane.[m]

The vacillating and trembling diaphragm in turn shakes the chest, following which there is a similar compression of the lungs, which breaks up the voice.[n] All this happens only during expiration, when the diaphragm is relaxed.

In laughter the mouth is wide open because of the muscles contracted by a repletion of humors or vapors, just as it is in a true yawn.[o] This is also due to the

d. Chapter IX.
e. Chapter VI.
f. Chapter X.
g. Chapter XIV.
h. Chapter XI.
i. Chapters XI, XXI, XXII.
k. Chapter XIII.
l. Chapters XIV and XV.
m. Chapter XVI.
n. Chapter XVIII.
o. Chapter XIX.

great need of frequent respiration, which holds the mouth open, and to the agitation of the chest, which contracts the wide muscle drawing down the jawbone. Sometimes one only shows the teeth, and plies the corners of the mouth, which comes about through the above-mentioned lighter causes, and through the contraction of the diaphragm, which also produces this effect on diverse occasions.

Laughter makes the face wrinkle (but especially on the outside corners of the eyes) because of the folds that these muscles make again and again.[p] The eyes tear in laughter because they are full of vapors, and the ducts are then opened wide in joy as well as in sorrow to allow for the passage of the humors.[q] For we are saying that laughter comes from these two emotions. The veins swell in the forehead and neck, which embosses the face.[r] Coughing also begins when laughing while eating or drinking because a small bit or drop falls from the mouth into the gullet. Sometimes when laughter makes us force out air we spew it out through the nose when the mouth is blocked.[s]

The arms, legs, and entire body move when the chest is in turmoil, because from it come the muscles which go to the four extremities.[t] The abdomen suffers considerably from the frequent, violent, and long concussion or battery that the viscera, tissues, and membranes endure, tormented by the diaphragm, itself even more tormented.[u] One pisses and shits from laughing because the bladder and the rectal bowel are pressed upon by the epigastric muscles and by the diaphragm, under the force of which the two sphincters, unable to resist, are weakened by such agitation, as is all the rest of the body. Sweat comes because of the difficulty in breathing, and the turmoil which generates heat. It exits more abundantly through the face due to the thinness of the skin and the softness and moisture of its parts, adjacent to the brain.[x]

The considerable loss of humors, along with such difficulty in respirating that one nearly suffocates, can be enough cause for fainting in those who laugh with too much violence. As for dying from such an excess, it is not easy to do: for the contraction hinders the extravagant dissipation of humors.[y] Some, nevertheless, it is said, have died of it, but we shall see whether this laughter is of a different kind in the books that follow.

p. Chapter XX.
q. Chapter XXI.
r. Chapter XXII.
s. Chapter XXIII.
t. Chapter XXIV.
u. Chapter XXV.
x. Chapter XXVI.
y. Chapter XXVII.

The Second Book of Laughter

CONTAINING ITS DEFINITION, ITS TYPES, DIFFERENCES, AND DIVERSE EPITHETS

PREFACE

In the edifice of the human body, several things worthy of particular admiration present themselves which if one wished to explain and pursue carefully, one would hardly ever finish. For what is held in common with the animals enjoys a perfection in the human body that is so much more exquisite that he who will weigh with an inaccurate scale the most excellent wisdom of their creator will be justly adjudged impious.

I am not considering here with what ingeniousness, facility, and propriety our bodies are firmed up by the bones, bound together with a nervy and strong liaison, yet perfectly free in all its movements, be it for running forward, for turning around, walking in all directions, creeping and crawling on one's belly, equally at ease climbing and cleverly descending steps and ladders, mounting or scaling, jumping and darting about in a thousand different ways, and in each with such dexterity that it is as if without effort. I leave aside those who with marvelous and almost incredible agility slip their body again and again through a hoop, bending themselves like wicker in so many ways that wax is not more workable.

But what a great praise to the creator it is that in the face of man is found such variety that among so many thousands and thousands of men, no two faces are seen but have some differences, or else it is considered very rare and among the great marvels. What will one say of the great diversity in speech, as to voice alone, so different one from another that without seeing the person one can guess and recognize him by the sound of his speech if he has been frequented even the least bit? As for language, so diverse that in a country, nay, in a city, the local dialects will be quite different one from the other (although in the beginning of the world and up to the time of the undertaking of the tower of Babel, there was only one language everywhere), this is still another thing to be esteemed.

But there is nothing more marvelous than laughter, which God has given to man alone above all the animals because he is the most admirable. For if laughter were less frequent it would seem a miracle when the whole body is seen to move so suddenly and with such impetuosity at having seen or heard something insignificant and completely ridiculous. Now this must come about through the power that the soul has over the body. With respect to this, the saying of the most learned and pious personages is confirmed: that the rational soul (the most excellent of forms) can be separated from the body and subsist in itself, having in no way need of an exterior support, or of any subject; for this reason the soul is declared to possess an immortal nature.[1] For it is most evident that the form which has existence through the body is not able to have over it any great power. There are many things that indicate how much the body is inclined and quick to follow the movements of the soul, and even that it is sometimes resolved and undone because of it, as when the mind is transported by great violence.

Aristotle tells us in the first book of his renowned *Ethics* that the parts of the soul are principally two: namely the rational and that which does not use reason. From the rational proceed prudence, cleverness of mind, wisdom, memory, imagination, logic, and so forth. That which is not rational is divided into two parts: the first, which in no way obeys reason, as the vegetative, the other, which sometimes obeys, as that of anger and concupiscence, both very useful to man.[2] For concupiscence maintains life and preserves the species inasmuch as, by means of it, we eat, drink, and have children. Anger, or disdain, and indignation are given to it as companions (although being its contrary) for the purpose of repressing excessive cupidity. For as cold and hot mixed together make a good combination, so also coveting and disdain or anger, the one breaking up the other, make a very good mixture of modesty and virtue.[a] The coveting power of the soul is in pleasure, or voluptuousness, and displeasure, which is also called pain. These two passions, voluptuousness and pain, are preceded by desire and fear respectively. And so the emotions following fantasy or imagination are four in number: namely desire or appetite, voluptuousness, fear, and pain, which being sometimes excessive, move not only their own spheres but others also.

One feels clearly the troublings and impulsive movement that boiling anger works in the heart, and how, by tickling, carnal concupiscence moves the liver, besides the warmth and blushing it excites in the ears—I say nothing of what it stirs in the shameful parts. Why, amorous desires even alter the natural movement of the arteries, as we read of Erasistratus (most ingenious doctor), who learned through his galloping and trembling pulse of the ardent love of King Antiochus for Stratonice, his step-mother, as Appius recounts.[4] A similar story is told by Giovanni Boccaccio in his *Decameron,* the eighth story of the second day. What would we say of those in whom the genital semen is copious and hot and who pollute and befoul themselves while sleeping for having but dreamed of and had the mind attentive to some woman they might have seen during the day? Is it not believed that the eye of the sorceror, staring fixedly with a desire to harm and do evil, is able to cast a spell on the tender body of an infant? From which spell even cattle are not exempt, as Vergil has noted well in saying:

> I know not what evil-willing stare
> Goes casting spells on my tender sheep.[b]

a. Theodoret, *On Curing the Passions,* Book 5.[3]
b. *Eclogues* 3.[5]

But where is it more apparent than in the appetites of pregnant women, on account of which the body of the child being carried is very often marked and in it is imprinted the trait of what the mother desired? What? Are not the imaginings of the man or the woman during their copulation the cause of the features in most children? "For this reason," says Pliny, "there is greater diversity in the single species of man than among all the other animals. For the quickness and the lightness of the mind and of thoughts imprint diverse traits."[c] But the minds of the other animals are immobile (or slow and heavy) and all alike, each in its species. Of this Cicero rightly says that resemblance appertains more to animals, who have a mind that is not rational.[d] Yet, one observes that certain animals are born white from fathers and mothers that imagined white, as we know to happen with peacocks and rabbits that are kept in very white surroundings. There is also Jacob who put staffs of diverse colors in front of Laban's sheep, in the troughs where water flowed out, at the place around which the flocks would gather to drink, so that getting excited upon looking at said staffs, they would make their lambs spotted and speckled; of this, Moses is the very faithful author.[e] We read also that this was done in Spain, in the haras of mares. Besides several other serious authors, Quintilian proves that such is the power of nature in the controversy and suit in which there was the question of a Roman matron who had given birth to a Moor. And our Hippocrates delivered a woman from torture who was accused of adultery because she had had a very beautiful child who in no way resembled his relatives; Hippocrates gave the command that her room be searched in order to see if there were not some such painting, which was found, and there was no longer any doubt or suspicion.

I shall remain silent and pass over those who are so given over and enslaved to their belly that often upon merely imagining or conceiving of some delicacy, it seems that they are eating it; for which reason saliva and the taste of it come to their mouth. Several people have a great aversion to medicine, and when it is about to be given to them (even before they smell or taste it) become sick to their stomach and feel like vomiting; even before they taste the bitterness they feel it in their mouth. There are some people that go to stool only from having seen another take medicine, or the apothecary bringing it. This is what strong imagination can do. For there are some people so delicate and weak that upon merely seeing or hearing spoken of a putrid or dirty thing they throw up or become sick to their stomach.

Now all these things appertain to the soul and not to the body, as philosophers veritably hold, since it is the soul that exercises all of the life-functions. "The soul sees and hears," says Epicharmus, "the rest is deaf and dumb."[8] He who will contemplate a body that has been dead only a short time will be able to understand this easily. For all the instruments are there in entirety and there is nothing missing or changed; the body is perfect. Yet it lies idle, deprived of all action and work, completely powerless, from the instant that the soul (mainspring of all the preceding functions) is separated from it.

c. Book 7, chapter 12.[6]

d. *Tusculanes,* Book 1.[7]

e. Genesis, chapter 30, verse 38.

With good reason, therefore, do so many impressions, changes, and alterations take place in the body through the affections or movements of the soul. How many diverse effects follow joy? How many people are said to have died from such an event, as we have mentioned in the first book?[f] There are also people who are healed of a great sickness on the arrival of a sudden and unhoped-for joy. For the same reason the teeth of some people are set on edge upon seeing or merely hearing certain things. Others, if they see somebody bleeding, or look at a large wound, inasmuch as their mind is surprised and as though cut through with astonishment or commiseration, faint away. And fear, what force it is seen to possess at times! From a sudden fright a cold trembling runs deep through the bones, the hair stands on end, and the voice sticks in the throat: one bepisses and beshits oneself, and sometimes one dies from it or falls into a long and grievous illness. There are people so fearful and who mistrust so much their natural strength that they let themselves be won over by the sickness, so much so that they can nowise be cured, and die because of their opinion as if on credit. There are others who feign illnesses, and since they remain a long time in their conviction, having great fear and apprehension over it, they eventually fall victim to it.

One sees through experience, on the other hand, that because of fear some afflictions cease, such as the hiccups and the fourth fever[9] (as Rhazes says),[10] from a great and sudden scare.[g] Herodotus[11] writes, and several others after him, that Croesus's son, mute because of a natural impediment, upon seeing his father in danger of death, suddenly began to speak and cried out: "Do not kill the king"; and for the rest of his life he spoke most distinctly. This is because with the very great fear, accompanied by a very great desire to speak, he was able to produce such a great effect. And hope also profits sick people, so much so that the greatly desired doctor appeases with his mere arrival the cruelty of the pain. Whence comes the common saying (which must not be considered false or foolish) that he who cures the most people is he in whom the most people trust.[h] For the strength of the soul, which previously was succumbing to the sickness, is excited and raised because of hope, with which it now assaults the illness with such confidence that in the end it overcomes it.

What will one say of the fact that the imagination or firmly imprinted desire is able to move the body, not only of the living but also of the dead, as if by some miracle? It is confirmed by the witness of several, and accepted by the wisest jurists that the bodies of those who were killed bleed if the murderer is present, even though death causes the extinction of body heat and, with its coldness, clots and stops the blood. Shall we say with certain philosophers that some of the sensitive soul's forces (namely the desire for vengeance) still subsist after death in the blood until it decays? Lucretius the Epicurean poet and philosopher[12] seems to be of this opinion when he says:

f. Chapter XI.

g. Book 18 of the *Continuations*.

h. *Plures curat in quo plures confidunt.*

It is surely then that the semen abounds
In his vessels, when the needle probes them.
Then is there pleasure, when one reduces it
To the object that desire is pursuing.
The upset soul moves the semen-harboring parts,
Titillating them. And toward that from which it
Receives outrage it aims everything and tries to go.
For we see the blood thus flow
Straight to the part which has received a wound,
And show itself. If then perchance
The author of this misdeed approaches nearby,
It spurts out on him and flows once again.[i]

It is as if he were saying that just as the lusty emotion of the spirit desires to pour semen on one's lover, the love for whom has irritated and upset this spirit, so also does wounded flesh desire to cover with blood his enemy who is present. As for me, because of the authority of those who affirm it, I am ready to believe that if the murderer returns within seven hours, or thereabout, the blood can spurt out on him. For this, some give the following reason: that he whom one murders, when being killed, is entirely attentive to the murderer; he would, then, want to be avenged and thinks only of vengeance in great distress. And so anger is inflamed, from which the blood is suddenly heated, and which hastily and with all its might rushes to the wound as if to defend it. The humors fly there all together and because of their natural lightness squirt immediately all over the murderer, whose heat they pursue and support themselves with for a while. For which reason if during this time the murderer looks closely at the wound, the blood spurts on him because the body heat is not yet extinguished and because the internal agitation has not ceased, and also because it had already come out. But is it not necessary that, for the body to do this, some intelligence must remain in order to be able to recognize the murderer? This could easily be the case for someone who is not completely dead, though he would be considered to be so since he is on the brink. Otherwise it could not come about naturally that the wound enjoys such descretion as not to spew out blood on just anybody over the next few hours; and the above-mentioned reasons uphold this.

Some of the scholastic theologians,[13] in following the preceding arguments, hold that the humors coming out of the wound (as was said) cause the effusion of the blood when it calls upon them, and that they then seek it out. This comes about through the express will of God for the greater horror and detestation of sin. For which reason God says to Cain in Genesis: "the blood of your brother cries out to me."[k] Monsieur Papon,[14] most learned and prudent jurist and light of our times, has most elegantly treated this question in his book, *Decrees.*[l]

We could relate here several other marvelous effects of natural reason, by which (not without amazement) is amply proven the unspeakable power that the soul has

i. Book 4.
k. Chapter 4.
l. Book 4, Title 9, Decree 5.

over the body, were this not abundantly sufficient. Yet, it seems most useful to us to furnish still a few more marvelous stories, and for the most part prodigious.

Avicenna[15] writes of a man who made himself a paralytic whenever he wanted to, and who was not bitten or stung by venemous creatures unless he forced them to bite him, whereupon (for the completion of this marvel) they would die from it immediately. The remarkable natural condition of a priest named Restitut is recounted, who as often and as many times as he wished (and he was often asked to do it) emptied himself of all feeling and lay as if dead so that he could not feel those who were pinching or punching him, not even if one might be burning him, but persisted without feeling any pain, except afterwards, from the wound that remained from it. And that this was not from restraining himself, but rather from his body's being immobile, since he was not feeling anything, was proven by the fact that he was not found to be making an effort of any kind. But he said afterwards that he could hear the voices of the men as if at a distance, provided they were speaking loud and clearly. Saint Augustine[16] writes that he knew a man who could sweat whenever he wished. It is also well known that there are people who cry when they want, and even produce great quantities of tears, which is commonly attributed to women. But what surpasses all marvels is that some people have been seen that, having swallowed an unbelievable quantity and diversity of things, took out as if from a sack whatever they wanted all in one piece by shifting things around in the area of the stomach. Some let farts that do not smell, as many as they want and of diverse sounds, so much so that they seem to sing from their arse.

I know that many will refuse to have any faith in these stories, but (to return finally to our task) when I consider the force and the power of the rational soul, so genteel, over this earthly and unrefined body, certainly nothing seems unbelievable to me, less improbable, than that the body be considerably moved by all of the soul's movements. For man is composed primarily of body and soul: the former must obey, the latter, command. Then we distinguish mind and understanding, where we recognize a dual commanding, one outrightly mastering, the other, cunning. The mind exercises over the body the dominating mastery, of which the noble historian has most properly spoken when he said: "We use the commands of the mind and the service of the body." Understanding exercises its cunning, civil, and royal command over concupiscence. Now, considering the excellence of the celestial and divine soul, it was necessary that its receptacle be quite weak and delicate, so that it would not be hindered in any way, but be able to use it freely, like a pliable instrument. Thus it is that people with great minds are most often soft-fleshed, very thin, weak and sickly, which noble Cato noted well in his distichs, saying:

> He has a great mind, as if in recompense,
> To whom Nature has not given a hardy body.[17]

On this same subject Plato said in his *Timaeus:* "God could have made the body of man so massive that he would have been less subject to all the evils that come to him, but he preferred to make him weak so that he would be more disposed to contemplation."[18] It is written that a barbarian, when asked what he thought was the most remarkable thing in this theatre of the world, answered (not as a barbarian but as a wise person) that man surpasses completely all capacity of admiration. For he is not only prince among the animals, and of a divine splendor by virtue of his reason and understanding, interpreter of all Nature, but also of the nature of a Proteus, or of a chameleon; of a frail and unsteady strength, he transforms himself into everything he wishes again and again. This is found to be very true when one observes that the mind's vehement movements dissolve and undo the body, and that the slightest emotions cause highly diverse transformations, just as devil-fish and polyps change their diverse colors at every occasion, according to their surroundings. In the same way Indian hens again and again taint the fleshy growth hanging at their throat with diverse colors according to their passions and fantasies. Somewhat similar is what is daily observed in young girls who have a nimble, clear, and shining complexion: they often change in their appearance. This is why they are called "dailies," because they are sometimes more, sometimes less beautiful.[19] And that happens to them according to the passions of their spirit: joy, sadness, hope, despair, fear, worry, love, hate, anger, malice, shame, envy, pity, jealousy, and others that move the soft and tender hearts of females easily, and express in their faces the signs of their affections. Those who have a heavy, thick, and dull skin are almost always in the same state unless some grave emotions trouble them, which might make them become thin.

Now among the things which suddenly and considerably move the body because they have first touched or moved the mind, laughable matter is not the least, for such sudden, such diverse and remarkable movements are seen to be forced by laughter that scarcely any of the other things worthy of such admiration are found in man. Of the other passions there are hardly any signs that show up in the face, but from laughter how great and in what great number do they come, not only in the face but also in the entire body! For it is completely moved by them, since these things accompany laughter: the great opening of the mouth, the notable drawing back of the lips, the broken and trembling voice, the redness of the face, the sweat that sometimes comes out of the entire body, the sparkling of the eyes with the effusion of tears, the rising of the veins in the forehead and throat, the coughing, the expelling of what was in the mouth and nose, the shaking of the chest, shoulders, arms, thighs, legs, and of the whole body, like a convulsion, the great pain in the ribs, sides, and in the abdomen, the emptying of the bowels and of the bladder, the weakness of the heart for lack of breath, and some other effects. What increases the marvel is that something insignificant, completely foolish and light, is able to move the mind in such great agitation, and even more, the fact that laughter escapes so suddenly and promptly, and obeys reason and the will less than any other emotion, although it excites all these gestures by means of the very muscles which serve the will! Certainly this emotion is rendered admirable in every way, and for which reason, in order to earn this respect, laughter had to be peculiar to man so that being endowed with the most worthy of souls, he might feel the most excellent, admirable, and pleasant emotion there is.

We have, in the first book, sought and discovered, through a diligent and painstaking (I do not mean to say ingenious) search, the matter or object of laughter, its seat, and almost all the causes of its accidents. Having furnished such (what it was necessary to put forth first of all, to serve as a foundation), in this second book we shall first undertake grasping briefly (what we call defining) the essence of laughter; then we shall describe its differences or types, and deduce its epithets. Thus, one will have a perfect knowledge of it, and there will remain in our task but to recite a few of the admirable virtues of laughter, and to treat diverse problems related to these, which we shall refer to in the third book in order to explain everything more distinctly. The method we shall observe will be to infer in these next two books some new conclusions drawn from what we demonstrated in the first book. For they will thus illustrate it and make it clear, and from the first book these latter will borrow the certitude of their conclusions and the basis of their arguments. But let us get to the point, and take up again the subject of our work.

CHAPTER I
WHAT THE TRUE DEFINITION OF LAUGHTER IS

Isaac the Jew, very celebrated among the Arab doctors,[20] was the first of all those who have attempted to define the nature of laughter, for not one of the Greek authors has treated it in this manner. Here is the definition given by Isaac: "Laughter is a trembling and noise made by the muscles of the chest and by blood coursing in these parts through a natural agitation initiated by a movement of the soul when that which is introduced by joy falls upon the mind."

But Monsieur François Valeriole,[21] most articulate, most human, and most learned personage, has pointed out how absurd this definition is.[a] For laughter is, properly speaking, neither trembling nor noise of the muscles of the chest, especially since these muscles are not vocal, that is, dedicated to sound and to the voice, but rather to respiration for the most part, and some to the movement of the arms. And the noise which is perceived in laughter must be attributed to the muscles of the throat, which are called *larynx,* organ of the voice. As for the trembling, laughter resembles it somewhat in that the parts of the body moved by laughter suffer from some passion, which makes them recall other parts that do truly tremble, as we have shown in the preceding book.[b] But laughter is most improperly called trembling, since this is always unnatural and proceeds from illness; laughter, on the contrary, is natural and is not the sign of any sickness. I knowingly leave aside the pursuit of the other parts of the definition containing the efficient and material causes because they are sufficiently rebuked from what I said in my first book.

The definition given by Gabriel de Tarrega[22] seems more appropriate to me when he says: "Laughter is a sound-producing movement of the spiritual members in man,

a. *Enarrations* 9, Book 3.
b. Chapter XVII.

accomplished through the contorting of parts of the face for having obtained what man desires of joy and delight, and so forth."[c] But there are several things subject to reproof. Girolamo Fracastoro,[23] most learned philosopher and doctor, defines laughter in this way: "It is a movement composed of wonder and of joy, which is why there are contrary forces in laughter. For wonder holds the mind somewhat in suspense, while joy expands it; and thus it is that when laughter is continuous, it is not without danger."[d] Which definition the above-mentioned Valeriole refutes with strong and firm reasons. For it is false that laughter springs from wonder since it does not cause or constitute laughter, although it is sometimes found in it. Fracastoro would have come closer (in my opinion) to the essence of laughter if he had put light and false sadness instead of wonder. For sadness contains a certain tightening and a sort of suspension of the mind, which breaks up and stops the expanding and outgoing caused by joy. Meletius,[24] of the same opinion as the others, defines laughter as "a movement which stretches the muscles of the face, or a movement of muscular dilatation which is driven by the innermost intestines through the agitation of the soul."[e] This is also justly reproved.

After all these, the good Valeriole has woven his definition in such a way that I find little to add. He gives it like this: "Laughter is a certain hasty movement of the mind over something pleasant, in order to express the internally conceived joy, upon which the muscles of the chest, mouth, and face, are moved with impetuosity. Or, laughter is the dilating of the parts of the mouth and of the face because of the expanding mind, which agitates the pectoral parts with noise and impetuosity." In these definitions he has wisely taken *movement* in the sense of genus, especially since in truth laughter is a motion, and belongs to that class of things called *sequentials*,[25] for its essence is all action, and in the doing, as the philosophers say, as are also voice, sound, action, and passion, none of which has any permanence or stability, but exists only while it exists. Now laughter is the effect of a passion which it denotes, as we have demonstrated in the first book. It is therefore properly defined by movement and action. As for the other parts of the definition, it will be clearly seen which ones do not please me if my definition is compared to his and the others.

I define it in this manner, the most accomplished of all, in my opinion: Laughter is a movement caused by the jubilant mind and the unequal agitation of the heart, which draws back the mouth and the lips, and shakes the diaphragm and the pectoral parts with impetuosity and broken-up sound, through all of which is expressed a feeling over an ugly thing unworthy of pity. By these words I adequately embrace (unless I am mistaken) the whole of the nature of laughter. For all the things observed in laughter, and consequently called inseparable accidents of it (as we have shown in the first book), especially since they constitute its essence, are included in this definition. The first to be observed is the opening of the mouth and the drawing back of the lips, as if in a convulsion. This is caused principally by an

c. *Questions* 4.
d. *On the Sympathy and Antipathy of Things*, chapter 20.
e. *Of the Nature of Man*.

effusion of humors, but also aided by other accidents, all depending on the agitation of the diaphragm and chest. These parts are agitated by the unequal movement of the heart which dilates and contracts in turn, but more the former than the latter.[f] There is impetuosity in laughter because the humors and sanguine vapors are the principal instruments of such movements. And since the chest beats the lungs with the same unevenness, an interrupted sound proceeds from it, coming out of the mouth or the nose only. The thing both sad and happy, followed by the ugliness unworthy of pity, moves the seat of the affections so much that it is forced to express in the above-mentioned manner the conceived laughable matter.

Now, we have demonstrated in the preceding book that such is the matter of laughter and that in such a way is it apperceived by the heart; also, all the other parts of this definition have been amply treated there. Thus, this definition is absolute and perfect, containing the essence of laughter. I shall explain this in still another manner for greater confirmation. Every definition is completed in its genus and in its differences, which necessarily contain the causes of that which is defined. Movement here takes the place of genus, all the rest are the differences proper, distinguishing laughter from all other agitations of the body. Also in it are almost all the causes which produce laughter. For the thing that is ugly and unworthy of pity is the material cause; the efficient cause is the effusion of the humors; the instrumental cause is the uneven movement of the heart by which the diaphragm and the entire chest are moved; the formal cause is the extension of the mouth and lips, accompanied by the broken and seemingly faltering sound of the voice; and the final cause is the expression of a thing that is more joyful than sad. Now it is necessary that the matter of laughter be conceived or apperceived by the mind, which could not be ignored, although nothing has been said of it. For no action is made unless it is with respect to a known thing. This is why I knowingly and purposely omitted in my definition the attention of the mind, and also did not say that the conception by the mind is expressed through the laughter, since it seemed sufficient to have shown it in laughable matter.

We have condensed into little space the whole of the nature of laughter, collecting in a description all the things demonstrated in the first book. It follows that we must search out and explain all its types and differences, synonyms and diverse appellations, at least the principal ones, as well as those mentioned by good authors.

CHAPTER II
ON THE TYPES AND DIFFERENCES OF LAUGHTER

The most learned give us to understand that all laughter is not of one kind, but that there is one proceeding from nature, which is called natural, and another against nature which we may call unhealthy. The first kind comes about through the sole working of nature in bodies that are in good health and untroubled by any unhealthy

f. That is, it dilates more than it contracts.

affliction. Such is the one that we have described in the first book, and which our definition fits. For there is always, as for subject or matter, an ugly thing unworthy of pity, which, conceived in the mind, moves the heart (and along with it the humors and natural heat which are enclosed in it) to declare the risible emotion. Also agitated by this movement are the diaphragm, the chest, and the muscles of the face; whence it is that the voice must be broken and the mouth stretched in a certain manner.

The other kind of laughter is one that does not have said causes, and is not from a natural instinct, but rather is excited by some maleficent cause, as that which often comes about through reverie, and of which Hippocrates has said, if I am not in error, "The reveries or follies which accompany laughter are less dangerous; likewise that which comes from having drunk gelotophylic,"[a] of which Pliny has written: "Gelotophylic is a plant from Bactria and around Boristhenia. If one drinks it with myrrh and wine, it makes one see or conceive diverse objects at which one does not stop laughing until drinking pine seeds cooked in palm wine with honey and pepper."[b] I think that this kind of laughing closely borders on mad or manic, especially since mania does not excite laughter except when false images or ridiculous representations come into the mind, which is what Pliny said happens with the above-mentioned beverage. Now, the madness that makes man inclined to laugh is sanguine, of which Aetius[26] says: "If the mania or madness is from the blood only, here is what follows: they are moved to excessive laughter because they see often before their eyes some ridiculous little images or representations; their face is jubilant and they usually sing." This happens very often for almost the same reasons to sanguine people who, without having an external or evident reason, burst out laughing; which one imputes also to madness, since for the most part those who have too abundant an amount of mild humors are foolish. Also, one does say, "Laughter without cause is a sign of madness."[c]

All these different kinds of laughter, even though we said they were against nature, are nevertheless formed in such a way that only the natural kind is salubrious. Abuse alone will render this laughter unhealthy since, as for the movement of the heart and diaphragm, and all that follows from the true risible affection, it is found in this sickly laughter of an abused brain. There is another type that I call bastard or illegitimate, which is a laughter that is only equivocal since it expresses only the gestures and external manner of laughers without having the internal actions which precede true laughter. For there is agitation in neither the heart nor the chest, nor are humors sent out and spent, but only a simple retraction of the muscles of the mouth, similar to that in laughter, and which can easily be counterfeited. With this kind of illness Anaxandrides' son Cleomenes was afflicted, who, having gone mad, cut himself all up with a small knife from his heels to his vital parts, laughing all the while, and thus died, with his mouth a little contracted.[28]

a. *Aphorisms* 53, Book 6.[27]
b. Book 24, chapter 17.
c. *Risus sine re signum est stultitiae.*

Such laughter is no more laughter than a painted man is a man, but is produced through certain types of convulsions, as is that called dog laughter, nearly always fatal. Its causes are diverse, external and internal, for it comes during burning fevers, frenzies, head wounds, depression, etc. It also comes from damaging the nerve which goes to the testicles, and from the touch, bite, or sting of a certain spider. It is also believed that the usage of the herb sardonia causes it, and the eating and drinking of too much saffron. But it is better to treat this separately and a little more amply.

CHAPTER III
CONCERNING UNHEALTHY AND BASTARD LAUGHTER

The contraction of the muscles which move the cheeks and the lips cause the look and countenance properly called laughter, as we have shown in the first book.[a] Now, these muscles are drawn back, being filled with blood vapors and humors, as if they were undergoing convulsion, which we also explained in said book (following the doctrine of Galen),[b] comparing laughter to yawning, especially since the latter is caused by vapors which fill the muscles, and by means of this make them contract. One can also prove from Aetius[29] that laughter is caused by a sort of convulsion of the maxillary muscles, when in describing satyriasic leprosy he says: "the cheeks of these people are swollen and red, and since the maxillary muscles are in a sort of convulsion, the chin extends just as it does in laughers."[c] Thus, if the cratophyte or the masseter (which are muscles drawing the lower jaw upwards, providing for chewing), or those governing the cheeks, or the lower jaw, are convulsed and contracted, either from repletion or inanition (or from a neuter cause, as I maintain),[d] and if it is from one side only, there comes about what is properly called *torsion*, or distention of the mouth. If it is from both sides, the look will be completely identical to those who laugh. We call it elegantly by a Greek term, *cynic spasm*, inasmuch as angry and threatening dogs have this look.

I am not unaware of the fact that the *cynic spasm* and the torsion of the mouth are taken commonly for the same affection, but I wish to distinguish it in this way because there is another kind of entire mouth convulsion, and partial mouth convulsion. One is called mouth torsion, in which the mouth is all askew, a condition most evident if it is serious and extensive. As for the small, or light convulsion, it is only apparent when one speaks or laughs, for then the lips go crooked against one's will. Paralysis of the lips causes the same deformity but with the difference that if it is from paralysis, the lip turns up in the healthy part; if it is from convulsion, in the affected part.

a. Chapter XIX.

b. *On the Difficulties of Respiration.*

c. *Tetra,* Book 4, Sermon 1, chapter 120.[30]

d. It is in his *Opuscules,* where he proves that convulsions are caused neither by repletion nor by inanition.

Now this unhealthy and bastard laughter commonly follows high, burning fevers, frenzies, head wounds, and great losses of blood, convulsions, depression, and all causes which dry the brain severely. It is most often fatal, not in itself but because of the gravity of the cause from which it proceeds, which is a vehement and perilous illness, designated as such through the consequences of such an accident.

Among the external causes (which the Greeks call *procathartic)* producing the cynic spasm, or dog laughter, is eating ranunculus (called *batrache* in Greek and *ranuncule* in Latin), namely from that type which has leaves similar to wild celery, which is why it is called *wild parsley* in Dioscorides.[e][31] It is also called *sardonia* because it flourishes so in Sardinia. It is tart and (as Dioscorides writes, and after him Paul Aegineta)[f][32] deprives of their senses those who eat it, and through a certain tension of the nerves forces and draws back the lips so that they turn up at the edges, resembling laughter; from this sickness (certainly fatal) has come the adage of Sardinian laughter, through mishap. Pliny writes of said herb on this very thing in his work on natural history,[g] and Solon[33] in his *Polyhistor.*[h] Alexander of Alexandro[34] speaks of it in this way: "In Sardinia there grows an herb similar to wild celery, of which if one eats one dies with the mouth drawn back as if laughing."[i] Pausanias[35] in the *Phociacs* says that the island of Sardinia is free from every harmful herb except for one that causes death, resembling wild celery, and that those who eat it die laughing.[k] For which reason Homer and several after him have used the proverb, "to laugh with a Sardinian laugh" in speaking of those who laugh with an unhealthy laugh. The common herbicists, in order to describe the shape of this herb, together with its pernicious quality, have named it *wild celery of laughter.*

And what shall we say of saffron, reputed to be among the best spices, aromatic and cordial drugs? It causes a similar sickness (if we believe Dioscorides)[l] and is as dangerous in certain quantities, such as if one drinks three drams of it dissolved in water. It is certain that saffron fills the head considerably with vapors, and with its odor alone causes a throbbing headache. For this reason Galen, in his concoction of bitter ivy,[m] diminishes the amount of saffron for those to whom the odor gives a headache, and we advise removing it altogether, especially for the vertiginous. It is extremely volatile, something mule-drivers know only too well, and I can understand it, for the mules carrying saffron are made to follow all the others so as not to make the others light-headed; and never will they load a mule entirely with saffron, but rather, if they have a bale of it to transport, divide it among several mules.

Thus, since it fills and weighs down the head in this manner, it can easily cause convulsions and provoke dog laughter which could be fatal, as is also everything that

e. Book 2, chapter 171.
f. Book 6, chapter 14; Book 5.
g. Book 20, chapter 11.
h. Chapter 10.
i. *Geniales,* Book 5.
k. Chapter 15.
l. Book 1, chapter 25.
m. *On Medicinal Concoctions according to Regions.*

engenders vapors and flatulence in the body, which can penetrate into the nerves, if it is true what Paul Aegineta recounts[n] concerning Pelops's[36] opinion that convulsions are caused by the muscles' being filled with humors and heavy and active air, which he claims to be very cold and frozen and therefore inept in causing movement. Other times convulsions are a little wind one feels going up through the body from one of the toes, causing general convulsions, called *epilepsie* in Greek and commonly: *epilepsy, St. John's sickness, high sickness,* and *earth sickness.*

Among the external causes one does well to count the rupturing of the nerve going to the testicles, because for just such a reason those who are castrated[o] will sometimes convulse with dog laughter, and it is due to the consensus that the testicles have with the diaphragm, the principal instrument of laughter, as I have shown in the first book.[p] The basis for their consensus is the nerves which extend from the sixth conjuncture of the brain down to the testicles, and with which the diaphragm is also considerably furnished. Because of these very nerves one makes a sort of grimace with the mouth during the venereal act (which is also compared by Hippocrates to a mild epilepsy) when the genital parts feel a most pleasant tickling while forcing out the semen. Also for this reason comes in part the fact that after castration the voice is more high-pitched, for the testicles no longer heat (and consequently fortify) the vocal nerves and muscles through the alliance they previously had together through their nerves; and, contrarily, the voice starts deepening as soon as a boy hurls himself into love's games.

I think that one can rightly consider along with this convulsive and bastard laughter the one caused by the touch, bite, or sting of a poisonous insect. Strabo[37] writes[q] that in Cambysinia, on the Alazonia river, there is a sort of spider that causes some people to die laughing, and others to die weeping for their parents. Some call it (in my opinion) tarcotelle, others tarantula,[38] after the country where more of them are found, which is Taranto, a city of Puglia, or Apulia, in the kingdom of Naples. The people of that region bear witness that of those who are attacked by them, some laugh, some weep, some scream, some only sleep, and others stay awake; there are some that jump about, most vomit, some sweat, others tremble, and still others are constantly fear-stricken. There are a few that have other symptoms, but all seem mad, maniacal, and out of their senses. Such a variety of effects can be a result of their diverse personalities (as we shall say to be the case with wine in the book that follows) or of the particular spider's disposition, which is said to change his venom every day (even every hour). The principal remedy lies in musical instruments, for as long as they hear them play, they dance; if the instruments stop, they fall to the ground, completely lost, with a recurrence of languor. For this reason it is necessary for them to dance ceaselessly, so much that either by sweating or by undetected perspiring the matter and quality of the venom is resolved and extinguished.[39]

n. Book 3, chapter 20.
o. Castration makes it an external cause.
p. Chapter XVI.
q. *Geography,* Book 2.

Besides these types of laughter there is another which is grouped under unhealthy laughter. But it is not cynic spasm, and does not have the entire form of true laughter. It is that which has been observed in some because of an injury they received in the diaphragm, and which I wish to treat separately; besides, this chapter is long enough.

CHAPTER IV
ON THE LAUGHTER ACCOMPANYING AN INJURED DIAPHRAGM

In the first book we attributed to the nerves of the fourth conjuncture the laughter accompanying injury to the diaphragm,[a] but that this laughter is legitimate I did not grant there, nor can I claim it here. Yet it goes beyond dog laughter as well as that which is entirely feigned on the outside only, in that it seems to move the diaphragm and the chest. For in the kind which is completely convulsive nothing appears other than a turning up of the mouth and a retracting of the lips, as we have demonstrated a little earlier.

The injured diaphragm, then, is shaken and so agitated that it moves the chest and lungs with the same movement; for this reason not only can the mouth open, as happens in a convulsion, but also there can be interruption in the voice during expiration, both of which are considered to be proper accidents of true laughter. Now, that they result from an injured diaphragm, this Hippocrates indicates in calling this laughter *torybode,* that is to say, tumultuous. For he says that during the siege of Dat, Tycho was wounded by a catapult in the chest. And a little later that his laughter was torybode. Then, in explaining the reason for this tumultuous laughter, he says: "It seems to me that the doctor (or surgeon), while withdrawing the wood, left the iron tip in the diaphragm, and so forth."[b] Here the laughter was present right from the beginning, although not yet convulsive, for he went into convulsions only after three days (as Hippocrates later wrote), and while dying. Aristotle also says: "It is recounted that in battles when a blow would pierce the diaphragm, laughter would follow."[c] As for the reason, he thinks it is from the heat that the wound emits. For he had previously taught that when the diaphragm is injured, the mind expands and we laugh as the movement arrives instantly at the diaphragm which, although only lightly heated, nevertheless opens and moves the mind in spite of the will, and Aristotle thinks that such is the cause of the tickling. But this we shall treat in its proper place soon, and more amply.

Pliny seems to express the phrase of Aristotle when he says: "In the diaphragm is the principal seat of joy. One understands this principally through the tickling of the armpits, to which the tickling descends since man's skin is nowhere else any thinner,

a. Chapter XIX.
b. *Epid.,* Book 7, at the end.[40]
c. *On the Parts of Animals,* Book 3, chapter 10.

and since the pleasure of scratching oneself there is closely related."[41] For this reason, during battles and public fencing matches, the injuring of the diaphragm has brought about death through laughter.

It is much easier to show why a wound in the diaphragm is fatal than why it causes laughter. We shall, nevertheless, attempt to explain both. First, a wound there cannot heal because it cannot clot, due to the continual movement of said part, as Galen interprets Hippocrates on this, who said that when the bladder is pierced, or the brain, heart, or diaphragm, it is a mortal blow.[d] The injury is worse in that such a part has so close an alliance with the brain that frenzy or convulsions beset the wounded victim no differently than if the leucomae of the brain were injured. Add to that the great need for respiration, which he no longer enjoys with ease when the instrument of free respiration is impaired.

But laughter results from it (which certainly is displeasing and brings great pain) as if the diaphragm were being tickled. For it has such a high and delicate sensitivity that it cannot endure being touched. Yet it shakes as if fleeing the contact of another, and when wounded it tries (although in vain) to reject through its movement the harm that is troubling it; and it is still more shaken when the surgeon dresses it, otherwise it has less pain. Now the agitated diaphragm pulls from afar on the chest, to which it is attached on all sides. The chest, being moved intermittently and by an unsteady pressure, undergoes all the things that we have pointed out in the first book as being the signs of true laughter, namely, the opening of the mouth, the shaking or trembling voice, etc. Nevertheless, this is not a true or legitimate laughter, seeing that it does not proceed from the things which we said to be the principal causes, such as the agitation of the heart, which churns the diaphragm, and the laughable matter, which excites the heart with a peculiar affection, and this with an appetite solicited without touch. For these are the two principal causes in the nature of laughter: the laughable object and the heart, seat of the emotions, as we have pointed out in the first book.

Since, then, when the diaphragm is injured, laughter is not provoked from it except through touch, and not because there is matter for laughter, or because the heart is first affected by it, as should be the case (for it is not enough to be moved by it afterwards), this should not properly be called laughter. It is well enough a movement of the trembling diaphragm, especially since its function of respiration invites it to expand, and sadness or pain contradicts this. For this reason there is, just as in laughter, a shaking of the chest and lungs in it. But for true laughter the movement must begin in the heart, and there must be laughable matter. Furthermore, this must come about without touch. For laughter follows only apprehension and the concupiscible appetites, as we have shown above.[e] I think, then, that from these arguments it is sufficiently understood that laughter coming from a wound in the diaphragm is not entirely convulsive as is that called canine, and that besides the turning up of the lips, it has many of the accidents of true laughter.

d. *Aphorisms,* Book 6, 18.
e. Book I, chapter VIII.

There still remains the last kind of laughter, which is caused by tickling, and seems to be considerably akin to this one. For that which the injured diaphragm contributes, the same happens in tickling, which is defined as a light handling.[42] Besides this, the behavior that tickling causes seems to proceed from a consent or proximity of the diaphragm. For one tickles mainly under the arms, especially since the skin there is very thin, and its feeling is easily communicated to the heart, as some people say. But it is fitting to research the truth of the matter more diligently.

CHAPTER V
WHETHER LAUGHTER FROM TICKLING IS A TRUE LAUGHTER

We had to do much in the first book in order to measure up to the height and difficulty of the proposition of how laughter is caused by a simple laughable object. But it seems even more difficult and tedious to arrive at this one: how laughter is caused by tickling. Moses, the Arab doctor,[43] well understood that it was not easy when, relying on the authority of Galen, he says: "The reason for laughter caused by light and foolish things, or for any other laughter, cannot be explained; even less that which is caused by tickling the armpits or the bottom of the feet."[a]

Still, the difficulty should not in any way cause us to withdraw from the enterprise, but rather excite us and raise our courage as we remember the old proverb: "Difficult things are beautiful," or, turning it around, "Beautiful ones are difficult." Besides, we are committed by reason of our promise made in the foregoing book, having vowed to treat this question which comes more properly here. For we believe that we have left in doubt the fact that laughter coming from tickling is bastard and illegitimate. Now, having examined what can cause false laughter, we shall pronounce more boldly our sentence against it. I know well that to many this will seem absurd, and to others only a paradox; yet our opinion will be confirmed by the authority of the greatest philosophers and doctors.

First of all, Girolamo Fracastoro,[44] and before him Nicholas of Florence,[45] both personages consummate in wisdom, find that the laughter that comes from tickling is an imitation and copy of real laughter, without having its true title and nature. François Valeriola,[46] who is very learned and humane, takes issue with them, and is amazed that they went astray from the phrase of Aristotle. "For," Valeriola says, "since in the laughter coming from tickling, the mind is moved at having understood a pleasant thing (namely the gentle touch and handling of those parts), and since the muscles of the chest are heated and driven with no small impetuosity, which causes the noise, and since because of this movement great amounts of humors are spilled and sent forth, which upon rising cause the widening of the mouth and face, and since this is the true nature of laughter, included by us in the definition we have given, I see no obstacle in the true nature of laughter befitting it perfectly."[b]

a. *Aphorisms,* penultimate and last section of his book.
b. *Ennarrations,* Book 3, 9.

This is what the good Valeriola says, but I shall make it so that he will cease being amazed over it, and that he himself (perhaps) will change his mind, seeing that neither has Aristotle ever said that this was true laughter, nor can it, by its true definition (which has certainly been proposed by us), be inferred. For with regard to Aristotle, he has never stated whether the laughter caused by tickling was true or false, and we conceive easily from his words that such a laughter is similar to that said to come about from wounds penetrating the diaphragm, as he himself adds. For (as I shall immediately demonstrate) both are unpleasant and unfortunate.

But what then? Valeriola himself admits that the laughter caused by said wounds is not legitimate when he says: "This laughter is not true, nor is it caused by the paths of nature, although it has some of the more obvious traits of it, and a certain resemblance." Since, then, without adding to it any difference or limitation of true or false, Aristotle attributes laughter both to those who are tickled and to those who have an injured diaphragm, and since one of these is indubitably considered as bastard, why will as much not be said of the other, which is compared to it?

Now, that tickling is unfortunate, displeasing, and disagreeable, as is the occasion of true laughter, many things confirm; but primarily it is a fact that no one wants to be tickled. This is why it is said of those who feel it more strongly that they *fear* it. With this expression things that are harmful or inimical are commonly referred to; for one speaks of *fear* in talking about that which is particularly odious or disagreeable, and that which can bear harm. There are some who fear more than others the evening damp, the cold, the sun, spices, garlic; some fear cheese, wine, the smell of apples, strong odors, and (what is more rare and amazing) some hate bread. In certain passages of the first book I made use of the common manner of speaking, which must not be scorned, especially when it has more meaning and energy than is ordinarily thought. By the above expression one makes it clear that certain things bother or harm certain people who have a tendency to be offended by what does not annoy others, or annoys them very little, or only afterwards. Tickling is like this, for there are some who do not feel it, or who are not at all moved by it; others are so transported by it that they would willingly endure anything except to be tickled. I am certainly so sensitive about it and fear it so much that I consider it a great injury and offense for which I would willingly take vengeance, if this could be done respectably. But one is only tickled by people who are friends, and in fun, and most often without their knowing that one really dislikes it. It is always a great discomfort when one is forced to endure it for a long time, and so it is not altogether strange, what someone told me about a gentleman who wanted to stab one of his friends who was tickling him too much; but he was not strong enough, exhausted by the laughter, and another friend took away the dagger.

Now, that some people are greatly harmed by tickling is shown quite clearly by the fact that they can be reduced by it to such an extremity of torment that death will result (of which I gave an instance in the first book)[c] no less than from a wounded diaphragm. For one wishes and grants that tickling appertains to the

c.Chapter XXVII.

diaphragm, and it seems that in both cases death's coming about from false laughter is caused by the same thing: namely, because the man suffocates from it for lack of respiration, which is always impaired when the diaphragm is injured or otherwise distraught.

What, then, shall we say concerning tickling? Certainly this question deserves more ample argumentation, and preparing myself for this, I shall take up a little later what I pointed out in the first book, where I sought the proper seat of true laughter and the name of the faculty that produces it. For it seems that we left there a portion that belonged to tickling. Let us, therefore, pick up the path from there in order to arrive at the bottom of this inquiry, summarizing the whole very briefly, as follows.

In explaining the virtues, or faculties, of the soul, we postulated two sensitive appetites, one involving touch, the other being without it. The first is followed by pleasure or displeasure and pain, which is accomplished by the action of the nerves, and it is not the source of any thought or cogitation since it will never cease under an order from reason alone. The second is necessarily accompanied by cognizance, and such an appetite is a movement of the heart, for which reason we pursue or refuse the object it has grasped. We have classed with it the emotion that causes true and legitimate laughter. It would be a great absurdity to categorize it as essential to bastard laughter (as well as that which proceeds from a wound in the diaphragm), seeing that such laughter has no need of cogitation or of thinking and being attentive. Similarly, that which comes from tickling cannot depend upon the concupiscible appetite that does not involve the sense of touch, but rather upon the other, under which one puts pain and pleasure or delight. For tickling is accomplished through touch, and causes pain or pleasure, or both together, as in scratching when one itches intensely, and in the scarification of the gums in terrible toothaches. And what is to hinder the part that is tickled from participating in both at the same time, just as the matter of true laughter proposes something sad mixed with much that is pleasant? For there is no other kind that is more akin to true laughter than that which is excited by tickling, especially since tickling is accomplished through a light touching in the places where the skin is thinner, more relaxed, and more delicate, such as on the lips, under the chin, in the armpits, between the toes, etc.

Foreign tickling brings some unpleasantness and distress to the parts not accustomed to it, but since it is light, it causes some sort of false pleasure; this is also because it does not truly hurt, and because nature enjoys diversity. Now there is diversity, for the hand of the tickler is suspended, sometimes touching, sometimes withdrawing. Thus it is that if one squeezes somebody, or hugs him tightly in the place one is tickling, he will not be tickled. Christopher of Vega,[47] a very great philosopher and doctor, in his *Commentary of Galen concerning Afflicted Parts,* after having spoken of the cause of tingling in parts of the body that are asleep as being the humors that rush therein with impetuosity and vehemence (which brings on pain, intermixed with pleasure), adds that a similar sort of movement comes about in the humors of those who are tickled "when," he says, "suddenly the concave parts of the body, armpits, groin, and chin, are shaken, in which the humors, contained within in abundance, are troubled, and cause inundation, by reason of the emotion which precedes it."

But why is it that we bear so impatiently this conjunction of pain and pleasure, excited by a fondling touch? There are areas of our bodies so delicate and sensitive that they flee contact with everything: such as the eye, but still more those parts that are ulcerated, or simply without their skin covering. There are some who cannot endure the unevenness involved in tickling, and so they withdraw, even though they do not experience great pain from it, because the touch of those tickling is benign and suspenseful. There are others who do not perceive the uneven manner of this handling, or if they feel it, since they are less weak, tender, and sensitive, do not find it distressing.

Tickling can also displease because we cannot bear two contraries at the same time: if not in the other senses, even less so in touch. Nature would better endure each one separately—now pain, and then delight. What will you say about the fact that one coming promptly after the other causes much harm? One experiences it often enough when one puts freezing cold hands close to a fire. How great a pain one feels in the root of the fingernails! Certainly still less will Nature sustain two contraries together without distress.

There are several other questions concerning tickling, such as: 1) of the two contraries in tickling, which is superior, delight or pain? 2) which part first moved by tickling excites bastard laughter? 3) why can one not tickle oneself (even though it is said commonly: he is tickling himself to make himself laugh)? and other problems or queries, which we shall consider in the next chapter as succinctly as possible.

CHAPTER VI
SIX PROBLEMS OF TICKLING

We have pointed out that tickling is caused by pain and pleasure together, and that there is in it a both sad and gentle feeling, just as true laughter is made up of things that bring both joy and sadness. But in this case does not one of the contraries win over the other, so that there is more pain than pleasure in tickling? It seems so, since tickling is unpleasant. Yet it causes laughter (although this laughter is not legitimate), which comes from the rarefaction and dilatation of the part afflicted, as it is said.

Now, pleasure causes expansion; pain, tightening and contraction. Since, therefore, true laughter is provoked by something less sad than happy, it is absolutely necessary that this bastard laughter be the effect of a pleasure greater than the sadness. It is true that this pleasure is unpleasant (as I have said) because the very sensitive parts refuse foreign contacts, light though they may be.

What is the principal seat of the laughter caused by tickling? That is, which part must be moved in order to cause this bastard laughter? There are several places where we can be tickled, of which the main one is the armpits. Now, it is necessary that this feeling of unpleasant pleasure be transmitted to the diaphragm from all of the parts being tickled. For the diaphragm seems to be the principal instrument of laughter, by which the chest shakes, the lungs produce an interrupted sound, the mouth opens, and the lips draw back. Aristotle agrees with this, for he assigns all tickling to the diaphragm when, in explaining the function of this organ, he says: "That the heated diaphragm promptly causes a reflex is proven by what happens through tickling. For those who are tickled laugh suddenly because the movement races instantly to the diaphragm which, even though somewhat heated by it, does nevertheless prompt and cause a reflex against our will." He adds: "And the reason why only man among all the animals is tickled is the thickness of his skin; and he alone, of all the animals, laughs. For tickling is a laughter caused through the movement of the part communicating with the armpit."[a]

Why is it that no one can tickle himself? Is it because tickling is a sudden reaction of the surprised soul, as some answer? No. For even those who are conscious of it can be tickled, and those who have been tickled for a long time cannot be said to be surprised. What is more, there are some who merely upon being threatened with it, and upon seeing the one who wishes to tickle them approach, shiver as much as if they were actually being tickled. But the reason is similar to that seen in the touching of wounds and ulcerated parts. Afflicted people touch their wounds, apply dressings to them, and sometimes pull fragments of bone from them with less pain than a surgeon would cause. For no one is foreign to himself; this is why he endures less any outside touch. Yet from our sense of touch comes another similar movement. Aristotle speaks of the problem in this way: "We will not be tickled by another if we have seen him beforehand, or if we see the tickler. Thus, no one can be tickled if the touching that one brings is not hidden or unknown. Now, laughter is a failure and a fraud, especially when one laughs if wounded in the diaphragm. We do not laugh at every occasion, every hidden and fraudulent thing. Thus, it can happen that one and the same thing will and will not cause laughter."[b]

This is what Aristotle says, whose first reasons we approve of more, and which seem in fact to weaken the second ones. There is a similar question: why do we willingly quaver more if another touches us in a certain way than if we ourselves do it? Aristotle explains this also, saying: "The seat of the sense of touch feels more keenly something external than something of its own, for that which is natural and inherent is not perceived by the senses. All the more so, what is done clandestinely and quickly seems more terrible: and fear is a sort of cooling. Now, external touching has these two conditions as more than proper and familiar. Finally, each thing is moved by another, as much as or more than by itself, which is evident also in tickling."[c]

From what we have pointed out up to now, the essence and the causes of tickling are quite well explained, which otherwise are most difficult and risky to deal with.

a. *On the Parts of Animals,* Book 3, chapter 10.
b. Book 25, Problem 6.
c. Book 35, Problem 1.

Let us pursue, therefore, the easier of certain questions that remain on the same subject.

Why is it that of the parts of the body, some are affected by tickling and others not, even though the sense of touch services all of them? Is it because of the thinness of the skin, which is not everywhere the same? Is it because one tickles most in those spots where one is least accustomed to being touched? For one feels more the tickling done in the armpits and on the toes (especially on the skin between, which is very soft) than elsewhere. Besides these reasons, Aristotle makes up a few that do not account very well for the fact,[d] or else I do not understand them.

But why is it that among men some fear or hate intensely to be tickled while others fear little or not at all? Just as all do not take pleasure in the same thing, and do not get angry over the same thing, so also all do not fear, hate, or flee the same thing. Trembling is very akin to the grimaces caused by tickling. Now there are some who tremble and grind their teeth merely upon seeing or hearing a sheet torn, others upon hearing a saw or a file scrape or be sharpened; still others upon hearing a pumice stone cut, or a pebble crushed by a millstone, or an ear of wheat stroked against the nap; yet others are in no wise affected. So also it is with tickling: some cannot stand it, others think nothing of it in the least.

One also wonders if man alone feels tickling. Aristotle assures us of it, and says that it is because of the thinness of the skin, and because man alone laughs.[e] Yes, but we cannot admit these reasons, since the laughter which comes from tickling is not a true one. Someone will say that Aristotle meant this very thing, since shortly afterwards he says that such is the laughter caused by an injured diaphragm. His words are: "it is reasonable that laughter is never caused in other animals through injury to the diaphragm since they are deprived of the virtue of laughter." These words sufficiently confirm our interpretation, in which we said that laughter from tickling was similar to that resulting from an injured diaphragm, namely, bastard and illegitimate. But why would animals not have the virtue and faculty of false laughter through tickling? And this especially since their skin is thicker and mostly covered with fur? But we find the skin very thin and sensitive in several places on dogs, cats, monkeys, and other animals. And what? Man clearly feels tickling through several layers of heavy and thick clothing. Is the naked skin of the more sensitive animals thicker than so many clothes, which feel not in the least, and hinder our feeling as little as when we are naked? And does one not see that when dogs are tickled on the stomach and inside their thighs where the skin is soft, they wag their tails and make a grimace similar to dog laughter?

Certainly I dare say that just as domestic and docile animals imitate man in several ways, so also do they have a crude manner or imitation of laughter when they are tickled. But not in such a manner that the diaphragm is moved. Thus, the chest is not shaken by it either, nor does it emit an interrupted sound. For all this is peculiar to man, who has the chest formed differently, and a different connection between the

d. Book 35, Problem 8.

e. *On the Parts of Animals,* Book 3, chapter 10.

heart and diaphragm, as we have shown in the first book. Likewise, his soul has many other powers over the body in order to move it, which body is more delicate and sensitive than any other, having a more exquisite and refined sense of touch (barring the excellence of the other senses of the other animals), since he is the most prudent of all. He should, therefore, judge best the first qualities, along with their natures: a most difficult judgment.

Through so many reasons I think that I have sufficiently proven that man alone is greatly affected by tickling, and that he expresses the feeling he has from it through a striking sign: a laughter which is truly false, but that makes much noise.

This is what we had to explain and demonstrate concerning tickling, in which we were more prolix because of the diversity of the matter forcing us to it, and because we did wish to treat it in proper fashion. Let us come back to our subject of the types and differences in laughter, in order to see if there are more.

CHAPTER VII
ON THE OTHER DIFFERENCES IN LAUGHTER AND ON ITS EPITHETS

Having begun to treat the kinds and differences in laughter, we first distinguished the bastard from the legitimate; then we explained the bastard kind in several types. For there are several sorts of it, one of which we said was tickling. Those that follow will more properly be called epithets than types of laughter, or else accidental differences observed in a same laughter. They can be infinite, and I shall stop only at the better known, gathering up summarily those found in the most worthy authors, or those most frequently used in common speech.

In the species of man there are as many different faces in the world as there are people, as many differences in speech and in voice, and (if you please) as many different laughs. Some men, when they laugh, sound like geese hissing, others like grumbling goslings; some recall the sigh of woodland pigeons, or doves in their widowhood; others the hoot-owl; one an Indian rooster, another a peacock; others give out a peep-peep, like chicks; for others it is like a horse neighing, or an ass heehawing, or a dog that yaps or is choking; some people call to mind the sound of dry-axled carts, others, gravel in a pail, others yet a boiling pot of cabbage; and some have still another resonance, aside from the look on their face and the grimacing, so variedly diverse that nothing parallels it.

This is why following out all these differences individually would be as useless as it would be impossible. Nevertheless, one can understand and know that the principal differences proceed from two sources: one is from the diverse voices, by reason of the confirmation of the throat, tongue, palate, and other parts serving the voice; the other is from the diverse agitations of the heart and diaphragm. For to a clear, resonant, and high voice corresponds a similar laughter, just as to the somber, rough, and broken voice, the laughter is proportionate to these qualities. Those who have long breath give out a long laugh, the others, a short and often repeated one.

He who has more mobile and more supple instruments of respiration has a quicker one; in others it comes late, and like a constraint. But what need is there to explain such things? Everybody can observe separately the infinite kinds of laughter. We have the intention of adding to those mentioned above only the accidental differences and the principal epithets of laughter as read in the good authors so that each can understand their meaning.

It is most proper and fitting that laughter be called a trembling, inasmuch as the interruption of the voice, similar to a trembling, is of the very essence of laughter, as we have pointed out in the first book.[a] This is why every laughter is surnamed with a very proper and common epithet, *trembling.* Lucretius spoke of it fittingly:

> With a trembling laughter do all, moved, cachinnate,
> With tears moistening mouth, cheeks, and eyes.[48]

Now the first kinds of true laughter ought to be *modest* and *cachinnation.* The modest is that which we first described in the foregoing book,[b] and which we are accustomed to call simple and small laughter. Cachinnation is immodest, excessive, insolent, and too long; it expends our strength and is accompanied by all the accidents we described towards the end of said book. Similar to cachinnation is that which the Greeks call *syncrousian* because it tumbles and shakes intensely. For it is an excessive and immodest laughter. Some think that it is *sardonian* laughter, perhaps because Hesiod interprets the expression *sardonian laughter* as meaning an ample laugh, or deep and broad, as when someone laughs throatily.

But *sardonian* properly signifies a feigned and simulated laughter, on which consult Erasmus[49] in his *Adages,*[c] and before him, of the modern writers,[50] Alexander of Alexandro in his *Genial Days,* where he says: "The expression *sardonian laughter* is used to designate those who act joyous while machinating evil and who, beside themselves with anger, with a caress veil and cover their malevolence."[d] Such a laughter is lying, simulated, and traitorous, full of bitterness and ill will, or (at least) falseness, and with it one acts kindly to those one does not love, as with the laughter commonly called *hostile* laughter. The one that long ago was called *hospes* in Latin used to be called *hostis* (signifying enemy), from which the French have retained the words *hote* and *hotelier.* Sardonian laughter is also used by some people for a laughter of folly, arrogance, injury, or mockery. Now this epithet of laughter is found written in several different ways among good authors. In Cicero and in Lucian we read *sardonion,* in Homer *sardanion,* in Vergil *sardoum,* in the interpreter of Lycophron *sardion,* in Plutarch *sardianon.* Estienne the grammarian[51] informs us that it is also spoken of as *sardoicon* and *sardianicon.* He who wishes to know its origin

a. Chapter XVIII.
b. Chapters XVIII, XIX.
c. *Chiliad.* 3, *Centur.* 5, Adage 1.
d. Book 5, chapter 15.

more thoroughly than we have described it above in the third chapter should read the *Adages* of Erasmus, under the expression *sardonian laughter.*[e]

Now, that the look on the face can be feigned, along with several of the other signs or accidents of true laughter (as if it were not done in imitation), we have sufficiently demonstrated in the first book.[f] It is by means of the muscles both of the face and of respiration, which are controlled voluntarily, one can so well imitate full and wholesome laughter that one would not be able to tell. This feigned and counterfeit laughter, not unhealthy like that which resembles dog laughter, proceeds most often from an evil resolution and a dissimulated malice. Such was the laughter Homer speaks of in telling of Ctesippus (one of the suitors of Penelope), when he threw the foot of an ox taken from a basket at Ulysses, who was seated in his house disguised as a beggar, and who warded off the blow by turning his head sideways and laughing sardonically:

> He smiled to himself in a sardonic laugh,
> For his spirits were greatly upset.[52]

With respect to this passage, Eustathius his interpreter[53] informs us that he who laughs with a sardonian laugh only draws back his lips, and is otherwise internally distraught with anger or sadness. We touched upon canine laughter, which is thus called because the laugher only uncovers his teeth. The metaphor or comparison is taken from dogs showing their teeth as a sign of anger. For such is the laughter of those who do not laugh from the heart. From this comes the funny expression of the parasite in Plautus,[54] complaining about the young people who did not at all laugh at his jokes, and that they did not even imitate dogs that would at least show their teeth. This type of laughter is described by Homer, in speaking of Juno:

> By her lips each could see that she was laughing,
> But her nubile forehead was not seen shining.[55]

He speaks of it again when he attributes it to the valiant Ajax going out to fight in hand-to-hand combat, or in a duel;[g] this is why it has since also been called *Ajax* laughter, when one laughs with rage, felony, or ill-will. Hesiod[56] writes that Jupiter laughs the same way when angry with Prometheus for having furtively stolen fire.[h] It is considered inevitable when danger is imminent for somebody, while he is playing and laughing, sunken in pleasure or evil deeds.

Also to be considered akin to feigned and simulated laughter is that called *megaric,* which is when one laughs even though thoroughly depressed. From all these arguments one can easily understand that such laughter is voluntary, and that there is nothing but the facial expression, called *smile,* and thus it differs considerably from

e. *Chiliad.* 3, *Centur.* 5, Adage 1.
f. Chapter XXI.
g. *Iliad* 8.[59]
h. *Works and Days,* Book I.

the sardonian mentioned in the third chapter of this book, which is convulsive and restrained in movement.

Very similar to *cachinnation* and *syncrousian* is excessive laughter, called *Catonian*, which is extremely inordinate and shuddering. For it is said that Cato the Censor[57] laughed only once in his whole life, and then excessively, when he saw an ass eating thistles, and entirely spent from the laughter, he screamed out: "His lips have similar lettuce." Angelo Poliziano[58] uses this epithet nicely in his epistles, saying: "Oh subject facetious and worthy of Catonian laughter!"

There is also a laugh called *Ionic*, proper to weak, delicate people wholly given over to their pleasures. For the delights of the Ionians among the Greeks have been taxed, as has been the pomp, superfluousness, affectedness, and flabbiness of the Sybarites among the barbarians. In the same vein one speaks of a *Chian* laughter, from Chio, isle of great delights.

I find another laughter, called *agriogele*, of the jabberer and blabbermouth, who amuses himself with nonsense and banter, laughing fearlessly, without keeping himself in countenance.

We have spoken above of tumultuous laughter, which Hippocrates calls *thorybode*, and which is nowise legitimate, but convulsive, as in *inept* laughter, so named by Quintus Serenus in his *Curatives of the Spleen*.[60]

I think that there are several other designations and epithets of laughter, which I shall leave to the curious to seek with greater ease in Pollux[61] and other approved authors. It is necessary to return to the main path, and to pursue what remains for us to do. That is (in my opinion), to explain several questions commonly asked about laughter, which I shall answer as best I can by basing myself constantly on the demonstrations given up to now. And then I think that I shall have put a cap on all that can be said concerning this beautiful subject.

The Third Book of Laughter

CONTAINING THE PROBLEMS AND PRINCIPAL QUESTIONS ONE CAN ASK CONCERNING LAUGHTER

PROEM

The royal prophet David marked a beautiful pause in his thoughts, ideas, and desires when he cried out, speaking to the almighty, eternal, and incomprehensible God, "I will be satisfied when your glory appears to me."[a] And this is precisely because our soul is made in the image of its creator, divine and immortal, and with a capacity so great that it can understand by itself all that is in the world, composed of the earth and of the heavens, and of all that is in them. For all this, being limited and infinite, is consequently comprehensible by means of philosophy, which is knowledge of things divine and human.[1]

But as for the essence of God, because it is infinite, it cannot be understood by the human mind. For the vessel must always be able to hold what it is supposed to contain. Now the soul is but a speck compared to its immense creator, who, being larger than everything, has neither place nor space. But compared to other creatures the soul is like a little God that understands all things made for man's use, and is comprehended only by itself. This is why in this lower domain, where the soul is like a pilgrim, there is nothing that can satisfy it; it remains, rather, insatiable, even though most of the time everything comes to it as it would wish. For either the thing desired does not last, or one's desire of it passes, or the mind turns to imagining something else. He who has a defect in his person, or who is bed-ridden with a serious illness, would rather be the poorest man on earth, without relatives, without friends, without honors, if only he could have a healthy body. It seems to him, at the time, that he would wish nothing else but to have his desire satisfied. But, having once obtained this, he desires friends, honors, and riches, thinking that without such things he would live miserably. Then it seems to him that when he has such a status, such friendship, or such an income, he would not be able to desire more. Yet, having finally managed to have all these, and enjoying all his fondest desires, others come to him; and if he were king of a great country, even against all hope he would still want the other kingdoms of his neighbors, and the others around them, so as not to have any neighbors, but to be the peaceful monarch of the entire world.

a. Psalm 17.

The soul still could not be full and replete since it is able to contain far more than that. For it is able to imagine and project, from this world which is known to it, another world that is not, and to desire to have two of them, or even three or four or an infinite number. For it can embrace all this, and from one arrive at others. He who has no children desires infinitely to have some, and says that he would be happy with a boy or a girl. Having daughters, he no longer desires anything but a son, and would be happy to die (he says) if only he could have somebody to inherit his possessions. Having the son, he begins thinking about making him a great success, and does this during the rest of his life until he sees him well provided for. This no sooner happens than he wants to have other sons for fear that if this one dies he will be without a bastion in his old age. When he has several of them he begins thinking about advancing them all as well as he possibly can. And if one of them becomes an abbot he would immediately wish to see him become archbishop, and (it seems to him) he would desire nothing more, saying that his house would be sufficiently honored and well off from it for everybody. Does he get his wish? His son must now climb higher, and wish to be pope. And the pope still could not be content, even if he is much farther along than when he was a simple priest.

Thus, he who is much in love would wish nothing in this world but to enjoy his love. For the beauty and the grace of his beloved seems infinite to him, and he could not desire any greater good. Does he enjoy her? Not long afterwards some other woman or maiden seems more beautiful to him, and to have more grace, or to be more inviting; and so, little by little (if he is not well instituted in the fear of God, and reformed in his morals) he takes measures to be able to enjoy the second, thinking himself the happiest and most satisfied man who ever was if only he can manage to do it. For which reason he postpones and puts after this pursuit all goods, honors, and dignities. What happens? Just like him who chases a hare all the day long, working his person very hard, also his horse, and his dogs, because, whatever it costs, he wants it, and when he has caught it does not think it worth five sous, but he had to catch it, since he had desired it and undertaken it; so also this other one in hot pursuit, while enjoying his beloved, dreams of a change.

As much must be said of all things that our mind desires, thinking at that point to have its fill and to be completely satisfied when it has what it intensely desires. But the mind is still able to contain more, and, always being able to grasp more, it continues to desire, even though one often says: "I am content, I want nothing more, I have all that can be desired." For who is he so well blessed and to whom God has given so many graces and goods, be they of mind, of body, or of fortune, that does not want to be still wiser, more handsome, and more advanced than he is? Of that which cannot be otherwise, such as the size of the body and the proportions of its limbs, one will well say: "I am satisfied with it." Yet would one not want to be taller, handsomer, stronger, and more graceful? And does one not see an infinite number of women and girls who are beautiful and have a beautiful complexion nevertheless powder themselves, arrange their eyelashes and eyebrows differently from the way they are naturally, and change their complexion and their hair almost every day? If they could also change the shape of their forehead, nose, mouth, chin, and other parts of their face, or even of their whole body, oh, how willingly would they work at it, just as they make themselves taller with heels, their body thinner by corseting it, raising the hips, their feet smaller and tinier with extremely narrow shoes that ruin their feet, causing corns and bunions. This is more understandable in women (to whom a smaller foot is attributed as a mark of their beauty) than in men, who are very ill-advised to thus twist their toes and irritate their feet, already in danger of gout, also called podagra, which results from it very often a short time afterwards.

Let us come now to the goods of fortune. Who is he, so well blessed, well off, sovereign, and at his ease, that will refuse an inheritance offered to him, or that comes to him, saying: "I have enough, I do not want any more"? And yet he will very often say: "I do not want anything more, I have enough"; but this is when nothing is being offered to him, and when he no longer hopes to receive anything else, and not because the desire is lacking in him. This would be unnatural for our minds if it were otherwise, as can be understood from what has been said.

Properly and correctly speaking, he is full and replete, satisfied and content, who would not accept anything offered and which he was able to have, be it in possessions or corporal good, in honors, favors, friendships, knowledge, intelligence, or other human commodities, just as one calls full and replete him who has a stomach so full and satisfied that if he were presented with all sorts of food and drink he would accept nothing. His stomach has its limits also, and could not hold more without forcing, straining, and injuring itself, after which it would feel ill, and have only displeasure.

But our mind is so ample and avid that nothing can fill it with earthly things, precarious and transitory. There is always room for more, especially since it is larger than all of that together. For it must be greater than that which it is able to contain. Therefore, our mind will never be satisfied unless the glory of God appears to it, which, being infinite, will so fill our soul down to its smallest part that it will not be able to hold anything else.

And there is the beautiful pause that David marked in his thoughts, ideas, and desires, which are nevertheless not at all to be despised; rather, many in it are very laudable, such as the curious desire to philosophize to the very bottom of things. Of this it is never full, ever since it tasted a little of it, savoring it very much. And it is the operation that, more than any of its other actions, proves it to be more divine, just as man the philosopher certainly inherits much from divinity.

Now, this is what made me advance my argument so far into this matter of laughter, the nicest and most exciting that has ever been touched. For from one proposition I am led to another, and with a curious desire I go searching constantly, as though insatiable, all that I can grasp. I think that surely I shall never finish, and that there will always be more to say or add, but I want nevertheless to satisfy my fellow men a little (these are the curious ones, and of a philosophic mind) by gratifying them with a brief explanation of several problems or questions they might put, having read my preceding arguments. I know well that they will be more bored by them than satisfied or content, but I am not undertaking to fulfill their desires and to satisfy their appetites (an impossible thing, after what has been said above), but only to stave off their hunger (as the proverb goes) with some coarse food. For we shall never be happy with being perfectly enlightened with what our mind wishes to hear and know, so long as we do not have the vision of God, in which is all wisdom and perfect knowledge of more than we are able to understand or imagine. But while awaiting this felicity we amuse our minds in a proper manner and spend our time in this world searching for the causes of marvelous effects. And this is the felicity that the good Ovid so eloquently praised in his *Fasti,* saying:

Happy are they whose first concern
Is to go to heaven in order to know this.
I think that they have their heads
Raised above the worldly vices and delights,
Their magnanimous heart has held in contempt
Venus, wine, war, and the cries of lawsuit,
Vain ambition, the hunger of great treasures;
And fard-laden honor has pressed them in vain.[2]

Now, in this contemplation we are guided in part by our senses and in part by the arguments that our soul is able to make over the objects communicated to it. So much, in fact, is this the case that he who is the least ignorant can be considered the wisest, or he who has some plausible answer, opinion, or judgment for the problems brought to him. May God give us the grace to be always content with reason, and to moderate our passions in all things, to whom alone all praise, honor, and glory belong, for ever and ever. Amen.

CHAPTER I
WHETHER OR NOT ONLY MAN LAUGHS AND WHY

The school of philosophers affirms that laughter is proper to man, that is, that it is natural for every man and for each man; and always understood here is the power to laugh, for (as they also say) what is put in definitions signifies potency and not act.[3] Experience verifies this. For besides man, no animal laughs, unless perhaps it is a bastard laughter, simulated and counterfeit, such as those we call canine and sardonic.

Now the virtue and power to laugh is fittingly conceded particularly to man so that he might have the means to refresh his mind from time to time, overworked and tired due to serious occupations, such as study, contemplation, affairs of business, public administration, and others proper to man. For of all the animals only man is born apt to study, contemplation, negotiation, and all sorts of affairs; which occupations make him a little gruff, severe, sad, difficult, brusque, angry, and depressed. And since it is fitting for man to be a sociable, civil, and gracious animal, such that one might live and converse pleasantly and benignly with another, God has ordained, among man's enjoyments, laughter for his recreation in order to conveniently loosen the reins of his mind, just as he has given wine to men in order to temper and lighten the severity and austerity of old age; as Plato used to call it, it is the medium elixir and the mildest of all sweet drinks that can nourish men.[a] Laughter, too, is very pleasant because it keeps a certain mediocrity[4] between all the passions, as we have demonstrated in the first book. And not only does this affection please us, but it is also the safest of all because there is not any extreme expansion of the heart (which is most dangerous) as there is in great joy, nor is there vehement constriction, as in great sorrow. For this reason several people with a weak heart faint easily from joy or sadness, and some die from them, but one does not read of many people dying of laughter.

What would you say, paying close attention, about great sorrow coming from great joy? It is a common observation, from which came the saying: "From great joy, great distress," and the old Latin maxim: "Sadness occupies the other side of joy."[b] Why is this? The heart, being greatly dilated, undergoes a great dissipation of humors, by reason of which (even though no other occasion of sadness comes about) one becomes sad. For when there remains but a small amount of humors in the heart, it contracts so as to keep the little it has. Now each and every time the heart contracts in this way, the person becomes sad and remains dumbfounded. This the common man understands very well when he says of somebody who is quite sad: "He has a sad heart."

From these arguments one can understand (as I see it) why it is that Nature has given the risible affection to man, who is busy and attentive to tiring and difficult things (which make him melancholic), as the wisest of all animals. And since Nature undertakes nothing rashly, and since also it does not appear that she ever wanted anything that was not consonant with reason, she had to accommodate man's form to be well inclined to laugh, and to fabricate industriously in the human body instruments capable of producing laughter. For she did not fashion all the animals in the same manner, but gave to this one the power to laugh while denying it to others. Which, nevertheless, we firmly believe to be within the full power of God, if he wished to use his absolute power; but his majesty most often makes use of the ordinary, picking and choosing the materials naturally proper for his purposes. This is what Galen, inasmuch as he ignored the divine omnipotence, recognized in God alone, attacking Moses most viciously.[c] The creator, therefore, has thus formed our soul that among several faculties it has the power and aptitude to laugh. And this is (I think) what the philosophers say, that the power to laugh depends on the form of man, and that it is hidden in his soul, or that it flows directly from it, as we say commonly of the properties of a thing.

Now the formative virtue, which presides in the semen (where it is only potentially the nature of the animating agent, as our metaphysicians say), prepares and

a. *Laws*, Book 2.
b. *Extrema gaudii luctus occupat.*
c. *On the Usage of the Parts*, Book 2, chapter 14.

builds from it a body very proper to the soul which is coming into it. And it is the admirable genius of nature to fabricate and construct a shop and tools fitting the manners and conditions of each soul. It has thus fashioned, built, and composed the human body in such a way that it obeys easily as soon as the mind is moved by the laughable object, and expresses it with an external laugh. We pointed out in the first book that the heart and diaphragm are its principal instruments,[d] adding also that in man the pericardium is connected to the diaphragm (principal seat of joy, according to Pliny[e]) with a wide mass of tissue,[f] very different from that found in animals, from all of which we gather that man alone is able to laugh.

Vesalius,[5] a most excellent anatomist, has well observed that in man the entire bottom of the pericardium and a large portion of its right side is very firmly and very widely rooted in the nervy center of the diaphragm on the left side, and that this is peculiar to man.[g] For in monkeys, dogs, and pigs, the pericardium is very far from the diaphragm. I have dissected several such animals, and others, in which I find that the mediastinum intervenes, forming the link between these two parts, and it is two or three fingers long. For this reason the heart does not have a similar power in animals to move the diaphragm as it does in man, in whom the pericardium is connected immediately to the diaphragm in a wide and thick juncture, and a strong link.

Aristotle gives us to understand that laughter comes from a movement of the diaphragm,[h] but does not sufficiently explain the cause. For what he says about the cause of laughter being a tickling seems suspicious to me. Nor do I accept what he infers: that the reason why man alone is tickled is the thinness of his skin, and that of all the animals he is the only one to laugh. As if he thought that laughing and tickling were interchangeable, so that one won out over the other or that one was the cause or dependent of the other. But we have shown in the second book that the skin is very thin in several animals that still do not laugh when tickled.[i]

There are important people who count astonishment among the causes of laughter,[6] by which one could easily (so it seems) exclude dumb animals from laughter. But this idea has been very learnedly refuted by the most knowledgeable François Valeriole,[7] because astonishment does not cause laughter, but only holds the mind in suspense.[k] Furthermore, man is not alone in being astonished, if we believe Pliny, who attributes it to deer.[l] And doves and woodland pigeons (as also are partridges), upon seeing at night the light of the fire made to catch them, are so taken with astonishment that they can be taken in the hands. And I hear that woodcocks and geese are of the same nature.

d. Chapter XVII.
e. Book 2, chapter 37.
f. Chapter XVI.
g. Book 6, chapter 8.
h. *On the Parts of Animals,* Book 3, chapter 10.
i. Chapter VI.
k. *Ennarrations,* Book 3, 9.
l. Book 8, chapter 32.

Someone could object here, since we are saying that the risible faculty is relegated to the sensitive appetite deprived of touch. Why, if it is common to animals, will they not be able to laugh also? Or why do we not rather put it with rational intelligence, since that way animals would be excluded from having the risible faculty? The solution to these problems depends on what we pointed out in the first book, where we explained the parts or faculties of the soul. For in order to cause laughter, aside from the sensitive appetite, it seems that consciousness and imagination are required, since the emotions can be moved only by a thing conceived and known.

Now, nature has given to animals consciousness of the things appertaining to the necessities of life, to the conservation of their species, and to the defense of their bodies. If one attributes to some of them the intelligence of things other than these, this is exceptional, or in error, or refers to the above-mentioned areas of consciousness. But to man is due the knowledge of all things, through the senses and emotions, so that nothing is hidden from him who is closest akin to God. The reason why we are not of the opinion that the power to laugh is to be put under the rational faculty of the soul is that laughter most often does not obey the will, as we have pointed out more amply in the first book.

There is, therefore, no better reason than the one just mentioned, from which we are able to understand why man alone laughs. It is, on the other hand, strongly confirmed by the definition we gave, and upon careful examination one will easily understand that all the requirements for laughter are not to be found in animals.

CHAPTER II
WHETHER OR NOT MAN ALONE WEEPS AS HE ALONE IS ABLE TO LAUGH

The philosophers teach us that contraries haunt a same subject. That laughter is the contrary of weeping, there is no contradicting. I understand weeping not as the sole and simple effusion of tears, which can come about in laughter (as we said in the first book) or in injury to the eye, but rather this whole change one sees in those who are afflicted with sorrow while they weep. It is necessary to note here in passing that which Isaac[8] points out to us: that weeping surely expresses a movement contrary to laughter inasmuch as it springs from a dissimilar emotion of the heart, but that it is not an active contrary (as one says in metaphysics) as heat is the contrary of cold. For these latter interact among themselves reciprocally with their contrariety.

But weeping is not so contrary to laughter that it does not sometimes receive it with itself. For one sees people weep with laughter, and someone can laugh while sad (but it is a bastard laughter) as we shall be saying later. Let us come back to our argument. If the power to laugh is peculiar to man, why will we not also say that weeping is peculiar to him? Yet logicians do not say this when they assign the nature of man to the fourth mode; as though weeping did not appertain as well to man alone. But it can be tacitly understood if what we said a little earlier is true: that contraries have a same subject.

For experience teaches us that there is no animal that weeps, none that blows his nose, that spits, or that picks wax from his ears. Man among all the animals, because he has a large brain, not only in proportion to his body, but also with respect to his weight (for a man has a brain twice the size of an ox's), abounds considerably in said excrements, which he releases from his eyes, nostrils, mouth, and ears. This is not because his brain is cold, as it is said, but because it has need of large quantities of blood in order to engender a great amount of humors, which are necessary for its principal functions. And since in all this blood there is scarcely any material proper to this, or to the food for the brain, there is much left over, which is called excrement. And so one must not be surprised if, when the brain is compressed, it ejects great quantities of tears. It is true that weeping is easier for those who by their constitution and nature, or by reason of their age, sex, or culture, are weaker and moister, which is why we see phlegmatic people tear promptly, along with children, elderly people, and women. Why, there are women so prone to weeping that tears distill on their eyes if their brain contracts the slightest bit, so that common people think that they can cry whenever they please, and that there is feigned weeping, just as there is feigned laughter. It is also said in jest that women have sponges full of water between their shoulders, and that from there a tube runs up the neck and to the eyes. Thus, if they wish to cry, by only pressing their shoulders together they force up some of this water, which goes into their eyes through its canal.

To man alone, then, is weeping proper; it cannot be accorded to animals because they scarcely understand or conceive the things that lead to weeping. And if they sometimes understand, there is not in their brain (which is small and dry) the wherewithal for tears. Some animals, when they are very sad, howl, as do dogs. And several among them have given great proof of their sadness in diverse times and places, as it is recounted how some die on their master's grave, still howling pitifully, unable to be chased away, unwilling to eat or drink. Pliny says that one dog never departed from the body of its master (who was put to death by justice), howling sadly, surrounded by a circle of Romans. And when someone threw it some food, the dog brought it to the mouth of its dead master. Then, when the body was thrown into the Tiber, the dog started to swim, trying to lift him and hold him up. A great many people everywhere contemplated the fidelity of this animal.[a] Cats also have a wailing similar to man's. Likewise, woodland pigeons and doves wail, and, once contented with a husband, never let out another cry; but once he dies, they never again perch on a green branch, and do not cease wailing. Vergil spoke of them:

> The dove on an elm high in the air
> At every hour of the day wails ceaselessly.[9]

a. Book 8, chapter 40.

One says also of the crocodile that he imitates so well the voice of a man weeping that he attracts people to himself and eats them. Whence came the proverb *crocodile tears* to designate a feigned look of sadness.

But no animal truly weeps, although some shed tears, as is reported. For Plutarch affirms that deer and wild boars shed tears, and that the tears from deer are salty, and those from wild boars are sweet.[b] He explains the cause of this diversity. The Arab doctors make much of a stone they call *Bezaard,* as being the best antidote for poison and venom in the world, and say that it is from the tears of oriental deer which, having eaten serpents in order to be rejuvenated and strengthened, go into a river where they remain submerged up to their head until they feel the virtue of the venom dissolve. During this time they shed a tear sometimes as large as a filbert or hazelnut, which solidifies and hardens so that it falls when the deer leave the water, at which place it is found. See what Avenzoar[10] the Arab author writes about it,[c] and Theomnestus,[11] the serious author of veterinary or horse medicine,[d] and Pliny in his *Natural History.*[e] Scribonius Largus,[12] the very ancient Roman doctor, seems to mention it for venomous animals when he speaks of the ill-smelling excrement found in the corner of the eye, and which touches the nose of the deer; he says that Sicilian huntsmen gather it up diligently.[f] Cardan[13] in his *Subtleties* corrects Scribo in this, saying that this stone is usually found in Pely, in eastern India, and not in Sicily.[g] Jules-César Scaliger[14] seems to have spoken better and more convincingly in his *Excercitation,* 112, against Cardan: "It is not found in a deer until it is seven years old. After that age it forms against the bone at the corner of the eye, and becomes prominent, sometimes extending all the way down to the mouth, and harder than the antlers. Externally, it is round, very shiny, dark in color with even darker veins. It is so smooth that it slips from the fingers and slides in such a way that it seems to move. It is very effective as a remedy for venoms. It is given to plague-ridden people with a small amount of wine, after which they perspire so much that their entire body seems to melt. Some deny that it is the tear of the deer, but rather a true stone; but one can see (if it is whole) the spot where it was taken from the bone."

We wanted to elaborate a little on this stone, as much because of its reputation as because it is considered to be the tear of a deer. But these are not true tears like those man alone sheds, but are called such out of similitude, neither more nor less than howling and wailing are called weeping, and the turning up of the mouth, or bastard laughter (as we call cynic or doglike), is called laughter by similitude.

Weeping, then, is peculiar to man, as well as laughter, although there have been people who have never wept, for some have also been found who never laughed. Pliny writes that Phocion was never seen to weep or laugh.[15] Democritus, on the other hand, used to laugh, and Heraclitus to weep, at everything that happened.

b. *Symposium,* 7, chapter 2, in *Natural Causes.*
c. Book 1, Treatise 3, chapter 6.
d. *The Veterinary,* Book 1.
e. Book 8, chapter 27.
f. Chapter 163.
g. Book 7.

These are marks and indications of an unhealthy nature, as he says, just as they are with Antonia, wife of Drusus, who never spat, and with Pomponius the consular poet who never burped, all of which things nevertheless seem proper to man.[16] We shall later show by what causes that can come about. For it is most fitting to explain, aside from the frequent things, those which happen rarely, and treating them is even more enjoyable because they are akin to miracles.

CHAPTER III
CONCERNING THOSE WHO HAVE NEVER OR VERY SELDOM LAUGHED AND WHENCE IT COMES

If we are to believe stories that have been told, several people have never laughed. First of all, Crassus, grandfather of the Crassus who died in the war against the Parthians, was called *agelast* (as they say) because he never laughed.[a] It is also written that Phocion was never seen weeping or laughing, as we said just above. The emperor Numerian and Philip the Younger were never seen laughing.[17] Angelo Poliziano writes that in his country of Italy there is a family with a surname of not laughing.[18] Apollonius Tyaneus[19] certifies that Nerva would reign because he had never been seen laughing or playing. It is said that Cato the Censor laughed but once, and that then it was upon seeing an ass eat coarse thistles, which we mentioned earlier.[b] We also find that Lucia and Marcus Crassus (the one who accused Carbonius) never laughed but once in their whole life.[20] It is written of Philip Caesar that he was of such a severe and sad mind at five years of age that he could not be made to laugh by anybody.[21] They say also of Socrates (very celebrated for his great wisdom) that he always had the same expression, neither too happy, nor too troubled. Plato was so modest that he was never seen laughing, unless quietly. Dioces, son of Phaortes, who because of his equity was elected king of the Medes, never permitted anybody to laugh or spit in his presence.[22] Trophonius was an oracle of Jupiter in Lebadia (others read Lelidia) in the country of Boeotia, in a crevasse in the earth, about whom this marvel is told: that whoever went to ask his opinion never again laughed afterwards, having a constantly troubled and sad mind.[c] From this fable can be taken what is said of Saint Patrick's well in Hibernia,[23] as Erasmus[24] says: that those who have been taken to it never again laugh because from it (some say) is seen or heard what is done in hell, since this well is the entry to it. Some also affirm that Lazarus, brother of Martha and Magdalene, once revived and brought back from hell,[25] was never seen laughing.

What can be the cause of this? I would willingly say that all these people have been very sad and melancholic, either naturally or by accident. For thick and earthly

a. Pliny, Book 7, chapter 19.
b. Book 2, chapter VII.
c. Alexander of Alexandro, Book 6.

humor (such as we say the melancholic juice to be) is slow to move and to alter, especially since it is dry, coarse, and heavy. For this reason all melancholy people are more or less fixed, firm, stiff, and stubborn: they scarcely concern themselves with other than serious things, take no pleasure in ridiculous ones, and are not moved by them. For these are light things, and have no analogy or proportion to these grave spirits. Pliny speaks of their condition very well: "This tension of the mind sometimes becomes stiffness and natural wretchedness, hard and unyielding, and removes human emotions. The Greeks, who had experience with much of it, call such people *apathetic,* that is, exempt from passion. In fact (what is astounding), most authors of wisdom were thus afflicted, such as Diogenes the Cynic, Pyrrhonius, Heraclitus, Timon, etc."[d] This last one was so sad that he fled the company of men, like a werewolf; for this reason he was surnamed *misanthrope,* that is, hater of men.

It is manifestly clear from this how true is what we said in the first book,[e] that severity was the great plague and destruction of laughter. For those who are reduced to the apathy of the Stoics, empty of all joy, are in no way tempted by laughable things. And this is because they are not moved by any emotion of the spirits, having hearts that are neither soft nor agile, but hard and stiff by nature. Likewise those who daydream and always have their mind elsewhere, the dreamers, the abashed, the fearful, the suspicious, or those who desire something inordinately, like people in love, transported with madness. For such people pay no attention to ridiculous things, nor are they in any way moved by them. There are even some who arrive at such a firmness and stiffness (not to say rudeness) that they cannot easily be sad or happy about anything. On the contrary, those who are very inclined to laugh are soft and resilient, phlegmatic or sanguine, gentle and peaceful, piteous, joyful and jolly. Such people are suddenly moved on any occasion, and so they seem to be satisfied and varied in their emotions. This comes from a natural sensitivity which easily receives every impression, especially since (as metaphysicians and doctors both say) every fine and loose substance is sooner altered than is the thick and dense. One must therefore not be amazed if some are of such a severe and austere nature that they are never moved by pleasant things, and consequently never laugh, or else laugh much later, since it seems that the mind of melancholy people wanders, and is almost outside, alienating itself from the body, off building castles in the air, as the saying goes.[26] For this reason they are very taciturn, dismal, and musing.

Nothing, however, hinders such people from being strong, valiant, courageous, and magnanimous, for (if we believe Aristotle), in all courageous and valiant animals, the heart is small, thick, and hard; in fearful and cowardly animals, it is large, soft, and agile, as in the rat, the weasel, the hare, the rabbit, the deer, the ass, etc.[27] These arguments confirm what we said in the first book: that the constriction or beating of the heart has much to do with the easy or difficult reception of emotions.[f]

d. Book 7, chapter 19.
e. Chapter IV.
f. Chapter XI.

For as we said then,[g] a soft, delicate, and agile heart is promptly overwhelmed by a great joy, to the point of fainting and even dying. The hard and stiff heart, on the contrary, is more moved by a sad thing than by a joyful one, over which it loses its natural warmth more quickly.

Here is how it happens. Upon meeting something pleasant, the heart promptly dilates. Because of this, a large amount of humors escapes in those who have a large, agile, and soft heart. The small and hard heart dilates with difficulty, and its humors are not easily moved, since they are compressed in a narrow vessel. In a larger heart the heat is less vehement (as we pointed out in the first book, following Aristotle),[h] and there is a smaller quantity of humors in proportion to the other. For this reason there is also less difficulty in moving and agitating the humors, since in a larger space they are not compressed.

Now, not only courageous and magnanimous people were for the most part melancholic, but also the most brilliant and wise, who were mainly authors of wisdom, as we said above, citing the story of Pliny's. Aristotle speaks thus in his *Problems:* "Those who have been renowned for their great minds, either in the study of philosophy or in public administration or in composing poetry or in exercising the arts, have all been melancholic, and some of them to such a point that they have been transported into madness, as among the heroes and great figures (called *demi-gods*) are mentioned Hercules, Ajax, and Bellerophon, one of whom went totally mad, and one of the others frequented deserted places. Homer speaks of them:

> This one, hated by all the gods,
> Wanders alone through fields and solitary places,
> Eating out his poor heart, and fleeing like
> A wild animal, only the remnant of a man.

Several others among the ranks of heroes have been found who have likewise been sick. And lately we have heard that Empedocles, Socrates, Plato, and several other well-known people have been of this nature, as well as many poets. For this sickness bothers many such people because of this predisposition of the body, and some are inclined by nature to this affliction, but almost all were such at birth, etc."[i]

As for prudence, it is thought to be caused by dryness, just as moisture and softness make for foolishness. For because of this men are definitely wiser than women, and men of age wiser than children. For this reason Heraclitus seems to have spoken correctly when he said *dry, light, wise mind.* Plato also meant this when he said that because of moisture of the body the soul forgets what it knew before being attached to and imprisoned in the body, but day by day the body dries out more and more, and the soul shows itself to be wiser and more learned. For this reason, children, by nature drier, account for the gifts and graces of their mind sooner than most people; in fact, some too soon, whom we say to be of a precocious nature (that

g. Chapter XII.
h. Chapter XI.
i. Book 30, Problem 1.

is, mature before their season), and that they will not last or live a long time. For in such bodies there is little moisture, and moisture causes long life.

If, therefore, it is dryness that leads the mind to prudence, just as moisture causes madness, it follows that extreme dryness will make for great prudence, and medium dryness will bring about as imperfect a prudence as it will participate in great moisture.[28] Now the soft, such as women and children, are not only less conscious and less wise, but are also easily moved by every occasion, be it sad or happy. This is clearly evident in children, who rejoice or get angry at many things that would not move them at all if they were older.

Inconstancy comes from the same cause, because softness seems not apt to act, and most apt to be passive. Now, every affection is a passion. If, then, there have been some prudent and ingenious men who have not been at all, or very little, moved by the passions of the mind (even by those which dilate the heart, like laughter and joy), it is probably because they were melancholic, that is, of a cold and dry constitution, from which I also conjecture that they were slight and thin, with small, hard, and stiff hearts, which were more easily moved by sad than by joyous things.

The fact that heat, besides copious moisture, contributes much to joyfulness, Aristotle points out, saying: "Heat causes assurance and gaiety, and consequently children are usually more joyful, and older people more sad. The former are warmer, and the latter cold. Also, after making love almost all men are tired mentally and become sad, because not only are they dried out, but also they are made cold by the subtraction of a substance necessary to the parts."[k] If, therefore, someone either naturally or accidentally has dryness joined to coldness, such a person will always be sad, and not apt to be joyful. Which condition or constitution is considerably foreign to good human nature, and predicts a short life and bad health. Yet Pliny has well stated that these are signs of an ill nature, as with Antonia, the wife of Drusus, for never having spit, etc.[29] For one does not think the nature of each thing particularly good when it properly exercises what is proper to its species. If, therefore, laughter is appropriate and granted to man, he who abstains from it completely does not at all have the symmetry and moderation of human conduct or constitution.

Besides this, corpulence indicates this sufficiently. For everyone approves and praises *eusarcie,* that is, being moderately plump. Now this condition is found only in moist and warm bodies. The contrary holds for the melancholic, who for this reason are skinny (as they say), dry, and hard, having practically nothing but nerves and bones. I also add that the manners resulting from the temper[l] of the body (as Galen has most amply demonstrated, following Plato and Aristotle, in a treatise he wrote specifically for this) are by far much more excellent and pleasant in sanguine than in melancholic people. For the sanguine people are naturally gentle, gracious,

k. Book 30, Problem 1.

l. M. Joubert uses this common expression to mean conduct or constitution, as one speaks of temper in iron and steel in a sense similar to constitution, and wine is said to be tempered when "with constitution" is meant.

pitiful, merciful, humane, courteous, liberal, polite, affable, easygoing, accommodating, hardy, amiable, friendly, and cheerful, through which conditions and virtues the true nature of man is naturally expressed. The cold and dry, alienated and foreign to the human condition, are, on the contrary, for the most part both naturally sour, rude, cruel, inhuman, and atrocious, miserly, unsociable, brusque, difficult, fearful, stubborn, inexorable, solitary, etc. For this reason, if someone advances that among the *agelasts* there have been not only very prudent and ingenious, but also good people, and of praiseworthy manners, let him listen to the answer Socrates gave to his disciples concerning the physiognomian,[30] whom they mocked because he had judged their master (who was thought to be the most continent and chaste of men) a rake. "I used to be such," (he said) "by nature, but philosophy has since taught me other manners." And so we pay attention only to natural complexion and inclination, and say with Aristotle that the above-mentioned great figures were almost all such by nature.

By this argument, quite prolix and varied, it is apparent neither why some are inapt to laugh, nor whence it comes that some are more prompt in it, and others slower. It is our manner of arguing that has constrained us to this, since contraries opposed to each other are better clarified, and since from contraries comes much instruction. But because there may be some residues from this question (I mean from that which posits that laughter is more common to some than to others), let us pursue the remaining aspects briefly and separately.

CHAPTER IV
WHENCE IT COMES THAT SOME LAUGH MORE OFTEN AND MORE SUDDENLY THAN OTHERS

I think that it is clear enough from what has been said that those who are well born and of happy complexion laugh more easily. This is a result of the praiseworthy blood: pure, clear, clean, and more fine than coarse. For blood that is impure and bad, coarse and troubled, or even in small quantity, must necessarily be seconded by the opposite kind. This is why unseasoned and sick people, or those who have recently recovered from a disease, the unhealthy and melancholic, do not willingly laugh. And this is because some have little blood, others have it too coarse, and in others it is unclear. This is also why those who give themselves completely to study and contemplation, or to some great enterprise, are almost all *agelasts,* sad, rude, severe, and have knitted brows, because the vital strength having been weakened by the consumption of spirits, they have little blood left, and that little is as coarse as the atrabilious kind.

Children and young people, on the contrary, who have no worries and are in good health, are found to be quick to laugh, with joyous, open, gay, and pleasant faces. For the same reason women generally laugh more often and more easily than men, and fat people more than skinny people. For fat people and women engender much good blood, from which comes much oil, if one takes care of oneself, in peace and tranquility of mind. To this class should also be put those with a wide chest, and those who abound in heat. For they seem more inclined to laugh, and when they give themselves to it easily, they are transported with cachinnation, especially since through this conformation great amounts of humors are able to rise.

Now, that laughter is caused by the abundance of heat and of blood, can be confirmed by the authority of several. Meletius[31] is the first of all to speak of this, in his book *On Human Nature:* "Laughter," he says, "is called *gelos* by the Greeks, and *gelos* comes from *hele,* which means heat. For those who are hot are considered to be very inclined to laugh. And elsewhere *haema* (which signifies blood), said to be from *aetho* which means 'I am burning.' For it is the hottest of all the humors made in our body; and those in whom blood abounds, their mind is more joyous." It also seems that Homer would say that laughter comes from much heat when he calls it *asbestos* laughter, that is, laughter which cannot be extinguished.[32] Hippocrates attributes to the elements the cause of some men being sad and others happy. For (as he would have it) those who have purified blood are most often laughing and vermilion-faced, and have a beautiful complexion.[33] And the reason why the great amount and goodness of blood commonly make man joyous is because such a humor is, more than any other, consonant with nature. Which is why nature, happy and delighted with it, acquiesces more to laughter. Furthermore, from a benign, clear, and fine blood is made a great amount of clear, shining, and bustling spirits.

Now, it is the spirits that agitate the heart after the object perceived has moved them; this they endure without difficulty. It is manifestly clear, therefore, that the wisest and most expert physiognomians[34] are very well advised to think that excessive laughter indicates an abundance of blood, and that the causes of joy are all those that engender great amounts of blood. Thus it is that scarcely diluted wine (in modest quantities, of course) broadens the forehead and makes man joyous, since from wine comes good blood. This is why the expression, "Wine rejoices the heart of man," is well said, for wine clearly takes away all sadness and unhappiness. Whence Zeno[35] used to say (as it is told), just as bitter lupine becomes sweet from having been soaked in water, so also man is sweetened by wine. And Galen in the above-mentioned book[a] states that wine drunk soberly removes us from all unhappiness and sadness. And it is amazing that upon drinking too much, some laugh and others weep, since one and the same thing cannot from its nature produce contrary effects.

We shall further sound this question in the next chapter (principally with the views of Aristotle) because it seems pertinent to our subject.

CHAPTER V
WHY IT IS THAT FROM WINE SOME LAUGH AND OTHERS WEEP

Wine drunk without measure engenders diverse manners, rendering men either more gentle and accommodating, gracious, humane, facetious, pitiful, pleasant,

a. *That Manners Follow the Complexion of the Body.*

joyful, buffoonish, and playful; or, completely to the contrary, audacious, fearless, furious, angry, mutinous, quarrelsome, and belligerent; others become gloomy, heavy, and sleepy. How wine changes them step by step can be fully understood by considering drunks. For if wine begins to work in one who is by nature cold and taciturn, called *Saturnian,* a little gaily giving his head a spin, it makes him have even more words than a charlatan, rendering him cocky in babble and conversation, even articulate and eloquent, of which the poet spoke:

> Who, after drinking much,
> Is not articulate, pleasant, and talkative?[a]

If he continues carousing he becomes audacious, ready and deliberated; then, in pursuing this train, he becomes outrageous and petulant; then, enraged and wild. But in the end, completely won over by wine, he becomes dazed and stupid.

It is true that just as some in continuing to drink change their behavior and become completely different according to the amount of wine, so too there are others so accustomed to it in every kind of behavior that they cannot in any way be changed. For as so-and-so acts for the whole time that he is drunk, so is another naturally: namely, one talkative, another out of his senses, another pitiful or weeping. So much so that if the real personality of these people were not known, one would often be mistaken and in error, thinking this one to be drunk who is not, and that one to be sober who is quite drunk.

Wine, therefore, changes manners, according to the subject it encounters. For, as they say, some become weepers, like the one whom Homer makes speak in the following way:

> It is said that great tears come from my eyes
> When Bacchus overcomes me with his liqueur.[37]

Others are very sad (without weeping, however) and taciturn, even those among the melancholic who are excessively pensive, and are as if in a trance. There are some that wine makes brutally amorous, so that they will not be ashamed to fuck in front of people as a sober man would wish not to have fucked even furtively, because of his ugliness. Cheremon[38] said concerning this that wine applies itself and is accommodating to the manners of the drinker, and that it renders contrary not the things that are the same, but those which are dissimilar, as fire softens certain things and hardens others, namely, it melts ice and hardens salt. Thus, wine makes the clumsy more clever and slows down or dulls the agile. Or as a bath unstiffens and renders pliable certain hard and stiff substances by making them more supple, and weakens soft and moist substances, making them weak and faded, so also wine, by soaking the insides of man, changes him in diverse ways.

From this one can easily understand how wisely Plato advised that children under eighteen years of age not drink any wine, pointing out that wine was given to man

a. *Foecundi calices quem non fecere disertum.*[36]

by God only to combat the harshness and austerity of old age, as a remedy for rejuvenating and making us forget misfortune, and that a gruff mind having been mollified was more accommodating, just as iron is softened in the fire.[39] For old age is hard, austere, and full of chagrin, not because of the actual years but because of the constitution resulting from such age. For as adolescence is hot, and abounds with blood, so old age has little blood, and is cold. For this reason wine is appropriate for old people, from whom it drives the coldness with a fittingness and symmetry proportionate to their warmth. But in those who are still growing it is very harmful because it overheats their boiling and spirited nature, stimulating and needling them, as if possessed, to excessive and inordinate movements.

Now, that some people are compelled to laugh, and others to weep, must not be attributed only to the complexion of the body, as we have proposed, but also must be rightly attributed to the nature of wine. For those who fill themselves with it, if it is excellent and fine, and if they are of a good constitution, and have lots of blood, they are so carried away with laughter and are so discountenanced, undergoing diverse gesticulations or bodily attitudes, that they make those who see them laugh. For from such wine the natural warmth is augmented in quantity, because of which the blood enclosed in the vessels is agitated by it. Those, on the contrary, who drink common wine that is thick, turgid, and comes from the bottom of the barrel (even if their own constitution gives them defective blood, having in it much bitterness, sourness, and black bile) are not moved to laughter, but rather to quarreling and rioting, fury and rage, and sometimes to weeping. The reason is almost the same as for those who are sick with melancholic humors, of whom one sees some weeping, other laughing, all thus constrained by the nature of the illness.

But since these points, besides pertaining to the treatment of laughter, can greatly clarify the arguments we have opened, it is necessary to speak at greater length on them, as we shall do in the ensuing chapter. Meanwhile I do not wish to neglect what has been seen in this very city of Montpellier just a short time ago. A widow, advanced in years and not subject to illness, because she ate some pumpkins for supper one evening, was during the whole night taken with laughter and singing, without any other apparent sickness or change. Nevertheless, several remedies were administered. The next day it went away. She said she had dreamed she was laughing, and did not otherwise remember anything that had been done or said to her. Monsieur Hollier, a very wise doctor from Paris, tells in the commentaries of his practice (in the same place where he speaks of urinary suffocation) of two daughters of the president of Rouen that were seen laughing for an hour or two, very dissolutely, so much and so frequently that their uteri moved up. And we have seen such cases ourselves.

CHAPTER VI
THAT OF MELANCHOLIC PEOPLE SOME LAUGH, OTHERS WEEP

We have shown a littler earlier[a] that natural melancholy that is still within the bounds of health is inimical to laughter even though it is able to render people ingenious, prudent, and magnanimous. But the illness called *melancholy* and *mania,* inasmuch as it is against nature and depends on the burning up of humors, produces diverse effects in men's spirits, of which we shall only touch upon those that serve our purposes: laughter and weeping.

Of melancholic people (says Paul Aegineta),[b] some always laugh, others always weep. Hippocrates judges less dangerous and more curable those who have the madness of laughter, for he pronounces most dangerous that which is studious.[c] Of these two effects, a rare example seems to have been given by two excellent philosophers, Democritus and Heraclitus, one of which always laughed at whatever happened, and the other wept. But the most prudent Hippocrates attests in his epistles that, having been called by the Abderites in order to cure Democritus of his alleged madness, he found he was not mad, nor distracted, but rather the wisest man of his time. Now the reason by which it happens that of crazy people some are joyous and inclined to laugh, others (who make up the majority) sad, dismal, and weepers, Aristotle explains through the example of wine,[d] which we used above.

Such is the fact: the illness called melancholy (it is the alienation of the mind without fever) is caused by the abundance of melancholy humor, which is the dregs and silt of the blood. If this humor, or any other one, is burned up and becomes black bile, it triggers madness, otherwise called rage. There are diverse forms of it, which have different characteristics, depending on whether the humor is cold or hot. For the cold one causes much harm and anguish of the mind; and the hot one gives assurance and delight. If, then, the melancholic humors causing the illness known as melancholy become warm, the man becomes more joyous and audacious. In mania or rage, while the humor is being consumed, some delight and fury is observed; once the humor is burned, and as it were reduced to ashes, inasmuch as it burns less, the madness is not as acute as it was before. When the burning finally ceases, the man is full of anguish, sadness, and chagrin, and wants to be solitary. At this point the type of madness call studious is accomplished.

One sees, therefore (says Aristotle), diverse and uneven melancholic people because the force of the melancholy is diverse and uneven.[41] For it can be intensely cold, and extremely hot also. From this it is apparent that it can take on diverse qualities in between, and in diverse degrees. Now the type of laughter caused by melancholy must certainly be among the unhealthy ones, of which we have spoken in the second

a. Chapters IV and V.
b. Book 3, chapter 14.[40]
c. Book 6, Aphorism 53.
d. Book 30, Problem 1.

book.[e] And such (or very nearly so) is the laughter caused by pain, in which nothing pleasant appears and joins with the sad to produce the laughable. This is why we rightly call it bastard, because one sees that in its matter the other part is lacking. But we must talk about it in the next chapter more particularly.

CHAPTER VII
WHETHER OR NOT SOMEONE IS ABLE TO LAUGH WHILE IN PAIN

There are certain kinds of laughter which seem to proceed from pain, as it is apparent in those who because of an injured diaphragm have a fatal laughter, or who are bitten by a tarantula, etc. To such a laughter can be compared the one given out in spite of oneself when struck on the back or on the shin, where there is little flesh, which I have often experienced. From the blow one feels a very sharp pain, and yet one laughs as one does when one is tickled. This is because such a pain, being communicated to the diaphragm (as is plausible), causes one make a laugh-like grimace, no different from the one made when one gets into a very hot bath, or a very cold one. For hotness and coldness are equally unpleasant and cause us to tremble upon encountering them. Thus, when one touches a wound, or hurts oneself slightly while playing, one complains about the pain, as if laughing. Tickling also, although it is unpleasant, forces us to laugh. Yet laughter can be provoked without touch by some pain or disturbance, not of the body, but of the mind. Thus it is that this sardonian laughter, full of bitterness, which we treated in the second book, comes principally from sadness, anger, and spite.

One will be able to say that this is a feigned laughter, counterfeited as we wish, for such a shaping of the mouth and expression of the face can be counterfeited voluntarily, as it has been sufficiently demonstrated in the first book. This is true; but sometimes there also comes from the chest a forced and involuntary laughter when the mind is extremely anguished because of some upset. I can confirm this with a beautiful example. When the Carthaginians petitioned for peace, and it was difficult to raise the money they needed to pay, having exhausted their finances through the long war, and while the court was full of sadness and mourning, they say that Hannibal laughed. Hasdrubal reprimanded him sharply for having laughed during this public misery and calamity, particularly as he was the cause of this mourning and lamentation. To which Hannibal replied that if one could see the demeanor of the heart as one sees with the eyes the demeanor of the face, it would be clear to him that this laughter he reprimanded did not come from a joyful heart, but one nearly broken by the pain it feels.[42]

But how can this be? He who will have grasped clearly what we demonstrated in the first book[a] will be able to understand it easily. For there we proved that laughter

e. Chapter III.

a. Chapter XIV.

is provoked by joy and sadness together, and that the aspect of the mouth (even of the entire face) is the same in weepers as it is in laughers. From which propositions already accepted one can gather and conclude that sorrow as well as joy are both able to cause laughter. Yet (as we have already shown), joy wins out in the risible affection since the thing is more joyful than sad.

Was it, then, displeasure alone that moved Hannibal to laugh? No, in my opinion, for there was at the same time hope, which always accompanies valiant and magnanimous men, just as cowards and pusillanimous men are normally in dread. Now we pointed out in the first book[b] that with hope (which is never lacking in men of courage) there comes about almost the same movement as with joy. For the heart dilates gently as if it wanted to embrace the object which hope presents to it, and the heart is moved at thinking of the good it is seeking as much as it is by a good actually present. Since, then, hope dilates and sadness with compression squeezes the heart, these two passions mixed together could have moved the laughter in Hannibal. We can add to this the reason that depends on Hannibal's confession: they say that he replied that his laughter came not from a joyous heart, but a nearly broken one, which is very plausible. For we demonstrated a little earlier that, of madmen, maniacs, and furious people, some weep and others laugh; and it happens sometimes that, because of a grave sadness and a rage, the heart will be greatly troubled by it on account of the melancholic vapors and mists that trouble it, not assiduously but at intervals. From this (without doubt) it is possible that it will severely shake the diaphragm. Now with the movement of these two organs can follow all the other things required in laughter. But this laughter which comes from pain does not merit being called true and legitimate since it only results from the impetuosity of the heart, without any reason or occasion that might be present. It is, therefore, bastard, since the entire definition of laughter does not pertain to it.

To the above-mentioned questions and problems of laughter, more familiar to some than to others, and very well known to still others, we shall add this one as the last: why one commonly says, "the spleen makes us laugh," which problem will immediately follow these words, since from the spleen there sometimes comes a bastard and sardonian laughter, as we shall explain in the next chapter.

CHAPTER VIII
WHY IT IS SAID THAT
THE SPLEEN CAUSES LAUGHTER

One commonly quotes these lines of Latin pentameter:

Laughter comes from the spleen,
And love from the liver.[a]

b. Chapter VI.

---

a. *Splen ridere facit, cogit amare iecur.*[43]

It is meant by this maxim that the seat of love is in the liver, and that of laughter is in the spleen. As for love, this was truly the opinion of Plato, which we refuted in the first book;[b] we at least interpreted it differently, saying that love is not to be relegated to the vegetative faculty, controlled by the liver, unless you take love only as a desire and appetite to engender. For love, properly speaking, is a particular affection and movement of the heart, neither more nor less than hatred, since contraries are naturally in the same subject. We have proved as much concerning laughter:[c] namely, that it follows an affection and movement of the heart, and we have pointed out what this movement is.[d]

Why, then, does one say *the spleen moves us to laugh,* as if the office and seat of laughter were in the spleen, or as if the spleen were the instrument of laughter? Pliny writes that some have thought that the extremely playful being was the result of the size of the spleen, and that those who had it removed did not laugh at all.[e] But anyone who is the slightest bit versed in anatomy will easily understand that it is completely absurd to think that one can remove the spleen without causing death, and soon afterwards. For in the spleen there are such important veins and arteries that it would be impossible (especially because of the place it occupies) to stop the flow of blood by any means. I leave aside how great is the need and service of the spleen in the entire body, so that I cannot be astounded enough at the imprudence of Erasistratus,[44] who has actually dared to write that it was useless since it does not seem (he says) to have any function or use. It seems that Aristotle did not fall victim to this false notion when he writes: "The spleen is necessary by accident, as are the excrements of the bowels and of the bladder. For which reason it happens (he says) that in some the spleen lacks its proper size, etc."[f]

It is certain that in removing the spleen one removes laughter, if you understand (since it is true) that man dies as a result of it. And so what is said commonly about the spleen, that it can be removed from lackeys, and that they become thinner for it, is made up, completely inept, and absurd. For they would die from it and consequently would become immobile. Pliny writes: "Sometimes in the spleen lies the hindrance to run, and for this reason it is seared in runners, who work the hardest; and it is attested that animals live after their spleen has been removed by incision."[g] I willingly confess that those in whom the spleen swells up and is hard are short of breath, and are not good lackeys because of their weight, but not that one can live without a spleen; that is nonsense.

But why has the cause of laughter been attributed to it? Because it is soft and limp, resembling a sponge, drawing to itself the thicker and more murky blood, which the spleen likes and on which it nourishes itself. Thus it is the cause of joy, accidentally. For the purer and clearer the blood is, the more joyous and gay is the

b. Chapter VI.
c. Book 1, chapter IX.
d. Book 1, chapter XIV.
e. Book 2, chapter 37.
f. *On the Parts of Animals,* Book 3, chapter 7.
g. Book 2, chapter 37.

mind, as we have pointed out before, because from such blood several humors are engendered, and since these are shining, fine, and very active, they do much for the promptness and variety of emotions. Melancholic humor is like filthy dregs, very remote from the principals of life, mortal enemy of delight and liberality, first cousin of death and sickness. If the spleen absorbs it well, the mind becomes more joyous, otherwise it is sad and pensive, as is seen in those who philosophize. Man is also by nature very inclined and attentive to contemplation, in that he has a lot of melancholic humor, for which reason he is considered the most prudent of all the animals. For we have noted above how such humor affects prudence and understanding.

Now it is most fitting for man to be happy and to laugh, and for this reason he has a spleen very covetous and desirous of these dregs; consequently his spleen is very black. For, having great power to attract melancholic humor, which is by the way copious in man, it cannot fail being very black. While, therefore, this works well, man is more joyous; but if the spleen does not attract as much melancholy (or very nearly) as there is of it, either because of its weakness or because there is more humor than it can suck up and absorb, the blood remains black (as also will the spleen) and the mind becomes sad because of it. It happens sometimes that because of obstructions the dregs attracted and enclosed within the spleen cannot be freely excreted, and then a hard tumor forms which we call *scyrrhe,* threatening with hydropsy, succeeded by loss of weight and paralysis of the whole body. This is why the Trojan emperor, detesting and reproving the unreasonable exactions, taxes, and subsidies, used to say that the fisc in the domain of the prince is like the spleen, because as much as it grows, the other members shrink, wither away, and weaken.[45] Those who are thus afflicted do not have the inclination to laugh because their blood is murky, thick, and troubled.

Nevertheless, Florus[46] did not speak incorrectly in saying that confirmed spleenful people cannot laugh or smell. But what shall we say to the poet Quintus Serenus,[47] who attributes to a large and swollen spleen the cause of a certain laughter? Here is what his verses sing:

> A swollen spleen is harmful to man,
> And yet it produces
> An inept laughter: so much so
> That it recalls fittingly
> The herb called sardonia
> Which while causing laughter, takes life away.

Did he not mean to say the mania or madness that proceeds from an ill-functioning spleen, from which much melancholic humor rises to the brain? For that would not cause sardonian laughter as we have described it in the second book, as the result of certain convulsions. Also, is there not danger in saying here that from an enlarged spleen convulsions can result, when it is true (what our Galen holds) that melancholic humor easily causes high-sickness, called *epilepsie* in Greek, which is a general convulsion of the whole body? And so Serenus the poet would have more properly called such a laughter *inept.*

Following, therefore, the common manner of speaking, the spleen makes us laugh, and always does it accidentally when it preserves the purity and cleanness of the blood. Other times it is the cause of the wicked sardonian laughter, by causing convulsions.

CHAPTER IX
WHETHER OR NOT A CHILD LAUGHS BEFORE THE FOURTH DAY AFTER BIRTH

Pliny, demonstrating the miserable condition of man, and that Nature is cruel to him, says very eloquently: "She abandons man immediately, right from the first day of birth, completely naked, to wailing and weeping, and no other animal is so handed over to tears, especially from the first moment of life. And as for laughter, even the most advanced is given to nobody before the fourth day. Yet, we have learned that a man named Zoroaster laughed the very day that he was born, and that his brain was throbbing so violently that it repelled the hand placed on his head, a presage of his future knowledge. Solon[48] says the same thing: that the first sound of those who are born is wailing, for the feeling of joy is put off until the fourth day. But we know one who laughed the same hour at which he was born, namely Zoroaster, who was very soon expert in all the great arts."[a] Others say man laughs the first day when awakened from sleep, which is doubly miraculous if what Aristotle writes is true: that for the first four days children neither laugh nor cry while awake, but that they do both while resting and sleeping.[b]

Girolamo Garimberto,[49] who wrote his *Problems* in Italian,[c] tries to defend and interpret the maxim of Aristotle, but whether or not he manages to do so successfully, others will judge. I shall be content to put forth what seems best to me, according to my own judgment, having researched it beforehand, why the first sound the infant makes is wailing. For one cannot properly say that the infant weeps at that time, since he does not shed tears. Certainly it is amazing that man alone among all the animals is able to laugh (which is his nature in the fourth mode) yet he alone among all the animals begins by wailing. Some give as their reason that infants upon being born, seeing ahead and guessing the miseries of this life, are complaining about their condition. And that animals, although they are born into a much worse state, do not complain, since they are not aware of it. For man has the most foresight of all the animals. Some among us say religiously that the occasion is such: because of the sin of our first parents we are all subject to sin and death, and all those who come into the world, foreseeing this calamity, seem to accuse them. And for this reason it is said that the males cry out A-A, as if complaining about Adam, and the females E-E, as if wishing to say Eve, whom they know to have been the cause of these evils.

a. Book 7, chapter 16.
b. *History of Animals,* Book 7, chapter 10.
c. Problem 109.

But actually infants do not pronounce any letter distinctly, but the difference is in that the males most often have a loud and strong voice, the females a thinner one, and *A* is more resonant, deep, and loud than *E* is.

Of all those who have treated this matter, Alexander of Aphrodisias[50] seems to me to have the best opinion when he says: "One must not listen to those who think that an infant is forced to complain and cry because the mind has lost its heavenly home and is starting to live in an earthly body. Rather, infants, as soon as they are out of their mother's belly, begin to cry, or (to speak more correctly) wail, because they then feel strange and unaccustomed things."[d] For from a warm and soft body where they were contained they come out into a cold or cool air. And truly, the internal organs of our body, even the brain (which nevertheless is said to be cold), are warmer than the air around us, even that of summer at high noon. Do they not wail also at being surprised and shocked by the light, which they have not yet seen? For unaccustomed things, even though pleasant in nature, trouble and move us when they present themselves suddenly and without warning. One can add here the touching of hard and rough things by a body so moist that it seems like dribble or new cheese, to which Galen compares it. For the infant is first of all received into the hands of the midwife, which cannot be as delicate as the body of the infant, even if they were of a fifteen-year-old girl, carefully kept by guardians. But matrons, on the contrary, are for the most part old and wrinkled with dry, skinny, hard, rough, and unpleasant hands. Then the infant is wrapped in a cloth that is not as soft (soft though it may be) as the body of the infant. Must one be astonished if this tender little body, upset by so many things, complains about them by wailing? He is so tender, and was so gently kept in the womb, that everything outside is hard and rough to him. This, then, is one of the principal causes of the first wailing.

But why does the infant not laugh until after four days, except (perchance) in sleeping, as Aristotle thought? Are we able to say that not even after this limit is reached are children seen laughing, until they have gained enough strength to walk also? For the limbs are very moist at first, and the muscles serving the will are hardly developed in their functions. To the extent that they dry out they perform their duties better. Since, then, laughter is caused by means of the muscles, the laughter of these tender little ones, which they imitate like little monkeys, will be imperfect and bastard during the first months. Add to that the fact that they do not conceive the laughable in their minds since they only know during the first months what is necessary for life, just as do animals. They are, therefore, not affected by any objects, be they delectable or unpleasant, or of any other nature, unless it is through touch.

What would you say about Aristotle's declaring that children for the most part do not feel when they are scratched during the first forty days?[e] From this one can infer that they do not feel tickling either, which provokes a bastard laughter at least, as we have already stated.[f] Why is this? Since they are very moist they have a confused

d. Book 1, Problem 61.
e. *History of Animals*, Book 1, chapter 10.
f. Book 2, chapter III.

judgment in the mind. This is what Hippocrates before all the others seems to have meant when he says: "Infants do not laugh even though they are tickled and stroked before they are forty days old, for their strength is impeded by mucosity."[g] We grant that they feel very exactly and precisely, as do all who have a sensitive body. But the excessive moisture confuses the awareness of what it is that is touching it. So also it is with their minds which, soaking and drenched in much wetness, scarcely discern anything in that which the senses perceive, as though it were overwhelmed and mixed up, or else submerged and covered with a deep gulf of humors; during this time the soul occupies itself only with the vegetative faculty, from which life cannot be exempted. It does receive the different colors and sounds, but it knows nothing about them, and is therefore not affected by them, being still slow to understand them on account of the above-mentioned hindrance. Just as a Frenchman who is among Germans, not understanding a word of their language, nevertheless hears them and sees them laugh, but does not laugh with them, or it would be with the lips only (just as a child does) until he understands and grasps the meaning of the words. The child, freed of this excessive humidity with the lapse of time, has a soul that is freer, and his corporal instruments obey him better. Then it begins to use true laughter, when the mind is able to conceive the laughable and to move the heart over it, along with the other instruments required in this affair.

Now, that the laughter of infants during the first months is not legitimate is very easy to judge if one pays close attention. For they only draw back the mouth, just as in dog laughter (or, if you prefer, as one does in smiling, which is sweet, caressing, and an amorous trait) without any agitation of the diaphragm and chest, without any shaking of the lungs, and finally, without any sound of an interrupted voice. And this laughter does not come to them any less when they are awake than when sleeping, as we have often observed, against the opinion of Aristotle, which Hippocrates also contradicts, saying: "Infants, right from birth, seem to laugh and weep while sleeping. When awake they also laugh and weep by themselves, with a start, before they are forty days old."[h]

As for laughter, it comes to those who are of a gay, joyous, and well-nourished spirit, and of an abundance of blood and humors. For when this matter rises it fills the lips in such a way that there is a retraction of them which is in truth more of a sign of joy than of laughter. Children can also model their mouth voluntarily and consciously, imitating the look of laughers without having or perceiving any reason for it. This is because children what to imitate the gestures of those who laugh at them and coddle them while smiling. "For the nature of man (says Aristotle in his *Poetics)* is to know how to imitate right from infancy, and he differs from all the animals in that he is very capable of imitating, and in that he acquires the first disciplines through imitating, and in that he takes much pleasure in imitating." Since, then, those who caress children make this face, the children, wishing to imitate them, seem to laugh. Likewise, they laugh while sleeping because of the

g. *Book of the Seventh Parturition.*
h. *Book of the Seventh Parturition.*

abundance of humors which draw back the mouth. For, being always at the breast, they use much food from which they engender a great amount of blood and, consequently, a great amount of humors, especially while sleeping, which, pushing out sometimes, just as they are able to move the head, arms, and legs during sleep, are also able to move the mouth.

But we shall speak of this at more length later; let us come back to our subject. We finally gather from this that children do not laugh before forty days of age, nor even for a long time after, until their body has some strength. Precocious or advanced laughter, therefore (which we have observed in some before their twenty-fifth day), is not a legitimate and true laughter, but feigned and counterfeit, in infants of great vivacity, of whom Vergil, the great philosopher-poet, spoke in his prologue to Pollio, saying:

Begin, my little infant,
Knowing your mother with a laugh,
Who has for ten long months had
Long and bitter discomfort.
Begin, then, little infant.
Those (oh parents) who have not laughed,
God disdains from his table,
And the Goddess, for company,
Wishes not to have in her bed.[i]

Angelo Poliziano interpreting this passage says that he who has not laughed is not maintained in life by the God Genius and by the goddess Juno.[k] For it was believed in ancient times that each person had his Genius and his Juno presiding over his life. This is what Vergil meant by this figure of speech, since the table is consecrated to Genius (god of good cheer, of whom it is said, "Pour out some wine for Genius") and the bed to Juno, just as Junius Philargyrus[51] points out in interpreting this passage when he says: "To children born of a noble house, a bed is given and put at the portal of Juno the midwife, who measures up even to Hercules, etc. The table and the bed, therefore, are arguments that the child must live, since they were put there right from the beginning. Now man has in him the property of laughter, therefore how can life be vital to him who does not laugh, as Ennius[54] says?" In this he taxes learnedly and subtly the interpretation of Servius,[55] the very famous grammarian, who in reading the pronoun *qui* in the dative singular, *cui,* attributes this act of laughter to the parents of the infant, as if Vergil had said:

For the parents who have not laughed,
God etc.

i. *Eclogues* 4.[52]
k. *Miscellanea,* chapter 89.[53]

And what purpose can the laughter of the parents serve, smiling at the child, in order to render it vital? Certainly Vergil is not so clumsy as to praise and to commend the child by congratulating him at whom the parents had laughed, but rather him who is able to laugh with happiness, as if giving proof of his health and vivicity by the most appropriate action in the nature of man. Therefore, the word *qui* must be nominative plural, and the word *parents* must be in the vocative, so that Vergil, speaking to them, explains to them why he exhorts the infant to laugh, as if he were saying:

O you, his father and mother, in life do not remain.
The children who have not laughed die soon.
Genius refuses them his table absolutely,
Juno, likewise, wants them not in her bed.

Those, then, who imitate laughers sooner are more alive, happy, and (as our Hippocrates says) *prothymoteres,* that is, have a prompt and agile mind. By this the abundance of pure and clean natural heat is indicated, from which proceeds (if it is well preserved) good health and long life.

CHAPTER X
WHETHER OR NOT ONE CAN LAUGH WHILE SLEEPING

Galen wisely says that the opinion of those who affirm that the soul of sleeping people is idle is rash and mad unless they believe such a necessity to sleep to be not total cessation but like an intermission in its vigor.[a] For those who are the most asleep and sunken in slumber move their arms diversely; some speak and others walk about, which is what Galen says he did himself once when he was obliged to walk all night. He walked almost an entire furlong (which is 125 steps) completely asleep and (what is more) dreaming, and did not awaken until he stumbled over a stone. I have heard about a young woman in Paris who used to go bathing every night in the river all the while dreaming, which she continued doing for a long time until her father, being notified of it, waited for her one time on the road and whipped her thoroughly to make her lose the habit, at which the girl awakened and was very astonished to find herself completely naked in the middle of the street. Another story is told (but it does not seem credible) of a schoolboy who, having had a quarrel the evening before with one of his companions, got up while asleep and went and killed his enemy in his bed in another room, then went back to bed without waking up, as it is supposed. For the next morning when charges were pressed, he was found asleep still, and when his dagger was seized and found bloody, he confessed having dreamed that he was killing the one said to be murdered.

a. *Concerning the Movement of Muscles,* Book 2.

There are several such examples by which it can be confirmed that besides the natural and vital faculties of the soul (which are said to be very powerful in sleeping people), the animal ones are also at work; I mean those dedicated and subject to our will, and accomplished by means of our muscles, such as walking, embracing, and speaking. Respiration is also voluntary although, being necessary for life, it seems a little involuntary, as Galen has demonstrated very well.[b] Laughter is almost similar to it since it is brought about with the help of the muscles, although it does not always obey the will and does not take from it the source of its own generation.

But whether or not laughter ought to be called natural rather than voluntary, we shall say presently.[c] We must explain here whence it comes that one also laughs while sleeeping, as experience attests. We said above on the word of Aristotle that children laugh before they are forty days old while sleeping and not while awake. But Hippocrates bears witness (which experience confirms) that they laugh while awake also; but laughter is more frequent among them in sleep. The reason for this was stated in the foregoing chapter: it is the quantity of humors and sanguine vapors which multiply while one sleeps, and because of which the muscles of the mouth, being filled with them from time to time (since this matter rises up, gushing into them), are drawn back by them just as in a convulsion.

Girolamo Garimberto[56] thinks that children laugh while sleeping because they are dreaming.[d] And such is the opinion of our women, which can be rejected with respect to children who are not yet forty days old if what Aristotle says is true: that children do not dream at all when new-born, and that most of them begin to dream after four years of age.[e] Yet he seems himself to admit in another passage that they dream much sooner, even before being forty days old.[f] Doctors agree with this as well as reason coupled with experience. For Hippocrates in Aphorism 24 of the third book, where he mentions the illnesses of new-born infants, puts among others the fears and terrors met while dreaming, which Galen confirms in his commentary. Rhases[57] and Avicenna[58] also, confirming the opinion of Hippocrates, affirm that children dream two months after birth.

The reason constraining us to accept this proposition is the following: animals evidently dream; now the child is nowise inferior to an animal with respect to fantasies (at least after he is weaned and over two years old) which without doubt are operative in them. They therefore dream before they are four years old, which we see from experience. For there are some who only walk or speak very little, but who while sleeping cry out, say words, kick and sock, sit back and then want to sit up (just as adults do who are dreaming), repeating what they did during the day. Some answer for Aristotle that there are no true dreams before one is four or five years old, but only actions midway between sleeping and waking. I would like to say that the

b. *Concerning the Movement of Muscles,* Book 2.
c. Below, chapter XI.
d. Problem 109.
e. *History of Animals,* Book 4, chapter 10.
f. Book 7, chapter 10.

great philosopher meant rather dreams that are remembered. For he wisely adds that children are unable to remember their imaginings afterwards. This is because their brain is so moist that the impressions and conceptions are soon erased from it.

And here is the difference that we propose between forgetting in children and in old people (for both have a short memory). Old people scarcely retain the things they take in daily and do not remember them a few days afterwards because in their dry and hard brain the impressions are lightly engraved, and consequently are soon erased; but what they knew long ago remains deeply imprinted, retained by the dryness. Children, on the other hand, learn very quickly, and as quickly forget; yet what they learn in the present (since it is being engraved more deeply) will be remembered longer than by old people. They will therefore be able to remember (someone will say) the laughable that they observed while awake. But what can a child of five or six months of age observe and remember since he does not know things, as we have demonstrated?[g] Now, if he understands and recognizes it while awake, why does he not laugh then? Does the object actually present not move him as much as the one represented to his mind by his memory?

But we must no longer delay here, since we hold that the laughter of small children is counterfeit and illegitimate, like dog laughter. The reasons put forth on Aristotle's behalf apply more, therefore, to the other laughter given out by adults during sleep. This is because while dreaming they recall to mind what they saw during the day, and by which they are scarcely less moved than by things that are actually present. For this reason those who are more inclined and given to laughter, and who laugh all day most inordinately, also willingly laugh while sleeping. This I have often observed in fat, joyful, and healthy women who scarcely ever do much thinking, while others weep while sleeping. And it is not more difficult to laugh at that time than to speak or to walk, which actions the soul likewise exercises by means of the instruments serving the will. There is no lack of object, for the memory is able to represent it, as we have just said, and have demonstrated in the first book.[h] Nor is the faculty at all drowsy, but rather agitated by the mind during sleep. Furthermore, the instruments required to form laughter, such as the diaphragm, the chest, the lungs, the muscles of the lower jawbone and of the lips, all clearly move for other reasons while one is sleeping. If, then, the instruments are equipped for it, and the recalled objects are not lacking, how will it be that one does not laugh while sleeping? The causes being disposed and ordered just as they should be, it is impossible that the effect not follow naturally, as the metaphysicians point out.

But whether or not laughter is absolutely natural or is voluntary, or a mixture of the two, we shall demonstrate in the next chapter, thus acquitting ourselves of what we promised earlier.

g. Chapter IX.
h. Chapter IV.

CHAPTER XI
WHENCE IT COMES THAT LAUGHTER ESCAPES SUDDENLY AND THAT IT CANNOT BE RETAINED

These are among the great marvels of laughter, how it escapes so quickly that it seems to come without our knowing it, almost sneaking out, and how sometimes, letting ourselves be overcome with laughter, we cannot stop or suppress it. For when we laugh until we split, carried away by cachinnation, it is not in our power to close our mouth or to have breath at our bidding, so that with the air lacking, sometimes one almost suffocates. And is it not because the humors exit in great haste and with a sudden unexpected movement? For this action seems entirely spirited, and consequently impetuous, since our Hippocrates has also named the spirits *impetuous*.

Now, since this racing humor, as much because of the fineness of its very elaborate substance as because of its most subtle heat, passes instantly throughout the body, and is carried everywhere, we must not be surprised if it goes so fast that it cannot be stopped. For it is not within our power to quiet the humors that are moved in the heart, and still less to repress or retain those coming out of it and impetuously transported, given that their violence is extreme. Furthermore, the movement of the heart is natural, and not voluntary, both that which causes the diastole and systole perpetually, and that of the affections or passions of the soul, as we have shown in the first book.[a]

But you will say: laughter is brought about by means of the muscles, which are instruments in the service of the will. I admit that; but when they are constrained to follow the movement of the heart, at that time they seem to be moving naturally, just like the heart. And such a movement can be called ravished, as is one of the movements of the seven planets.[59] Still, you will insist, saying that respiration is no less necessary and constrained than is the obedience of the muscles to the movement of the heart during laughter, and yet we say with Galen that respiration is purely voluntary, and not natural, although it is going on continually while sleeping and without thinking about it.[b] And the reason why we call it voluntary is that we make it long or short, frequent and hastened or rare and slow, as we please; and we can hold it a long time or even suppress it completely, as did the slave Barbarus.[60]

Now, stopping it when we please and then starting it again is a voluntary act and not an instinctual one or a natural movement. For (says Galen), if one is able to stop what one is doing at one's pleasure, and to do it again either sooner or later, greater or smaller, it is definitely a voluntary movement. Such a one is not that of the heart and arteries, for it does not speed up or slow down, become larger or smaller at our bidding, but their movements are natural. And that all respiration is voluntary, the above-mentioned Barbarus clearly proved, who (as Galen recounts), transported with anger, and resolved to die, threw himself to the ground and held his breath. He remained immobile for a long time, and finally sprawling out a little, thus died.[61]

a. Chapter VI.
b. *Concerning the Movement of Muscles.*

The same reason cannot be attributed to laughter, seeing that because the movement of the heart is completely natural and does not obey the will, the agitation and shaking of the muscles following it is involuntary.

It is true that reason, given to man alone, tries very often to quiet the affections and the movement that follows them; namely, it points out and demonstrates that such and such is not proper. To this persuasion the heart sometimes consents and obeys politically, as we said in the first book.[c] Other times there is not a reason in the world that would retain it, but just as a wild animal is carried away by its passions, very often it even wins over the will and reason itself. For the force of the passions is sometimes so vehement and the link of the faculties of the soul is so slight that one carries away the other. This is why metaphysicians say that the first movements are not within the power of man.[d] If, therefore, reason is able finally to command the considerable commotion of the heart, laughter ceases immediately. And if it does not in any way acquiesce, the will will try to hold the muscles and constrain them not to obey the emotion. But most often both the will itself and the muscles, its instruments, are ravished and carried away in spite of themselves. And as for the muscles, it is always for as long as the laughter lasts. For such is the necessity of following and obeying, so that if they were unwilling and resistant there would not be the danger of suffocation, or of the membranes of the chest bursting and tearing open, as we said in the first book. And for this reason the moved heart easily draws up the diaphragm, which shakes the chest, and the chest puts in motion the other instruments of the will, although involuntarily.

Thus, this movement of the heart, which is purely natural, has itself served by the instruments of the will in spite of themselves, since they are constrained and forced by necessity. Nevertheless, we must be less surprised if such agitation is not able to be stopped by reason, but goes wild like an animal. For all the affections are involuntary and are moved by nature alone. To them the muscles accommodate themselves, if reason permits and there is deliberation, as in the anger to avenge oneself, in the fear of fleeing, etc. But in laughter reason is scarcely able to be the master in the end since necessity constrains the organs of the will to yield and comply to such an affection and to the movement of the heart.

Laughter, therefore, is voluntary, whether you want it to be or not, and is excited by the force of the heart, as we said concerning respiration. And it will even be voluntary because very often it stops at the command of reason when reason shows and persuades that such laughter is absurd, and also because the instruments of the will cause the act of laughter even though it is not by command of the will. Almost similar to this is what Galen proved concerning respiration: namely, that it can be called *voluntary-constrained*. Here are his words: "If one could not hold one's breath completely, would one still not say that respiration is not voluntary? For among the actions which are done through voluntary movement, there are some which are free, and the others serve the needs of the body. The first are done without any hindrance, the second not always, but at times, and with measure. For walking, speaking, and

c. Chapter VI.

d. *Primi motus non sunt in potestate hominis.*

grasping are absolutely free actions; going to stool and pissing are helps to certain needs of the body. Now there are people who refrained from talking for two or three years (as is said of the Pythagoreans) at their pleasure or will; but retaining one's stool or urine for a few years, or months, cannot be done, not even for a few days. For such matter presses us so much, and causes at times such anguish either because of its weighty quantity or its piercing acuteness, that some are not able to wait until they are in the privy. Thus, the act of breathing is similar to these; it even constrains much more, and its necessity is more hastened. For it is to be feared that one may die if one does not breathe, and it is an extreme agony to suffocate. And so one must not be surprised if it is very difficult to hold one's breath completely. Yet let no one think that, because we are able to abstain totally from speaking (if we wish) and unable to hold our breath, speech is a voluntary act and respiration is not, etc."[e] This is what he writes about it, and imitating him we can say that the movements one sees in laughter are voluntary (even though they are made by force of necessity) with the exception of the heart's, which express the emotions.

Now if this is true, in laughter there will be a mixture of both natural and voluntary movements, just as in the voiding of excrement from the intestines and from the bladder. For the bladder and the bowels reject and repel their contents through a natural movement, if the will permits and if the muscles of the abdomen assist this natural movement by compressing the intestines and the bladder. In respiration there is nothing natural aside from necessity, which is never counted among the efficient or the instrumental causes.

CHAPTER XII
WHETHER OR NOT THE NATURAL MOVEMENT OF THE ARTERIES IS CHANGED BY LAUGHTER, AND WHAT IT IS

It is certain that the arteries fittingly imitate the movement of the heart. Yet one is able to doubt that they are instruments of the diverse movements seen in laughter, such as the widening of the mouth, the agitation of the chest, arms, etc. For if the arteries serve the heart, and the veins the liver, it seems that the arteries must accommodate themselves to expressing the passions of the heart. But we pointed out in the first book that they are not the cause of the movements bringing about laughter, but that these things are done through the aid of the nerves, which serve the will.[a] And so it follows that the ·rteries have no part in the production of laughter.

But the question is whether or not in laughter the arteries are also moved beyond their customary displacement, which problem we promised long ago to explicate. It will therefore be good to say something about it.

e. *Concerning the Movement of Muscles,* Book 2.

---

a. Book 1, chapter V.

Galen, demonstrating how the pulse is changed by the passions of the soul, says: "During anger the pulse is high, strong, vehement, rapid, frequent. During joy, strong, rare, and slow, not differing at all in vehemence. During sadness, small, languishing, slow, and rare. In fear, quick and vehement, rapid, slight, erratic, and uneven. From inveterate fear it is similar to sadness's, etc."[b] From these words it is clearly evident that the movement of the arteries is altered by the passions of the mind, which we can also confirm through reason in this manner. The arteries are moved by the heart in a movement completely similar to its own. If, then, the heart is diversely moved by the emotions of the heart, as we have written in the first book,[c] the pulse in the arteries will also vary with the emotions, and, contrarily, the change of the pulse with the passions will argue for a heart moved similarly. And from this proof we also confirm that all the emotions are due to the heart.

Now, that from the arteries one can guess the passions of the soul hidden in the heart, the very expert and ingenious doctor Erasistratus has demonstrated well when from a slight pulse he recognized the love of Antiochus for his stepmother.[62] This is why Galen questions whether there is an amorous pulse. Since, therefore, the principal cause of laughter is from the number of emotions, the pulse is without doubt changed by laughter, so that in imitating and following the movement of the heart, it will be more frequent, more hastened, and somewhat uneven.

But what is the pulse proper to laughers? Galen has well pointed out that all the affections of the mind change the pulse and that in the simple ones it is simple and almost always even; in the mixed and confused ones, uneven. This is borne out in agony and fear, shame, and laughter, which emotions scarcely differ in the movement of the heart. Dread, or agony, is a passion mixed from fear and anger. Fear draws the blood and humors inwards, for which reason the external parts of the body are cold. Anger forces them outwards, thins them and heats them. Now in those who are afraid, their pulse is very small and weak; in angry people, on the contrary, it is very strong, powerful, and vehement. Thus, in fear their pulse will be uneven, mixed from contraries, and similarly in shame, for it is a movement akin to anger, by which he who feels guilty becomes angry with himself over the misdeed committed, and almost punishes and scolds himself, fearing censure, judgment, and reprehension from another. And so first the humors rush inward, then suddenly they turn outwards again, for if they did not it would be purely fear and not shame. Shame or verecund feelings happen all of a sudden when animal virtue does not expect something awful, as Galen says,[d] and come about because of a certain weakness and natural fear when one cannot endure being next to a more dignified person, but would like to be absent, and desires (if possible) to withdraw immediately. And so, as if fleeing a bit, the said virtue retires within without any cooling. For when reason suddenly excites and exhorts the liable part of the soul (that is, the one that is astonished and ashamed), it comes back and moves outwards.

b. *On the Causes of the Pulse,* Book 4, chapter 2.

c. Chapter VI.

d. *On the Causes of Symptoms,* Book 2.

The movement of laughter is scarcely dissimilar to these, as we have proposed. For laughter is made up of a false joy and a false sadness, as we have shown in the first book.[e] There are, therefore, contrary movements, one of which goes outwards and the other inwards; and because the one that widens wins out, much heat is poured forth with the blood and humors. As for the pulse of laughter, it is uneven, just as it is in the emotions mentioned above, skipping and with interruptions, as is plausible, and in this respect it is very close to shame and dread. What is more, anger, although considered to be simple, is excited by contrary movements that are akin to these. For the blood first of all gathers in the heart with great force, where it boils for a short time, then it goes out hotter than it was. The first of these movements is just as it is in sadness over the hurt one has received because of an injury, and so the blood gathers and retires. The other is of a spirit that demands vengeance, and for this it turns outwards. Shame does the same thing, except that it is done by other means, and more gently.

Thus these four emotions have a similar analogy or proportion to the pulse, namely, laughter, shame, anger, and fear, which are akin also in several other accidents. For the redness of the face, the tears, the sweat, and the expulsion of excrement from both the bowels and the bladder, the hindrance of free respiration, and a few other accidents are no less present in these emotions than in laughter, from which they also differ in several things, and especially in this: that no one ever died of anger, if we believe Galen[f] (of sudden death, one must understand, on the spot and immediately), but of fear, several. Also, some have died of shame, as they say; but of laughter, very few people, as we shall state at the proper time.

CHAPTER XIII
WHY IT IS THAT GREAT LAUGHERS EASILY BECOME FAT

We have sufficiently shown above[a] that laughter comes about easily with an abundance of heat and of blood, and that it is very common in those who are well-born, in good health, fat, and replete. Now we must say why it is that from laughing frequently one becomes fat. For it almost comes down to the same thing and is reversible, that those who laugh more easily are inclined to become fat, and that fat people laugh more easily.

In order to explicate this question, we must in the first place know what the efficient cause is, and the matter constituting fat, for from there the essence of the problem will be grasped. The matter making up fat is the softer, fattier, oily and aerated portion of excellent and pure blood, which, being more copious and not being consumed in the food for the members, and neither undone by a searing heat

e. Chapter XIV.

f. *On the Causes of Symptoms,* Book 2, chapter 5.

---

a. Chapter IV.

nor converted into a choleric humor or into semen (for it is the same matter, that of choler, sperm, and fat), upon meeting the membranes, or pellicules, and the skin, thickens and solidifies principally by reason of its density. This is the effect of heat and not cold, as I demonstrated in a paradox against the opinion of Galen.[b] For the cold does not deserve to be called the author of so praiseworthy a thing as fat. And it truly is heat that is able to separate the aerated and oily portion of the blood, and to move it or carry it here and there under the form of a heavy vapor until it stops, thickened because of the density of the membranes and not because of the cold, which is lesser in such spermatic parts (as I proved in another of my paradoxes) than in the sanguine. This same heat does something else in the matter of fat. For it heats, and in heating thickens it, rendering it a color similar to that of the parts to which it is connected. In doing this it is necessary that this heat be mild and tempered. For acrid and boiling heat dissipates and consumes matter.

Yet those who are by nature choleric, when they give themselves up to rest, without worry and without sadness, and if they eat well and take good care of themselves, easily become fat, and lose their natural slenderness. From this we are able to gather that it is not the burning and dry heat, but the soft and moist heat, that is the efficient cause of fat. Now if this is true, and this same moist heat (which accompanies copious blood) makes us inclined to laugh, as we have said above, from this same source will proceed the ability to laugh and the accumulation of fat. For it is the abundance of blood and of heat that makes us quicker to laugh, as on the contrary the cold and dry melancholic people are inept in laughter. This same heat, enveloped in a great and gentle moisture, makes fat in abundance inasmuch as it is not stinging, having been softened by a great amount of humors, and inasmuch as abundant material is not lacking.

Now, laughter contributes to the generation of fat in this manner. Laughter is seen to dilate the pores and to deplete the entire body. By laughter the blood is also thinned, dissolved, then reduced to a heavy vapor. Because of the frequent agitation and concussion, this vapor (which is the heavier portion of the blood) is ravished from nearly all the members and carried away throughout the body. Thus, much fat is made since the aerated moisture reduced to vapor passes easily throughout the depleted body, and from the heat generated the blood is worked through the membranes and the skin. Certainly there is in several people great alimentary moisture, but because it is not diminished, or because their body is too sealed, very little fat is made and almost all of it goes into muscle.

Now laughter does both, for it depletes the body and diminishes the humors, and aside from that it conducts vapor here and there without dissipating it. From this, one is finally able to gather why it is that joy and laughter often make the body fatter. The same argument points out why those who are hot by nature, such as choleric people, are quick to laugh and put on fat easily, if they accumulate much moisture at times. For it is the same material, that of fat and that of choler. After these, the phlegmatic laugh more easily (and because of it become fatter), for they

b. *Paradoxes* 7, 1.[63]

have in quite copious supply the matter for fat, and the heat required in this affair is sufficiently excited in them by laughter. Those who laugh the least, and who scarcely ever become fat, are the cold and dry people, properly called melancholic. For they combat with two qualities the causes of fatness, which are heat and moisture. Choler contradicts laughter because laughter, as we have shown, is provoked by heat.[c]

Laughter, then, is common in those who put on fat most easily, and conversely, in those who put on fat easily, laughter is common. But whether or not dissolute laughter is healthy must be seen separately. For someone (perhaps) might think that from a healthy thing, or one which signifies good health, nothing unhealthy could come. Yet laughing has very much harmed several, and has caused some to die, as they say. For this reason we consider worthy of inquiry the subject of what good and what evil can accompany laughter, which we wish at this point to uncover.

CHAPTER XIV
WHAT GOOD ACCOMPANIES LAUGHTER, AND WHETHER A SICK PERSON CAN BE HEALED BY DINT OF LAUGHING

Since being joyful and ready to laugh indicates a good nature and purity of blood, it thus contributes to the health of the body and of the mind, as experience coupled with reason shows us. For if laughter has been able to save some people from grave illnesses, as we have proposed in the first book,[a] how many other commodities which are less evident may it bring us?

"The joyous heart," says Solomon in his Proverbs,[b] "is a good remedy, but a crushed spirit dries up the bones." This is why those are the most wise and take best care of their health who live joyously, laugh often, and do not burden themselves with a load of thoughts and affairs, killing themselves for the goods of this world, as is commonly said. They prudently follow the most sound advice of Marsilio Ficino when he exhorts his friends thus: "Live joyously," he says, "the heavens created you out of joy, which they have made clear to be their way of laughing (that is, their dilatations, movement, and splendor), as if they were at play." And a little later: "So that you may live truly without worry, do not harbor even the worry that you will never be heavily worried, or seek by which diligent method you will principally be able to avoid worries; for this unique worry burns the heart (miserable, alas) of man more than any other worry. He who knows how to use this remedy lengthens his life, since the length of it depends for the most part on natural warmth."[65] Concerning this subject it is commonly said that laughing and being joyful stops us from getting old. But in order to show briefly the great good and profit that comes from laughter,

c. Chapter IV.

---

a. In the Preface.[64]
b. Chapter 17, verse 22.

we shall explain that proof among all which rightly seems the least simple: that is, that one can even avoid through laughter the imminent danger of death.

The story is told of a sick person who was very ill, and to whom the doctor, having ordered a potion of rhubarb and seeing that the patient had gotten worse, revoked his prescription and did not want the medicine to be given to him. After this the apothecary, having left it on the table of the patient, and having gone out of the room (with the other assistants) following the doctor in order to find out what he thought of this sickness, left the patient to remain alone in the room with an old monkey. The monkey leaps up on the table, takes the goblet, uncovers it and tastes the medicine made up of bitter and sweet.[66] Having tasted it the monkey makes a face, quivering its ears. Then it tastes some more of it and finds it not too bad. Finally he ventures to drink it all. But having tasted more bitterness in the bottom than on the surface, he throws down the goblet with such a great anger and such a funny look on his face that the patient, watching these monkeyshines, started laughing so hard that afterwards he started to be of good cheer.

One also reads about another one who was cured by laughter provoked by another monkey because of its bearing and facial expression that wanted to imitate the doctor. The doctor had had some urine taken and left it next to the stove. Shortly thereafter he leaves the room feeling sad about the patient who had lost his speech and seemed not to see or hear anymore. The assistants leave with the doctor to see what he thinks. During this time the monkey takes the bedpan and puts it on the fire. Then it takes it by the edge with one hand and with the other holds the bottom, just as it had seen the doctor doing. But right away it found the pan so hot that it threw it on the floor with such grace that the patient watching this little act started laughing very hard, and right after recovered his speech.

Another story is told of another monkey that was also the cause of curing his master, a doctor by profession but abandoned by the other doctors; and it is said that this happened in our city of Montpellier. This doctor was a foreigner without a wife and children, served by people who were waiting for his demise. And so when they saw that he was very ill each of them grabbed something. The monkey, seeing all this movement in the household, took for itself the furred red hood that its master wore on solemn occasions. It put the hood on before the patient with much grace, and the patient took such pleasure in contemplating all these monkeyshines that he was forced to laugh so violently that the commotion, spreading throughout his entire body, moved nature so much (because of the continuation of the pleasure he was taking in it) that he recovered his health. This is because the bond which was impeding the forces of nature was broken by the impetuosity caused by the laughable, neither more nor less than in Croesus's son, by nature mute, whose fear broke the bond of his tongue, as we said in the second book.[c] For from the fear (composed of sadness and anger), the boiling heat in the heart, coming back out and pouncing on the bond of his tongue, was able to break and dissipate the said bond, just as

c. In the Preface.

tetany is cured, according to Hippocrates,[d] by a palindrome (that is, a running back again) of natural warmth. And so in these illnesses the pleasant acts of the monkeys (an animal laughable in itself) excited and raised up the nature that was burdened, broken, and as if suffocated by sickness. The pleasure acquired from laughter can do this very easily. For such joy moves the languishing and crushed heart, spreads the pleasure throughout the body, and makes it come to the aid of Nature, which, seizing upon these means and proper instruments, finds itself once again healthy, and strengthened by such help, combats the sickness with great vigor until it vanquishes the illness. For it is, properly speaking, Nature that cures illness. The doctor, the medicine, and the aid of the assistants are but the helps which encourage Nature.

The dignity and excellence of laughter is, therefore, very great inasmuch as it reinforces the spirit so much that it can suddenly change the state of a patient, and from being deathbound render him curable. But it is said that some have died of laughter, and I know some who have become ill because of it. So laughter is not always healthy, as it is neither of itself unhealthy, but among the things which in medicine are called *not natural*.[e] Galen calls them things which necessarily alter our body, and conserving causes. They would (perhaps) be more elegantly called necessary and inevitable things, sometimes healthy, sometimes unhealthy, according to their use or abuse. But let us continue and see finally what ills can accompany laughter.

CHAPTER XV
WHAT THE ILLS CAUSED BY INORDINATE AND RELENTLESS LAUGHTER ARE

There is nothing so useful and so pleasant that it cannot become harmful and dangerous if continued for too long a time. For with respect to pleasure and delight, no one (as far as I know) doubts that the most tasty and delicious foods end up being insipid and hated when too much of them is had. From this came the Greek proverb, "Redone or cooked cabbage is death."[67] For the same reason, as we said in the first book,[a] laughable matter, although most enjoyable, loses its grace and no longer makes us laugh when it is too often repeated. Also, with laughter (although by nature pleasant and enjoyable), when it is excessive, the abdomen suffers so much from it that it seems to have been beaten, that it is splitting and bursting open; the jaws, the chest, and the lungs become very tired and overworked. Then laughter is displeasing and causes much pain.

Similarly, things which by their nature can be profitable are not only useless or unpleasant but even harmful on the same occasion, that is, when one has too much of

d. *Aphorisms*, Book 5, 21.
e. *On the Art of Medicine*, chapter 85.

---

a. Chapter IV.

them. So one must not be surprised when it is said that laughter hurts some people. For it often brings the danger of suffocation when it is excessive and inordinate, causing vehement coughing and a sort of strangulation. Furthermore, it troubles and upsets the food recently received into the stomach (when laughter comes while eating or soon afterwards), to the great detriment of the entire body. For the stomach digests food better while at rest and at its own rate. We therefore do not recommend right after a meal the movements involved in delivering the mail, hopping, skipping, dancing the wheel-around, and similar vehement exercises which ought to precede and not follow eating in a good agendum of health.

Now the lungs, the chest, the abdomen, and consequently the rest of the body are exercised by reading aloud clearly, and by crying out, as Celsus[68] says;[b] less, however, than by excessive laughing, which cannot be endured by a stomach full of food, and which because of it becomes weaker when, overloaded with its contents, it is struck and shaken by the agitated diaphragm; for it suffers pain from it no less than if it had been beaten with rods. For this reason it comes about that the food is rushed into the bowels and ravished from the warmed members, escaping before it is digested, as much because of the vehement commotion as because the stomach, fatigued and aching, simply cannot hold it. From this come coarse expressions, and among the oft-repeated ones comes that of the weakness of the stomach. If, then, one wisely orders people with a weak stomach not to read or sing or speak loudly and for long intervals until a long time after their meals (because such actions hinder digestion and fill the head with vapors, which make it heavy, as experience shows us), how much more is excessive laughter to be feared, which moves and terribly overworks the stomach and the lungs? Now the ills proceeding from an upset stomach are not to be scorned, for they are so diverse and so great in number that he who could count them

Could also count all the flowers
Of springtime, and how many grains of sand
The sea, troubled in its wanderings,
Along the coast of Africa carries.[69]

Here is an illness of great consequence, as will be seen better after our arguments, and it comes mainly when laughter is importunate, at a less than proper time, and without measure. There is among the other disadvantages which inordinate laughter brings, at whatever time it happens, one that is the fusing of the humors, and their spreading throughout the body, and this is most often dangerous. For when they remain in one place and do not move because of their weight, which renders them slow to act, all they do is weigh down the body. But fused and agitated, they can be carried to the extremities of the arms and legs, where they can cause gout. And of course we forbid people with gout to drink wine because it has great power to fuse, and is a very good penetrating agent,[c] as our practitioners say. For the same reason (it

b. Book 1, chapter 2.

c. *Vinum est penetrator optimus.*[70]

seems to me) too frequent and dissolute a laughter causes gout in some people. For it fuses and dissolves the heavy humors by apparently heating up the body with its agitation, which also causes the effusion of said humors throughout the body, and the considerable openness of the pores caused by this same laughter favors this.

Another reason for which inordinate laughter is often dangerous is because it considerably resolves, weakens, and renders effeminate the body it has weakened. It thus chills accidentally, since the heat is dissolved. In this it can do great harm to sick people that are weak (even if they had a hot sickness before) by dissolving altogether the languishing forces. For those who have a chilling sickness it is fitting in every way, but for the hot kind which by nature unnerves or weakens, excessive laughter is harmful.

Besides this, sudden and vehement laughter is harmful because nature cannot endure sudden or violent change, as Hippocrates says,[d] since all that is excessive is contrary to her. But what is done little by little is solid, and especially when one goes from one to another. Concerning this the wise Plato did well to order people to abstain from immoderate laughter, saying: "One must not be excessive in laughter, for such laughter is followed by a great change. It cannot be admitted, then, that someone representing people of great authority laugh dissolutely; still less the gods. This is why we must not listen to Homer when he says:

> Unextinguishable laughter burst out among the gods
> When they saw Vulcan running across the heavens.

For he had become lame."[e] Insulanus,[71] citing this same passage from Plato, thinks that the cause of said dangerous change following excessive laughter is that following a vehement dilatation there usually follows a great constriction. Now the heart is fantastically dilated (he says) when we are shaken with laughter and trembling with joy, which is consonant with what we said earlier.[f] He also subscribes to the phrase of Marsilio Ficino[72] when he says: "At every age it is most profitable for life to retain a bit of our childhood, and always to search diverse pleasures and recreations, but not a long and dissolute laughter, for it dilates the humors in the extreme parts far too much."[g] To these words Insulanus adds that the greatest pleasures (above all those which make us laugh a lot) draw natural heat outwards, after which there follows a chilling and a weakness. For if it is only a matter of the great diffusion of the humors, that in itself causes weakness, since united strength is always more powerful.

Excessive laughter, then, is infinitely harmful, especially in fat people, because it causes the diminishing of natural heat, and if such a cause is augmented, death can result, which is nothing else than the extinction of natural heat. Also, sometimes one faints from laughing because of the great dissipation of humors, as we said in the

d. *Aphorisms,* Book 2, 51.
e. *Republic,* Book 3.
f. Chapter I.
g. *Concerning Life,* Book 2, chapter 8.

first book.[h] Now fainting is a little death, or a path to death, for it often precedes and death follows, because of a lack of aid. Thus it is that sometimes people are taken to be dead who have only fainted, but they actually die because they are not helped. If this is true, death also can come from laughing too much, and this is the greatest of all ills if it is true what is said: that death is the most awful of all horrible things.

But we shall speak of this in the following chapter after we shall have ended this one by telling why excessive laughter is more harmful to fat people than to lean, especially since it is more common, likely, and customary for them, as our preceding demonstrations have shown. For it seems that laughter should harm them less since (as we say often in our schools), "Over accustomed things no passion is generated."[i] But we have already proven that laughter causes one to put on weight, and besides, it is well known that excessive fat is a great threat and reprehensible both as a cause and as a symptom, as our doctors say. For it indicates that there is little blood in the vessels and consequently little heat or humors; and fat is often a cause of suffocation and stifling of natural heat by compression and overburdening. This is why our Hippocrates used to say: "Those who are naturally huge and fat die sooner than thin people."[k] Now, excessive laughter does them double harm: first it makes them still fatter, and puts them in danger of suffocation, and secondly it causes great loss and dissipation of spirits, of which they have but a small provision. It is sufficiently clear, therefore, through the many ills we have recited, that importunate, intemperate, inordinate, and dissolute laughter, as well as any other excessive thing, is dangerous, and for this reason must be avoided, since the unfortunate things of this world can harm us from being far too frequent or in too great a quantity.

CHAPTER XVI
WHETHER OR NOT SOMEONE CAN DIE OF LAUGHTER

Death is our last blow and the last line (as they say) of all things.[a] We cannot go any further when we arrive at the end, which is the article of death. Now we said before that one can faint from laughter, and have demonstrated it enough in the first book,[b] where we also put this question: whether or not it is possible to die of it. For it does seem difficult, especially since the great dilatation of the heart and effusion of humors (in which lies the principal danger of death) is suddenly followed by the constriction, as we have pointed out in the first book, along with the fact that these two movements follow each other alternately, which guarantees the laughter. For by

h. Chapter XXVII.
i. *Ab assuetis non sit passio.*
k. *Aphorisms,* Book 2, 44.

---

a. *Mors ultima linea rerum.*[73]
b. Chapter XXVII.

such means the loss and dissipation of spirits and natural warmth is effected little by little, and not all at once, and for this reason there is less danger.

Yet we know from having heard it that some people have died of laughter,[c] such as the young man the girls tickled until he died, those who have an injured diaphragm, etc.[d] But these are bastard and illegitimate laughters, as we have proven in the second book, for they are caused by touching, and true laughter comes entirely from the movement of the sensitive appetite without touch. But what shall we say of those of whom it is written that they died of true laughter? Someone, the story goes, had given some figs to Philemon.[e] His ass comes and eats them in his presence.[74] He cries out to his servant to come chase it away but his slave, who had gone to get some wine, arrived too late. Philemon then said to him that since he was so tardy he might as well give the wine to the ass also. Then, seeing that the ass was drinking it too, the good old man started laughing so hard that he suffocated over it. Verrius[75] witnessed that Zeuxis, the very excellent portraitist, died from laughing ceaselessly over the grimace of an old lady that he himself had painted. Monsieur Boissonade, a very learned and expert doctor from Agen, and a good and honorable man, told me that the tennis lady, that is, the mistress of the tennis games in the city of Agen, an elderly woman, died on account of laughing upon hearing something very unusual, strange, and ridiculous.

It is true that these examples are extremely rare. This is why we cast them into doubt in the first book, wondering how it could be that laughter brings death. So it remains for us to explain here more exactly how this comes about.

I think that the principal cause of death's coming from laughter is lack of respiration. For I would not easily grant that from a laugh there could be such a dissipation of spirits as is required for death, especially since in laughter the dilatation is suddenly overtaken by the constriction of the heart. Yet, in those men whom we supposed to have died of laughter, such a dissipation of humors could have come about in the manner that I shall explain.

Those who stretch their understanding in high thoughts and inventions through ardent study and assiduous cogitation suffer a great loss of humors. And if they are fasting at the time (which certainly is better, for study does not have as much vigor when the belly is full of food) their strength falters easily. For it is restored by eating and drinking, at the proper time and in proper amounts, otherwise it languishes no less because of an overload of food than because of dearth and famine. Thus, if one puts off eating for a long time, and if during this period the mind is occupied in thoughts of great importance or in meditation, one will feel weak and faint, as a person does who is laboring intensely while hungry, from which he would become all languorous and spent. Also, Hippocrates says: "Where there is hunger there must not be any labor."[f] For if one is always making a great expenditure of spirits and does

c. Book 1, chapter XXVII.

d. Book 2, chapters IV and V.

e. Diogenes Laertius attributes this story to Chrysippus the Stoic philosopher. It could have happened to both of them.[76]

f. *Aphorisms*, Book 2, 16.

not sometimes replenish them with as much, or nearly as much, as was spent, one soon falls into decadence, and finally into such a weakness that one feels as though his soul hangs by a thread. I have often experienced this when I was spending several nights with hardly any sleep, working my brain over commentaries and compositions, skipping as many meals as I could. It seemed to me at times that a little puff would have broken the thread with which I felt my soul to be attached to my body.

Just so it could have happened to the good fellow Philemon, who probably had spent several nights without sleeping, and at the time was dining rather late because, involved most attentively in some work, he did not feel his hunger, or else scorned it. So one must not be amazed if his soul, since it was languishing, and since it had hardly any more spirits after the great dissipation that studying had caused, was dissipated completely by excessive laughter, which annihilated his strength, breaking the link of his soul, already very extenuated in a body all worn out and consumed because of study. In a very robust, full, and solid man, in whom the soul is very idle in a rested body, this would never happen; but a thin, lean, slight, and delicate man (for such are most simple philosophers, devoted completely to contemplation and without any charges in the public domain) whom people say to be but a ghost, does not find it difficult thus to lose a grip on his soul, along with his spirits, which cannot be held back by his weak heart, which is extraordinarily agitated. One must add to this that Philemon was old, as the story goes. Now it is certain that old people have little heat and strength, thus it is easier for them to die suddenly of joy or of some other emotion than it is for young people.

And it is very likely that Zeuxis also was old, beyond what we read of him, since each makes himself with time more perfect and excellent in his art. If the grace and perfection of his work gave him the opportunity both to laugh excessively and to die, one can conjecture from this that the work was marvelous, and the portraitist very learned in his art. Also, the tennis mistress at Agen, because she was very old and (perhaps) fasting, aside from the fact that in women natural heat is weaker and the link between body and soul more fragile, could well have died of laughter.

I think that I have covered with these arguments the problems and questions one might raise concerning those who die of laughter. These are examples and incidents that are extremely rare, and which require several conditions for their execution.

I have finished in these three books the principal history of laughter, and all that has come to my mind up to the present concerning the matter. If ever I encounter in thinking upon it other material for the argument, I shall trace a fourth book. In the meantime I beg the readers who have the talent to philosophize better than I, not to disdain this work but to employ their industry a little to enrich it with their more learned and more solid arguments.

NOTES

INTRODUCTION

1. For a more thorough discussion of Joubert and his applicability to texts of the period, see my *Rabelais's Laughers and Joubert's "Traité du Ris"* (University: University of Alabama Press, 1979).

EPISTLE TO PRINCESS MARGUERITE

1. Marguerite de Valois (1553–1615), daughter of Henry II and of Catherine de' Medici. She is one of the "three Margarets," known also as "la Reine Margot," and the author of *Mémoires* and *Poésies*. She was the wife of Henry of Navarre, the future Henry IV of France. See Ep. (n. 14).

2. Roundness was a sign of perfection in the Platonic doctrine in vogue during the Renaissance, in connection with the myth of the Androgyne. See Ep. (n. 5).

3. The conception of the microcosm-macrocosm was very popular during the late Middle Ages and sixteenth century. Dating back to ancient Greece, it postulates that man is a universe in miniature, a sort of résumé or mirror of the universe, while the universe itself is a sort of man in projected form.

4. Improperly, because Joubert does not admit that animals have a face, strictly speaking.

5. Plato's myth of the Androgyne was a commonplace during the Renaissance. Having been recently revived by Marsilio Ficino's translations, the story is from Plato's *Symposium,* where Aristophanes recounts that "primeval man was round, the back and sides forming a circle." After making an attack on the gods, he was punished by Zeus by being cut in half. "After the division the two parts of man, each desiring his other half, came together, and throwing their arms about one another, entwined in mutual embraces, longing to grow into one."

6. A commonplace image used by Plato in the *Ion* to illustrate the divine presence in the poet, and which during the Renaissance served to represent the attraction of love.

7. This is a reference to the judgment of Paris. After contemplating the three goddesses, Juno, Minerva, and Venus, Paris awarded the prize of the golden apple to Venus.

8. In an attempt to be exhaustive, Joubert uses the traditional four elements as a framework in which all animals might be classified. Joubert apparently did not believe the commonplace notion of assigning fire as a natural habitat for the salamander.

9. See Ep. (n. 3).

10. This is an echo of Plato's theory of the divinely inspired poet, as expressed in his *Phaedrus* (245A, 265B), *Ion* (534), *Meno* (99), *Apology* (22), and *Laws* (3: 682).

11. Henry III, third son of Henry II and Catherine de' Medici, and King of France (1574–1589).

12. Catherine de' Medici, wife of Henry II, and mother of Francis II, Charles IX, Henry III, and François d'Alençon.

13. François d'Alençon, in charge of troops for the crown, often implemented the wishes of his brother.

14. This is a play on words in French, because *Marguerite* is a synonym for "pearl" (or "daisy"). The first of the "three Margarets" was Marguerite d'Angoulême, sister of Francis I. She wrote among other things a collection of poems entitled *Les Marguerites de la Marguerite des*

princesses, "Pearls (Daisies) of the Pearl (Daisy) of Princesses." The second is Marguerite de France, daughter of Francis I and Claude de France. She married Emmanuel Philibert, the Duke of Savoy. The third, the Marguerite to whom Joubert dedicates his treatise, is Marguerite de Valois, also called Marguerite de France. See Ep. (n. 1).

15. The ends of the earth.

16. See Ep. (n. 5).

17. Twice cited by Joubert in this dedicatory letter, Guillaume de Salluste du Bartas (1544–1590) was a protestant poet who wrote a vast religious epic on the creation of the universe, *La Semaine,* of which the first edition was published in 1578. It was a great success, and was reprinted several times before the end of the century.

18. Joubert's blessing and wishes were not to be granted, for Henry of Navarre, future Henry IV (1589–1610), was to repudiate Marguerite for reasons of sterility in 1599 after twenty-seven years of marriage without children. Henry IV fathered the future Louis XIII in a second marriage with Marie de' Medici.

19. Montbrison is a small city in southeastern central France.

20. Joubert is referring to the constellation Aries, pictured as a ram, between Pisces and Taurus. It is the first sign of the zodiac, which the sun enters around the twenty-first of March. Thus, the date of Joubert's letter is not January first but rather around Easter. Soon after this the calendar was reformed by Pope Gregory XIII, and the new system, besides inaugurating several other changes, set January as the first month of the year.

THE FIRST BOOK OF LAUGHTER

Prologue

1. Hesiod, Greek writer of unknown date, probably of the period subsequent to Homer, author of didactic poems, *The Works and the Days,* and the *Theogony.* Joubert is referring here to the *Theogony.*

2. Joubert's torpedo is an electric ray.

3. Guillaume Rondelet (1500–1584), called the father of ichthyology, was Joubert's major professor and author of *De piscibus marinis libri* XVIII and of *Universalis aquaetilium,* which were translated into French a few years after their publication in Latin (1554). He was also an anatomist.

4. A succulent herb *(Portulaca oleracea).*

5. A plant of Asia Minor *(Convolvulus scammonia).*

6. Quintilian was a Latin rhetorician of the first century A.D. who enjoyed much popularity during the Renaissance for his *Institutio oratoria.*

7. Alexander of Aphrodisias, last of a long series of Aristotelian philosophers, began lecturing in Athens around 198 A.D. He was the author of several commentaries, among which are his *Problems,* often cited in Renaissance texts.

8. Moses the Jew, possibly Moses Ben Joshua of Narbonne (died 1362), or Moses of Palermo, who lived during the thirteenth century in Palermo and translated the "Treatise on the Healing of Horses," attributed to Hippocrates.

9. Jules-César Scaliger (1484–1558) was an Italian humanist, scholar, and physician, author of a book of literary and rhetorical theory, *Poetice,* published posthumously in 1561. His brother is Joseph-Juste Scaliger (1540–1609), the famous philologist called the miracle and glory of his century.

10. Girolamo Cardano (1501–1576) was an Italian physician, mathematician, philosopher, and occultist, author of *De vita propria* (his autobiography) and other treatises among which *De rerum varietate* and *De subtilitate* make him an important philosophical figure of the time.

11. Girolamo Fracastoro (1483–1553) was a scholar, physician, mathematician, and astronomer, author of the philosophical treatise *De sympathia et antipathia rerum,* and a treatise on syphilis, *De contagione et contagiosis morbis.* At nineteen years of age he was given the chair of philosophy and logic at the University of Padua, and the Italians call him the father of modern pathology.

12. François Valeriole, or Valeriola (1504–1580) was a French physician and philosopher who became professor of medicine at Turin, and who wrote *Commentarii in sex libris Galeni de morbis et symptomatibus* and *Loci medicinae communes libris tribus digesti,* medical treatises much read and cited at the time.

Chapter I

13. This is reminiscent of Aristotle *(Poetics* 5): "the comic mask is ugly and distorted, but does not imply pain."

Chapter II

14. See I (n. 13).

Chapter III

15. Poggio Bracciolini (1380–1459) was an Italian humanist and comical writer, leaving us some facetious tales and a history of Florence.

16. *Fictio* is usually defined as the attributing of reasonable attitudes and actions to animals or objects.

17. *Beausemblant* is a synonym for *fauxsemblant* (false seeming) and is a form of allegory.

18. *Dissimulatio* is another term for irony.

19. See I (n. 13).

20. Much of Joubert's material in this paragraph comes from the second book of Baldassare Castiglione's *The Book of the Courtier,* a sort of handbook for proper conduct at court, but also a great document of the social institution of nobility at the time of the Renaissance.

Chapter IV

21. Cato of Utica, great-grandson of Cato the Elder, led an exemplary stoic life, falling on his sword at the defeat of Thapsus in 46 B.C.

22. Heraclitus, known as the weeping philosopher, was a Greek philosopher of the Ionian school of the fifth and fourth century B.C. whose work has come down to us in the form of fragments. Along with Democritus, the laughing philosopher, he is an important figure in Joubert's treatise and in several other Renaissance texts as an image of the emotion of sorrow.

Chapter VI

23. Joubert's division of the soul (natural, vital, and animal) is based upon Plato's (nutritive, sensitive, and intellective) as expressed in the *Timaeus* (69C–71A).

24. The philosopher referred to in the note is Thomas Aquinas, who claimed that there is nothing in the intellect unless it was first in the senses (*Summa contra gentiles*, 91, 96).

25. This particularly stoical note seems to reflect the contemporary attitude to suffering, cultivated in part as a reaction to the cruel events witnessed during the religious wars. It can be seen in portions of Montaigne's *Essais*, the first two books of which were published in 1580, the year following Joubert's treatise on laughter.

26. Joubert was less familiar with Euripides' *Medea* than the *Medée* of Jean Bastier de la Péruse (1538–1570), French poet and playwright.

Chapter VII

27. This curious marginal note, probably one of Zangmaistre's, underscores in spite of its ambiguity the primacy of "philosophy" in all areas of knowledge and experience.

28. Galen and Hippocrates represent the two great pillars of medicine as it comes down from antiquity. Galen lived during the second century A.D. Born in Asia Minor, he became a doctor and ministered to the athletes at Pergamum for six years before going to Rome, where his fame caused jealousy among the Roman doctors. One year later he left Rome, but was called back by Marcus Aurelius. He was particularly famous for his theriaca, a much-used remedy composed of various drugs and honey. During his entire life he was interested in anatomy, which he considered the very basis of the art of healing. Hippocrates (fifth and fourth century B.C.) was an itinerant physician. Much of our knowledge of him is based in legend. An important collection of medical works and treatises came down from his school, several of which are probably by Hippocrates. The importance of his work in furthering the art of medicine is undeniable, and a sort of cult developed around him during the Middle Ages and early Renaissance.

29. By "the other souls" is meant the other divisions of the soul.

30. Joubert's term *desirous faculty* corresponds to Plato's *appetitive soul*.

Chapter VIII

31. Democritus, of the fifth century B.C., was known as the laughing philosopher. He lived in Abdera, where the inhabitants, thinking him mad because he laughed ceaselessly, called upon Hippocrates to come and heal him, but the latter found him to be exceptionally wise when Democritus told him he was laughing over human folly and stupidity. Joubert uses Democritus and Heraclitus often as images of joy and sorrow. See I (n. 22).

Chapter IX

32. Zangmaistre is referring to Joubert's *Paradoxorum demonstrationum medicinalium decas prima*, the first of two "decades" or groups of ten of medical paradoxes. It is in the fourth paradox of the first "decade" that Joubert takes up the question of *aimatose* (sanguification), and refutes Galen's opinion that it was done in the veins.

Chapter X

33. By *doctrinal* and *composite order* Joubert (Zangmaistre?) means that order used in teaching material which is composed of several elements (composite).

Chapter XI

34. This is from Aristotle's *Parts of Animals* 3:4.

35. Pliny the Elder, of the first century A.D., wrote books on history and rhetoric which have been lost, and also a *Naturalis historia* in thirty-seven books which has been preserved. This was a much-read work, often cited by writers of the Renaissance. The particular reference is 7:53.

36. The story of Sophocles and Denys the Elder is also from this same section of Pliny's *Naturalis historia* 7:53. There are other versions of the death of Sophocles besides that of dying of joy over the success of one of his plays. One of them maintains that he died while reciting passages from the *Antigone*, while an epigram of the *Anthology* affirms that he died from having swallowed some grapes.

37. The name Polycrites is not found in the biographies.

38. Phillipides (third century B.C.) was an Athenian comic poet whose works are no longer extant. Joubert probably read of him in Plutarch's *Lives* under the biography of Demetrius. The translation into French of this work under the title of *Vies parallèles* by Jacques Amyot appeared in 1559, and a second revised edition of it in 1565. Thus, Joubert could have been familiar with either or both.

39. Aulus Gellius's anecdote of Diagoras is told in the *Attic Nights* 3:15.

40. Valerius Flaccus (first century A.D.) was the author of an epic entitled *Argonautica* which was incomplete at his death. This did not hinder its being read, and the particular anecdote is taken from 9:13.

Chapter XII

41. The principle of life, according to Aristotle, was the heart. That is, the heart was the efficient cause of animal life.

Chapter XIII

42. This note makes an important point in Joubert's theory: rarely does one die of laughter. It will be thoroughly developed later in the treatise.

Chapter XIV

43. This is the core of Joubert's thesis: the twofold nature of laughable matter causes a twofold emotion in the heart.

Chapter XV

44. This is a variation of the famous principle of noncontradiction used in formal logic.

Chapter XVI

45. This is an important point because Joubert hereby substantiates on physiological grounds what Aristotle says in theory about man's being the only animal that laughs *(Parts of Animals* 3:10).

Chapter XVIII

46. This is stated in book two of Galen's *De motu musculorum*.

47. This is from Galen's *De usu respirationis*, one of several books on the subject: *De causis respirationis*, *De difficultate respirationis*, etc.

Chapter XIX

48. Martial was a Latin writer of the first century A.D. whose writings are extensive. He is remembered for his twelve books of *Epigrams*, from which Joubert cites this line in translation (7:25, 6). The genre was much imitated during the Renaissance.

49. Aristotle says this in the section referred to in the note: "Why is it that, although both fear and pain are a kind of grief, those who are in pain cry out, but those who are afraid keep silence? Is it because those who are in pain hold their breath (and so it is emitted all at once and comes forth with a loud cry), whereas the body of those who are afraid is chilled and the heat is carried downwards and creates breath?"

Further on in this section Joubert finds material which he will develop in later chapters: "Why is it that in those who are afraid the bowels are loosened and they desire to pass urine?" Aristotle also describes here the effects of fear on the sexual organs.

Chapter XX

50. This is one of Zangmaistre's notes, indicating that Joubert will treat this particular subject later.

Chapter XXI

51. See I (n. 7).

THE SECOND BOOK OF LAUGHTER

Preface

1. The influence of Thomas Aquinas is seen here, particularly that of his *Summa contra gentiles*, chapter 79.

2. Joubert's term "anger and concupiscence" corresponds to Aristotle's irascible soul.

3. Theodoret was a Christian writer of the fifth century A.D., appointed Bishop of Cyrus in Syria. He wrote a history of the Church of the fourth century. The work Joubert (Zangmaistre?) refers to is the *Treatise on Curing the Prejudices of the Greeks*.

4. Pliny, not Appius, recounts the story of the physician Erasistratus (third century B.C.) who discerned and remedied the passion of Antiochus for his stepmother Stratonice.

5. Vergil, the great Roman poet of the first century B.C., was a very popular author during the Middle Ages and Renaissance, both for his *Aeneid* and for his *Eclogues*, from which Joubert cites in translation the line: "*Nescio quis teneros oculus mihi fascinat agnos*" 3:103.

6. See I (n. 35).

7. Cicero (first century B.C.) was one of the greatest Roman orators. His prose had an immeasurable influence on French style throughout the Renaissance, and large traces of it in Joubert's style filter through Zangmaistre's translation besides being evident in the dedicatory letter which Joubert wrote to Marguerite in French. Of Cicero's writings it is the *De oratore* that has had the greatest impact on the rhetorical tradition in French letters, but his writings cover a broad spectrum of subjects from philosophy to politics, and his letters, numbering over eight hundred, constitute a rich fund of knowledge of the most interesting period in Roman history. The passage Joubert cites is from the *Tusculan Disputations* 1:33.

8. Epicharmus was the first great Greek comic poet. He lived during the first half of the fifth century B.C., and also wrote treatises on philosophy and morality.

9. Fourth fever *(fièvre quarte)*. We have little information on the state of knowledge in the area of pathology during the Renaissance. Most sicknesses were treated as fevers, duly numbered: third, fourth, double fourth fevers fill the memoirs of the time. See R. Mandrou, *Introduction à la France moderne 1500–1640* (Paris: Albin Michel, 1974), p. 58; and H. Brabant, *Médecins, malades et maladies de la Renaissance* (Brussels: La Renaissance du Livre, 1966), p. 122.

10. Rhazes (850–923 A.D.) was a famous Arab physician often cited in medical texts of the Middle Ages and Renaissance. His treatise on smallpox and measles was well known. Robert Estienne published the Greek version of this treatise in 1548, with the corrections of Jacques Goupil, and Sébastien Colin published it in French translation in 1556.

11. Herodotus was a Greek historian (fourth century B.C.) of Asia Minor (Halicarnassus). He is known for his account of the Persian War.

12. Lucretius was a Roman poet born at the beginning of the last century B.C. He is known for his didactic Epicurean work, *De rerum natura,* in six books.

13. Such as Albertus Magnus, Duns Scotus, and Thomas Aquinas.

14. See the end of Joubert's dedicatory letter to Marguerite de France.

15. Avicenna (980–1037 A.D.) was an Iranian physician and philosopher who wrote works on medicine and philosophy. He was celebrated for his knowledge, and his works were part of the program for medicine in French universities until the middle of the sixteenth century.

16. See III (n. 28).

17. Cato (Dionysius) was a Latin moralist concerning whom no biographical materials are extant. He is supposedly the author of *Disticha de moribus ad filium,* which was a sort of catechism of morals used in the schools of the Middle Ages.

18. *Timaeus,* 71 and 75.

19. Zangmaistre uses the French *journalieres* ("daily").

Chapter I

20. Isaac Ben Todros (mid-fourteenth century), known as Isaac Tauroci, was a French physician. He is said to have possessed a profound knowledge of theology and philosophy, and wrote a treatise on the plague in Avignon *(Source of Life).* He also wrote a work on facial convulsion *(Avit ha-Panim),* and it is to this work, in translation, that Joubert refers. See E. Wickersheimer, *Dictionnaire biographique des médecins en France au moyen âge,* Paris, 1936. Joubert's statement, that Isaac was the first to give a physiological definition of laughter, is not true. Gregory of Nicea, to name only one, gave such a definition of laughter. It is curious that the name Isaac happens to mean "laughter" in Hebrew, and perhaps this fact had more of an effect on Joubert's historical attributions than on those made today.

21. See I (n. 12).

22. Gabriel de Taregua was a physician of Spanish origin of the early sixteenth century who practiced in Bordeaux and who had a considerable reputation. He wrote a voluminous collection of medical compositions, a commentary of Avicenna, observations on Hippocrates and Galen, and a summa of nearly 1200 medical questions.

23. See I (n. 11).

24. Meletius was a Greek doctor of the fourth century A.D. He wrote a treatise on the nature of man. Joubert knew the Latin translation of it done by Nicolo Petreius, published in Venice in 1552. In this work Meletius gives anatomical expositions of the different organs, followed by physiological reflections on them.

25. *Sequentials,* that is, effects.

Chapter II

26. Aetius was a physician of Mesopotamia of the fifth and sixth century A.D. He compiled a collection of what most of the doctors preceding him had said. This work was entitled *Tetrabiblos,* and contained in addition his own observations on diseases and surgery. Joubert could have consulted one of the Latin versions of the translation done by Janus Cornarius, the *Contractae ex veteribus medicinae tetrabiblos,* published in Venice in 1543.

27. The *Aphorisms* of Hippocrates were edited by François Rabelais in 1532.

28. Herodotus recounts the anecdote in his *History* 4:75.

Chapter III

29. See II (n. 26).

30. See I (n. 47).

31. Dioscorides was a Greek botanist of the first century A.D. He wrote a famous *Materia medica* in which five hundred plants are named and described. This work remained the principal source for medical students and botanists until the seventeenth century.

32. Paulus Aegineta was a Greek medical writer of the seventh century A.D. He wrote the *De re medica libri septem,* compiled from Galen and other sources. It is the sixth book of this work ("On Surgery") that proved to be the most interesting to physicians of the Renaissance and to Joubert in particular.

33. Solon was a Greek legislator of the sixth century B.C., and one of the Athenian statesmen responsible for a more liberal constitution. Joubert appears to be mistaken in his reference.

34. Alessandro Alessandri (Alexander ab Alexandro) was an Italian writer and jurist (1460–1523) who left a work on philology entitled *Dies geniales,* modeled after the *Attic Nights* of Aulus Gellius.

35. Pausanias was a Greek author of the second century A.D. who wrote a well-known *Description of Greece.*

36. Pelops was a Lydian physician of the second century A.D., famous for his knowledge of anatomy. He was one of Galen's tutors.

37. Strabo was a Greek geographer (c. 60 B.C. to 24 A.D.) who added to his descriptions of countries notices of their customs and interesting comparisons. He furnished the men of the Renaissance a well-rounded picture of the world as the ancients knew it.

38. The bite of the tarantula *(Lycosa tarentula)* was supposed to cause tarentism, which is defined as a nervous affection characterized by melancholy, stupor, and an uncontrollable desire to dance.

39. Joubert here manifests his belief in musicotherapy, as did Galen and Theophrastus. Iconography has preserved the "cortège des danseurs de Saint Guy" in an engraving of Josse Hondt, which is based upon a drawing of Peter Breughel. See Brabant, *Médecins, malades, et maladies de la Renaissance* (Bruxelles: La Renaissance du Livre, 1966), p. 135.

Chapter IV

40. The work referred to in the note is Hippocrates' *De morbis vulgaribus.*
41. Pliny, *Naturalis historia* 16:25.
42. *Handling,* that is, manipulation.

Chapter V

43. Moses Maimonides, not to be confused with Moses the Jew (I [n. 8]), was a famous rabbi and philosopher of the twelfth century A.D. He was a disciple of Averroes, and wrote the *Guide for the Perplexed.* He went to Egypt in 1165 and became a physician to the Sultan.
44. See I (n. 11).
45. Niccolò Niccoli was an Italian humanist of the fifteenth century A.D., well known for his accumulation and critical editing of manuscripts in Florence. Joubert is mistaken in attributing a treatise to him, however, for he left no written work.
46. See I (n. 12).
47. Christopher of Vega was a Spanish physician of the sixteenth century. He wrote commentaries on Hippocrates and Galen. Joubert mistakenly attributes to Christopher of Vega what is the work of Thomas-Roderigue of Vega: *Commentarior in Galenum tomus primus, in quo complexus est interpretationem artis medicae et librorum sex de locis affectis.*

Chapter VII

48. Lucretius, *De rerum natura* 5:1397.
49. Erasmus of Rotterdam (1459–1536) was one of the greatest humanists of the Renaissance. His voluminous works include moral treatises *(The Praise of Folly),* scriptural studies, letters, and collections of passages from the ancient authors *(Adagia).* He corresponded with an incredible number of scholars, writers, and princes of the time. Joubert's types of laughter are drawn mainly from Erasmus's *Adagiorum Chiliades.*
50. *Modern,* that is, writing after Christ.
51. Joubert is referring to Henry II Estienne, a member of the great family of printers and philologists of sixteenth-century France. Besides printing a number of Greek, Latin, and Hebrew texts, Henry II (1531–1598) composed a Latin and a Greek thesaurus, a comparison between Greek and French, a protestant pamphlet during the religious wars, and a work arguing for the supremacy of the French language over Italian: *Projet de traité sur la Precellence du langage françois.*
52. *Odyssey* 20:229–303.
53. Eustathius was the Archbishop of Thessalonica during the latter half of the twelfth century, and is known for his voluminous commentaries on the *Iliad* and the *Odyssey,* which were first printed in 1542.
54. Plautus (third and second century B.C.) was a Roman comic playwright twenty of whose plays are extant, most of which are based on Greek originals. His characters were

usually taken from the middle and lower classes. The play to which Joubert refers is the *Captivi* (3:482–85).

55.*Iliad* 14:222–23.

56.See I (n. 1).

57.The thistle-eating ass causing Cato's death is from the *Palliata* in the *Comicorum fragmenta.*

58.Angelo Poliziano (1454–1494) was an Italian poet and humanist. He delivered lectures at Florence, and his correspondence attests to his influence and popularity in Renaissance Italy, as does the constant mention of him by many of the great humanists of the day.

59.This is a typographical error on either the printer's, Zangmaistre's, or Joubert's part, because it is in the seventh book of the *Iliad* that Ajax's laughter is mentioned.

60.Quintus Sammonicus Serenus was reputedly a Roman of much taste and reputation of the third century A.D. He is said to be the author of a medical poem with the title *Praecepta saluberrima* or *Praecepta de medicina parvo pretio parabili,* in which there is information on natural history and on the medical arts. It is divided into sixty-five chapters.

61.Julius (Polydeuces) Pollux was a Greek grammarian of the second century A.D. He became a sophist and taught rhetoric in Athens. He left a dictionary of Greek words, the *Onomasticon.*

THE THIRD BOOK OF LAUGHTER

Proem

1.Joubert's definition of philosophy is obviously more comprehensive than that which our own century allows.

2.Ovid (43 B.C. to 18 A.D.) was the greatest poet of the closing Golden Age of Roman literature. His first work was the *Amores,* love elegies, followed by the *Heroides,* imaginary letters from loveworn ladies to their absent lovers or spouses. His masterpiece was the *Metamorphoses,* in fifteen books, dealing with mythology. Ovid's *Fasti* contain stories and legends from Roman sources. His erotic poetry is the *Ars amatoria,* in three books, and the *Remedia amoris,* in one. He composed his *Tristia* (in five books) and some *Epistulae* while in exile. His influence on medieval and Renaissance literature in Italy, France, Holland, and England is notable. The reference here is to the *Fasti* 5:555–60.

Chapter I

3.The philosophers referred to here are the scholastic philosophers; specifically, when Joubert mentions act and potency he has Thomas Aquinas in mind. See II (n. 13).

4.*Mediocrity* is used here in the sense of a Golden Mean.

5.Vesalius (1514–1564) was a Belgian anatomist and humanist who studied in France and Italy. He was famous for his work on anatomy, *De humani corporis fabrica.* He dared attack and contradict Galen, and because of this suffered the anger of his contemporaries. Joubert does not give the title of his work because of its popularity at the time.

6.Girolamo Fracastoro, for example. See I (n. 11).

7.See I (n. 12).

Chapter II

8. See II (n. 20).

9. The reference is to *Georgics* 4:511–15.

10. Avenzoar was an Arab physician who lived in Spain during the eleventh century A.D. His principal work was entitled *Teiseer,* and is a source for the *lapidaires.*

11. Theomnestus (fourth and fifth century A.D.) was a Greek writer on veterinary surgery. Fragments of his work were published in a collection of veterinary surgery first published in Latin by J. Ruellius in Paris (1530), and in Greek by S. Grynaeus in Basil (1537).

12. Scribonius Largus was a Roman physician of the first century A.D. He wrote several medical works, of which only his *De compositione medicamentorum* remains. An edition of it was first published in Paris by J. Ruellius in 1529, appended to an edition of the works of Celsus. It contains almost two hundred formulae, several of which are quoted by Galen in his *De compositione medicamentorum secundum locus.*

13. See I (n. 10).

14. See I (n. 9).

15. Pliny, *Naturalis historia* 7:19.

16. Ibid.

Chapter III

17. Pliny, *Naturalis historia* 7:19.

18. Possibly the Arisi family of Cremone.

19. Apollonius Tyaneus (first century A.D.) was a Pythagorean philosopher who was supposed by his contemporaries to have been a magician and a prophet. His only extant work is his *Apology,* to which Joubert refers.

20. Pliny, *Naturalis historia* 7:19.

21. This name is not in the reference to Pliny given by Joubert.

22. Diogenes Laertius, *Lives and Opinions* 9:21.

23. *Hibernia* is the Latin word for Ireland.

24. Erasmus wrote this in his *Adagia.* See II (n. 49).

25. John 11:1–44.

26. "Building castles in Spain" (faire des châteaux en Espagne) was and still is a common expression in French.

27. This is from Aristotle's *Parts of Animals* 3:4.

28. Any middle position between two extremes is to be regarded highly. *In medio stat virtus* is the precept of this philosophy of the Golden Mean. The idea of the soul's inhabiting only moist places is from the pseudo Saint Augustine's *Quaestiones veteri et novi testamenti* (23). Rabelais repeats it in his *Gargantua* (5): "En sec jamais l'ame ne habite." But Rabelais applies the principle to the consumption of wine, with highly satisfactory results.

29. Pliny, *Naturalis historia* 7:19.

30. *Physiognomian,* that is, physiognomist.

Chapter IV

31. See II (n. 24).

32. *Iliad* 1:599.

33. This is from the *De humoribus.* By the elements, Hippocrates meant here the four

humors corresponding to the four basic elements: blood to fire, phlegm to water, choler to air, and melancholy (black bile) to earth.

34. See III (n. 30).

35. Zeno, in the "Life of Zeno of Elea"; Diogenes Laertius in *Lives and Opinions* 7.

Chapter V

36. Horace, *Epistles* 5:19. The expression *carousing* as used by Joubert here is related to the German *garaus trinken*.

37. *Odyssey* 9:362–63.

38. Cheremon (first century A.D.) was a Stoic philosopher and historian. He wrote a "Sacred and Profane History of Egypt," but only a fragment of it is extant.

39. *Laws* 2:666.

Chapter VI

40. See II (n. 32).

41. *Problems* 30:1.

Chapter VII

42. I have not been able to find the source of this anecdote.

Chapter VIII

43. Again, I have not been able to find the source of this aphorism.

44. See II (n. 4).

45. Another instance in which I have been unable to find Joubert's source.

46. Florus was a Latin writer of the end of the first century A.D. He is the author of the *Epitome*, an abbreviated history of Rome.

47. See II (n. 60).

Chapter IX

48. See II (n. 33).

49. Girolamo Garimberto was an Italian humanist of the sixteenth century and author of *Concetti*, a collection of ideas from ancient authors, and of *Problemi naturali e morali* (1549), to which Joubert refers here.

50. See I (n. 7).

51. Junius Philargyrus was an early commentator of Vergil. His remarks are limited to the *Bucolics* and *Georgics*, and are less elaborate than those of Servius. See III (n. 55).

52. *Ecologues* 4:60–63.

53. See II (n. 58).

54. Ennius was a great Latin poet of the third century B.C., and is called the father of Roman poetry. His works, none of which have survived entire, inspired many of his successors to the point of citing him at length. These quotations have helped preserve his poetry.

55. Servius Marius Honoratus (third century A.D.) was a Roman grammarian and the famous commentator on Vergil's works, particularly the *Aeneid*.

Chapter X

56. See III (n. 49).
57. See II (n. 10).
58. See II (n. 15).

Chapter XI

59. Seven planets, because Neptune and Pluto had not yet been discovered in Joubert's time.
60. Joubert gives the details of the Barbarus incident later in the chapter.
61. This incident is told by Galen in his *De motu musculorum* (2). See Book I of Joubert's treatise, chapter VII, note d.

Chapter XII

62. See II (n. 4).

Chapter XIII

63. See I (n. 32).

Chapter XIV

64. Joubert called the preface of his first book a prologue; it is the second book that has a preface (and the third a proem).
65. Marsilio Ficino (1435–1499) was an Italian humanist whose translations and commentaries of Plato were an important impetus to neo-Platonism during the Renaissance (see Ep. [n. 5]). He taught philosophy in Florence and among his students was Lorenzo de' Medici.
66. In this and in each of the anecdotes that follow, the narration lapses into the present tense, probably in an attempt to render the account more vivid.

Chapter XV

67. This proverb seems to embrace a play on words based on the similarity between *rathanos* (cabbage) and *thanatos* (death). Thus, a "redoing" of *rathanos* by metathesis would result in *thanatos*. It is not possible that the Greeks of the ancient world believed this if we are to believe the long lists of its virtues as preserved by Pliny.
68. Aulus Cornelius Celsus was a Roman medical writer of the first century A.D. His work is the *De medicina*.
69. These lines recall the theme of *impossibilia (adynata)* so frequent in Renaissance poetry.
70. This maxim is similar to Hippocrates' idea as expressed in his *Aphorisms* 2:27.
71. Insulanus, Guillaume de L'Isle (Menapius), was a French physician and humanist of the early sixteenth century and author of several medical texts on fever. He also edited Ficino's *De vita libri tres*.
72. See III (n. 65).

Chapter XVI

73. Horace, *Epistles* 1:16, 79.

74. See III (n. 66).

75. Verrius Flaccus was a Roman grammarian of the last part of the first century B.C. He was also a historian and a poet, and wrote a compendium entitled *Rerum memoria dignarum*.

76. Diogenes Laertius was a Greek author of the third century A.D. who compiled an important work on the lives and ideas of the ancient philosophers, *Lives and Opinions*. Chrysippus was a Stoic philosopher (third century B.C.) who is said to have written 705 works, and whose erudition is proclaimed by Cicero.

INDEX OF PROPER NAMES AND TYPES OF LAUGHTER

LAURENT JOUBERT:
Treatise on Laughter

was keyboarded for electronic scanner
by Ladonice McGill,
and set on the Linotron 606
in Merganthaler Garamond No. 3,
by Akra Data, Inc., Birmingham, Alabama.
The printer was Thomson-Shore, Inc.,
Dexter, Michigan, and the binder was
John H. Dekker and Sons, Grand Rapids, Michigan.

Book design: Anna F. Jacobs
Production: Paul R. Kennedy